Pot Shards

ADST-DACOR Diplomats and Diplomacy Series

Series Editor: Margery Boichel Thompson

Since 1776, extraordinary men and women have represented the United States abroad under widely varying circumstances. What they did and how and why they did it remain little known to their compatriots. In 1995, the Association for Diplomatic Studies and Training (ADST) and DACOR, an organization of foreign affairs professionals, created the Diplomats and Diplomacy book series to increase public knowledge and appreciation of the professionalism of American diplomats and their involvement in world history. Donald Gregg's account of his years in CIA, the White House, and the U.S. Embassy in Seoul, the 53rd volume in the series, is a window into Cold War secret operations and diplomacy with a major ally.

RELATED TITLES IN THE SERIES

Jonathan Addleton, *Mongolia and the United States: A Diplomatic History*
Herman J. Cohen, *Intervening in Africa: Superpower Peacemaking in a Troubled Continent*
Charles T. Cross, *Born a Foreigner: A Memoir of the American Presence in Asia*
John H. Holdridge, *Crossing the Divide: An Insider's Account of Normalization of U.S.-China Relations*
Edmund J. Hull, *High-Value Target: Countering al Qaeda in Yemen*
Dennis Kux, *The United States and Pakistan, 1947–2000: Disenchanted Allies*
Terry McNamara, *Escape with Honor: My Last Hours in Vietnam*
William B. Milam, *Bangladesh and Pakistan: Flirting with Failure in Muslim South Asia*
Robert H. Miller, *Vietnam and Beyond: A Diplomat's Cold War Education*
William Michael Morgan, *Pacific Gibraltar: U.S.-Japanese Rivalry over the Annexation of Hawai'i, 1885–1898*
Ronald Neumann, *The Other War: Winning and Losing in Afghanistan*
David D. Newsom, *Witness to a Changing World*
Nicholas Platt, *China Boys: How U.S. Relations with the PRC Began and Grew*
Howard B. Schaffer, *The Limits of Influence: America's Role in Kashmir*
Ulrich Straus, *The Anguish of Surrender: Japanese POWs of World War II*
Nancy Bernkopf Tucker, Ed., *China Confidential: American Diplomats and Sino-American Relations, 1945–1996*

For a complete list of series titles, visit <adst.org/publications>

Pot Shards

Fragments of a Life Lived in CIA, the White House, and the Two Koreas

Donald P. Gregg

An ADST-DACOR Diplomats and Diplomacy Book

NEW ACADEMIA PUBLISHING · VELLUM

Washington, DC

Library of Congress Control Number: 2014941748
ISBN 978-0-9904471-0-8 paperback (alk. paper)
ISBN 978-0-9904471-1-5 hardcover (alk. paper)

 An imprint of New Academia Publishing

 New Academia Publishing
PO Box 27420, Washington, DC 20038-7420
info@newacademia.com - www.newacademia.com

For Meg
With my love and thanks
For the joys of many years

Contents

Preface

His hair was glossy, his handshake firm and dry, his glance hard and inquisitive. The few seconds in which I had his full attention left me with an indelible impression. That was John F. Kennedy at the White House, 1962, talking about counterinsurgency and the Vietnam War.

The CIA officer's hair and eyelashes were burned away, his skin was charred, but his eyes were open and his blistered lips moved. "This is what I've been looking for, a cool place, me with my clothes off, and beautiful ladies all around." A white phosphorous grenade had fatally burned the CIA officer. The scene was a U.S. Army hospital, Vietnam, 1971.

"I know how things work around here," said Ambassador Philip Habib. "They are going to kill him, but they may wait until they hear something from me. If you can tell me who has him and where he is by tomorrow morning, we may be able to keep him alive." The ambassador was describing the kidnapping of Kim Dae-jung. South Korea, August 1973.

Fragments of memory have persisted through the vagaries of time, like shards of pottery broken long ago. They are reminders of things from the all-but-forgotten past. When I was U.S. ambassador to South Korea, I would often stop my armored car at construction sites in Seoul to prowl around freshly broken ground, looking for ancient pot shards newly exposed. I have boxes of shards thus collected that can never be reconnected to what once was whole. I also have a vivid collection of memories that I will try to string together to create the narrative of this book.

I remember waking up one night long ago, a small boy filled with the fear of dying. I cried out and my parents heard me and came into my room. I was still snuffling, but they comforted me enough so that I asked through my tears if I would live to see the year 2000.

They assured me that I would, and I asked how old I would be when that date came. They told me that I would be 72 years old. That seemed so reassuringly far off in the future that I was able to fall back into sleep.

It is now well more than fourteen years into the twenty-first century, and I realize that if I am ever to "connect the dots" of my memory, I had better get started now.

So I shall begin.

Thanks and Recollections

First of all, I am very grateful to Andrew Szanton, my long-time editor, and to Margery Thompson, ADST publishing director and series editor, who have worked so well as a team, and have done so much to bring *Pot Shards* into publishable form. I am also grateful to my son John, twenty-five years a journalist, for his professional judgments along the way.

Next I want to mention Tapani Kaskeala, my great friend in Helsinki. I sent him the chapter "The Finnish Connection" as a gesture of friendship. Thanks to him it was printed in Finland's leading magazine in the fall of 2013. Thank you, Tapani.

Turning to Korea, I want to thank professors Chung-in Moon and John Delury of Yonsei University for using excerpts from *Pot Shards* in their book *Bound by Destiny*, dealing with my activities in Korea over the past forty years.

Then along the way, several close friends have read Pot Shards in its various nascent forms, and encouraged me by their comments. In particular I want to thank Lucy Blanton, Jane and Bob Geniesse, Alice Gorman, Jan Harrison, Lorrie Harrison, Carla Hawryluk, Sue and Jack McMahon, and Jane Wood.

In the writing process, as I dug back deep into the past, people re-emerged who meant a great deal to me at the time I knew them. I believe that their collective impact was one of the major factors that led me to write this book.

In Japan, Tsuruko Asano and Honda *sensei* (first name lost), both magnificent teachers, pushed my Japanese to the point that I could move freely and confidently in the cities, the small towns, and the mountains of Japan. Artist Kado Hiroshi, whose portrait of

Meg graces our dining room, opened up his home and his family to us as very few Japanese did in those days.

In Burma, Bibi and Nona, our two devoted Karen nannies, utterly dedicated themselves to the health and safety of Lucy, Alison, and John. Thanks to them our tour in Rangoon was very healthy, and all contacts with wild dogs and bad snakes were avoided.

In Vietnam, three of my comrades at Fort Apache—Rudy Enders, Felix Rodriguez, and Dave Wilson—remain vivid in my mind for their resourcefulness, their valor, and their humor. And the late Lt. General Jim Hollingsworth, with whom I worked both in Vietnam and Korea, epitomizes America's fighting qualities as does nobody else I ever knew.

U. Alexis Johnson in Tokyo and Phil Habib in Seoul were magnificent ambassadors, the likes of which seem long gone from this era of diplomatic mediocrity. I loved working for them. They knew the value of intelligence and used it well.

In the White House, Phyllis Byrne was my secretary, but she was far more than that. She was rock-solid during very difficult days.

I was honored to work directly for Vice President George H. W. Bush in the White House. And as his representative in Seoul, I was fortunate to be able to work with President Roh Tae Woo, who got along famously with President Bush. Their teamwork produced a truly productive period in modern Korean history.

At the Embassy in Seoul, I was magnificently supported by Ray Burghardt, the deputy chief of mission, and by my glamorous and talented assistant, Barbara Matchey.

For the next sixteen years at The Korea Society, Fred Carriere was the absolutely indispensible man, bringing with him a knowledge of the Korean character that is unmatched by any other American that I know.

And now, as chairman of the Pacific Century Institute, I am fortunate to work for and with Spencer Kim, a Korean-American who embodies the best of both those nationalities.

In bringing this page to an end, I must mention the late president Kim Dae-jung, whom I grew to know very well and whose vision for reconciliation between North and South Korea will sooner or later take place.

PART ONE

EARLY LIFE

1

Abenaki Scalps and a Street Fight in Circleville

What triggers memories of the past? I was born in December 1927, and perhaps because I grew up in the pre-television age, many of the strongest links to my childhood are aural, not visual. The voices of Franklin Roosevelt and Winston Churchill are as thrilling and familiar to me as Peggy Lee singing "Why Don't You Do Right?" with Benny Goodman in 1942. The sound of a steam engine's whistle instantly takes me back to long train rides to my grandfather's house in Colorado, having dreams of wild Indians in my upper berth in the Pullman car. And the cry of a loon is as hauntingly evocative today as when I first heard one in Canada's Algonquin Park when I was five.

My childhood, in a hilltop house in Hastings-on-Hudson, New York, was unusual. I was taught to read at a very early age by an aunt, who was a brilliant teacher of pre-school children. Before I could start formal schooling, I picked up tuberculosis at a 1934 YMCA conference in South Carolina that I attended with my father, whose life work was with the YMCA. He was Abel Jones Gregg, and he became head of boys' work at the National Council of the YMCA, and started the Indian Guides program.

Because I had TB, I was not permitted to start school until I was eleven, and so for the first decade of my life, as an only child, I was essentially with adults, who went out of their way to include me in their conversations, and to introduce me to their thoughts about the world.

The first foreign issue I became aware of was Japan's invasion of China, which began in Manchuria in 1931. When I did not clean my plate at dinner, my father would tell me not to leave "a Chinese meal" to be thrown away. As he explained what that term meant, I had my first inklings that the rest of the world was not as well off as we were.

Through his participation in international YMCA conferences held in the 1930s, my father became aware of Adolf Hitler's rise in Germany, and was deeply apprehensive about what it would mean. On one occasion, an American radio network played a recording of Hitler delivering a speech in Germany. My father had me listen to the broadcast. Hitler's voice had a high yapping tone to it, and I did not like it.

I knew both my grandfathers, both of whom lived into their nineties, and through them was introduced to our long and colorful family history.

My paternal grandfather, Harry Renick Gregg, was born in 1852 in Circleville, Ohio. He was full of clear recollections, some funny, some violent and some tragic. He was proud to tell me, when I was a very small boy, that we were a Scottish family, descended from the war-like MacGregors, who were outlawed by the English king in the early 17th century, for generally ferocious bad behavior. Our ancestors then changed their name, if not their behavior, to Gregg.

I last saw Grandfather Gregg in June 1950, when he was 98. We talked of the Civil War, which he remembered clearly. Most vivid was his memory of President Lincoln's funeral train, which passed through his hometown in 1865. He said that "the silence and the sadness" were unforgettable.

My maternal grandfather, Charles Atherton Phinney, was born in 1853 in Maine. He was a conservative, church-going man but had some wild and woolly ancestors, including "Narragansett John" Phinney, who took part in the "great swamp fight" in 1675 that was the culmination of "King Philip's War" against the Narragansett tribe.

And there was Mary Corliss Neff, carried off from Haverhill, Massachusetts with Hannah Dustin and her baby by Abenaki raiders from Canada in 1697. Mary has been acting as a nurse to Hannah, who had very recently given birth. The Indians quickly killed the Dustin baby, and the women plotted revenge.

Their chance came one night after several grueling days on the way back to Canada, when, on a small island where they thought their captives had no chance of escape, the Indian captors grew careless, and all fell asleep. Mary and Hannah took three toma-hawks from the sleeping Indians, and armed a young boy who had also been captured. Acting swiftly, they killed ten Indians, scalped them for the bounty then being given for killing Abenaki raiders, and escaped downstream by canoe.

Mary lived until 1722, Hannah until 1736. In 1874, a large mon-ument honoring the courage of Mary and Hannah was erected on the small river island in New Hampshire, where they killed their captors. My mother's middle name was Corliss, and she was one of Mary's direct descendants.

The family anecdote to which I feel most closely connected concerns my great-grandfather, John Gregg. I heard the anecdote from my grandfather on three or four occasions; once or twice in the 1930s, in the summer of 1944, and in June 1950 for the last time.

John Gregg was a huge man for his time, the mid-19th century. When he was buried, he weighed 240 pounds. He was well over six feet tall, and was immensely strong. He helped run a family dry goods store in Circleville, and people would gather to watch him unload wagonloads of produce. He was noted for lifting heavy barrels of sorghum over his head and carrying them into his store.

One day a large, tough-looking man came into the family store, sized up my great-grandfather and said "I've come to fight you. If I can lick you, I can beat any man in this part of Ohio." The stranger, an itinerant prize fighter, was told to leave, which he did, but as he departed he said: "You'll fight me before I leave town."

The stranger set himself up in Circleville's bar district, acted with great belligerence toward those he encountered, and "beat the daylights" (my grandfather's words) out of anyone who challenged him. Word of these doings quickly got back to John Gregg, along with the stranger's claim that there was a certain storekeeper in town who was afraid of him.

My great-grandfather had his lunch at a hotel near the family store, normally sitting alone at a table reserved for him. One hot summer day, the stranger with his fearsome reputation fully estab-lished, barged into the hotel dining room, and, uninvited, sat down with John Gregg.

The two men stared at each other, and the stranger sneeringly said "You're a lily-livered son of a bitch." (Each time my grandfather told me this story, the high moment for him was the repetition of that powerful epithet. Otherwise, swearing was strictly discouraged in the Gregg family home.)

John Gregg leapt to his feet, flipped the heavy dining table over on the stranger, pulled him out from under it, threw him through a window onto the street, jumped out the window, and beat him unconscious. He then picked up the stranger and carried him over his shoulder to a nearby doctor's office. He told the doctor that he would pay all medical bills, and asked that he be notified when the stranger planned to leave town.

When word came of the stranger's departure, John Gregg went to see him off. The stranger held out his hand, and said "Well, I came looking for it, and I got it." He then climbed into the waiting stagecoach, and departed. Such was life in Ohio in the 1850s.

My mother, Lucy Corliss Phinney, had a beautiful contralto voice and was offered a chance to study for an operatic career. Her conservative father was against this, and so she went to Radcliffe, graduating in 1913, and going into a life infinitely more dangerous than she or her father would ever have imagined.

My mother had studied "social work" at Radcliffe and began work at the Boston Society of the Care of Girls (referring largely to unwed mothers). Mother's work attracted the attention of a group in Montreal called the Women's Directory, which had been formed to fight what was then often referred to as "white slavery," the entrapment of poor, uneducated young women into prostitution.

In 1916, she moved to Montreal to begin this new phase of her work. Within three years she had become head of the Directory, and had been successful in focusing press attention on what she referred to as "commercialized vice interests," which could be more accurately described as vicious criminal gangs. Two attempts were made to kidnap and kill her, and she was urged to leave Montreal to protect her life. So she went to Colorado College, as dean of women, where she met my father when he returned home from France after World War I.

Dad graduated from Colorado College in 1913, and joined the YMCA. In 1916, as a member of the Colorado National Guard, he was sent to the Mexican border to pursue the Mexican border bandit Pancho Villa. In 1918, he joined the Army, and as a 28-year-old college-educated buck private, was sent to France.

In his last letter before shipping out, he wrote these words: "I am looking forward to my trip with a mighty anticipation. A Western boy sailing overseas to have a hand in the biggest event the world has ever seen. I am quite happy to go so that I can hold my head up during the years ahead."

I worshipped my father. When I was a sickly child, feeling deeply inferior to both my youthful, healthy contemporaries and my powerful forebears, Dad always encouraged me to feel that one day I "would make a difference" in the world. The unhappiest period of my life started in the fall of 1942, when Dad became ill, suffering internal infection from an abscess on his duodenum. Just as my health improved, Dad's worsened. Radical surgery was attempted, but failed. Dad died in April 1944, when I was 16.

World War II was raging, my lungs had cleared from any evidence of TB, and I had been given clearance to play all high school sports. I decided to enlist in the Army as soon as I was 17, to "have a hand" in World War II, thus emulating my father. My mother wisely insisted that I graduate from high school before entering the Army, and so I doubled up on enough courses to graduate in 1945, at 17. I "toughened up" that summer at a canoe trip camp in Canada, and was on a remote lake in Ontario when travelers from another camp shouted the news of war's end. I enlisted in the Army in September 1945.

2

Texas Talk and a Takeshita Takedown

The war had just ended, and an eighteen-month enlistment had been created to fill anticipated personnel shortages at a time when those who had seen long, tough service were anxious to be discharged.

I was assigned to the Signal Corps, for reasons unknown to me. This meant that I went through basic training at Camp Crowder, Missouri, near Joplin and Neosho. I was a member of Company E, 26th Training Battalion, ASFTC. I think that meant Army Signal Forces Training Center, but we trainees knew those letters really meant: "All Shit Flows Through Crowder."

Company E was made up largely of draftees, several years older than I was. My platoon was a pretty compatible bunch, whose last names began with the letters "E" through "K." "Evans, Fanning, Faw, Fiegel, Finochio…" were the first names shouted out at roll call every morning. Through basic training, I carried a Springfield '03 bolt-action rifle, serial number 3587548. I have no idea why that serial number has stuck in my head—but it has.

One of the other platoons in Company E contained a number of tough Texans, widely disliked by our platoon. One cold day in November, a snowball fight broke out between our platoons, and I scored a direct hit on the head of one of the Texans. He immediately retaliated by shattering one of my front teeth with a solid right hand, enhanced by a large ring well suited for inflicting facial mayhem.

I was *hors de combat* for a day or two. Upon my return to full duty I wondered what I would do when I next encountered the Texan who had hit me. I was told not to worry about it, as he "had been taken care of" by one of the hard cases in my platoon who felt that what had happened demanded a response. That particular Texan was not returned to duty in our company.

(That missing tooth plagued me for years. The Army replacement was rather crude, and the plastic brittle, so the false tooth broke periodically, usually at a bad time, leaving me with a "Hannibal Lecter" look. Even worse was that the substance used for false teeth in those days did not show up under the ultraviolet light used in dance halls and discos of the time. My daughter Lucy belatedly pointed this out to me one night as I danced with her, telling me to dance with my mouth closed so as not to scare young children. It's finally properly fixed, but I fear my disco days are over.)

The Texans also suffered a stunning defeat at the hands of a diminutive Japanese-American named Takeshita. He was in the rear rank of the platoon that marched in front of ours. I had a good view of him, as I was in the front rank of our platoon. Takeshita was so slender that his heavy cartridge belt slipped down over his hips unless he held it up with one hand. When we had to march or run at port arms, with both hands on our rifles, Takeshita was doomed, as his belt crept down from his waist toward his knees, forcing him to drop out of formation, pull up his belt, and run to catch up with his platoon.

Most of us felt sorry about this, but the Texans thought it was hilarious, and constantly teased Takeshita, tormenting him by deliberately mispronouncing his name, which in Japanese means "Under the Bamboo."

One payday as we were standing around waiting to be paid, one of the Texans went up to Takeshita, yelled "Hey 'Take a Shit-a,' I hear you're good at *ju-jitsu*—let's see you get out of this," and clamped the small man's head under his arm in a severe headlock.

Takeshita was choking, but we heard him say: "Stop, I don't want to hurt you," which evoked a guffaw from his assailant.

With that, Takeshita clamped his hands under the Texan's buttocks, lifted him off the ground and fell backwards, using his back as a fulcrum. The Texan's face smashed into the frozen ground with a thud we all could hear. The man was out cold, and Takeshita, once he got himself untangled, began to administer much needed first aid.

The unconscious Texan was carried off on a stretcher, bleeding profusely, not to be seen again. Such was the U.S. Army in late 1945, adjusting to peacetime duty.

The racial prejudice shown Takeshita, and to all Japanese-Americans, was very common at that time. In 1942, in the wake of Pearl Harbor, President Roosevelt interned about 110,000 Japanese-Americans living on or near the west coast, to prison-like camps in the desert, to thwart possible "treachery" on their part. This was one of the worst decisions of Roosevelt's presidency. In 1988, President Reagan signed a congressionally authorized apology to all Japanese-Americans, and over $1.5 billion in reparations was paid to those so unjustly confined.

We had a platoon sergeant, named Hatridge, also from Texas, who embodied everything we'd ever heard about pugnacious non-commissioned officers. The slightest infraction of his rules caused Hatridge to inflict severe punishment on the miscreant. One freezing November night I was made to dig a goldfish pond just outside the company orderly room, where I could see Hatridge sitting contentedly, chewing tobacco by a hot stove, where he could keep an eye on me.

Digging the pond was a miserable process. The soil was half frozen, and full of rocks. I was sweating profusely, but my hands were cold as I had no gloves. Hatridge released me about midnight, but told me the next morning that the pond was "ugly," so I had to fill it in. I've forgotten what I had done to have this punishment descend upon me, but I developed a certain respect for the sergeant, and felt proud when he told us, as we graduated from basic training, that we had all done well.

Writing about Sergeant Hatridge reminds me of another redoubtable sergeant encountered by my uncle, Renick Gregg, in 1916 along the Mexican border. The National Guard had been activated to pursue the Mexican insurgent leader, Pancho Villa, who in March 1916 had led a raid into Columbus, New Mexico, in which 17 U.S. citizens were killed. My uncle's platoon had a sergeant known, more or less affectionately, as "Sergeant Whiskey." My uncle, a tall man, stood in the rear row of his platoon when it lined up for roll call.

One day a new soldier joined the platoon and introduced himself as Ruby L. Joiner. A large and muscular man, Joiner stood next to my uncle and among other things said that he had played fullback at the University of Georgia. Sergeant Whiskey duly arrived to call the roll, and when he barked out "Ruby Joiner," to the surprise of everyone, Joiner responded "Here" in a high falsetto.

This went on for several days until Joiner's first Saturday in the platoon. On that day, Sergeant Whiskey appeared to be particularly badly hung over, and Joiner's falsetto reply infuriated him. "Step out here, you son of a bitch, I want to see what you look like," he snarled. Joiner silently parted the ranks in front of him, stepped forward, flattened Sergeant with a mighty uppercut, and returned to his place.

The sergeant arose and dismissed the platoon. The next day Joiner was promoted to corporal.

In early 2010, I was in southwestern Georgia, and told this story to several residents of the town of West Point. One of the men in my audience nodded and said, "With a name like Ruby, you had to be pretty tough, particularly in those days." Apparently, Sergeant Whiskey had the same opinion.

At the end of our nine-week basic training, we were taken to an upstairs room where we could choose what we wanted to do as members of the Signal Corps. Various posters were on the wall, describing what life as a telephone repairman, a truck driver, a pole climber, a Teletype operator, or a cryptanalyst might involve.

I chose the final option, not because I wanted to be a cryptanalyst particularly, but because I didn't want to take up any of the other offered options. In fact, I was not at all sure what a cryptanalyst did. The Signal Corps poster was not at all helpful to that end. It featured a big question mark.

For training, I was sent to Vint Hill Farms Station near Warrenton, Virginia. I found the ancient history of cryptography and secret writing to be quite fascinating. What became shockingly clear to me were the tremendous military advantages that had come to the United States and its British allies as a result of being able to read, from time to time, both German and Japanese secret communications during World War II.

We were drilled on the absolute necessity of not letting any foreign country have the slightest inkling that we were reading any other foreign country's messages. Our instructors gave us a horror story from just after World War II, when technicians from a European country that made advanced cryptographic machines were brought to the United Staes and given a briefing on our use of their machines. Shortly thereafter, we lost our ability to "read several countries' mail." Both the value of intelligence, and the need to keep it secret became ingrained in my thinking.

After training, I was assigned to the Army Security Agency's headquarters at Arlington Hall, just outside Washington. There I encountered two or three middle-aged women who had made wartime breakthroughs in our ability to read Japanese ciphers. They were treated reverentially by their co-workers, who knew how many thousands of American lives had been saved by their brilliant work.

Etymology was more interesting to me than cryptography, at which I was not particularly adept. The patterns and frequency of letters continue to interest me, particularly as I think back to how words came to have their meanings. And so I was discharged as a sergeant (T/4) in April 1947 with no thought of ever returning to the world of codes and ciphers.

Incidentally, the life of our most famous traitor Benedict Arnold has always fascinated me. The best book I have read about him is Willard Randall's *Benedict Arnold, Patriot and Traitor*. And it strikes me that the two opposing words "patriot" and "traitor," which define Arnold's life, have all the same letters except one; patriot has a "P" where traitor has an "R." Two words so close in structure are diametrically different in meaning. And yet in life, the dividing line between the two words can become very faint, as Arnold's life clearly shows.

My Army experience, short as it was, taught me a lot. At the intellectual level came the value and importance of intelligence, and the need to keep it secret. At the emotional and physical levels came the impact of intolerant parochialism and racial prejudice. Having a front tooth knocked out in retaliation for hitting a man with a snowball was a shattering experience (pun intended) that totally surprised me. And the prejudice shown to Takeshita as an individual was exemplified at the national level by the internment of so many Japanese-Americans by President Roosevelt.

The Army had not been racially integrated; in basic training we had no blacks in our company. We did have two Blackfeet Indians, with whom I played basketball. They were treated with aloofness, but were not shunned, as their athletic abilities won them respect.

In Washington, D.C., there was wonderful jazz, mostly in black parts of town. I was often the only white person in the audience, but I was always welcomed. On the bandstands, in small clubs, there were no racial barriers, and I was struck by the power of the music made by black and white men, sitting side by side. (Remember, this was 1946.)

These experiences demonstrated to me how prejudice is fueled by ignorance, but also how hostility fades and friendship can emerge through talk and a shared experience.

So, I've always had a powerful, good feeling about my army experience. I survived it, learned from it, and the fact that I had had tuberculosis no longer defined my early life. I felt that I had "caught up" with my contemporaries.

3

Fraternities and Philosophy at Williams

In September 1947, after a summer in California teaching horse-back riding at a YMCA camp in the high Sierras, I entered Williams College a few months shy of my twentieth birthday. I was one of a relatively few men in my class who'd had military service.

Fraternities had a stranglehold on student life at Williams, which was then all male and 98 percent white. Before we had attended a single class, we were "rushed" by the sixteen or so fraternities on campus. About 90 percent of the class was pledged to a fraternity at the end of this process. The other 10 percent had suffered a bitter rejection, often based on religious criteria. On August 18, 2013, I led a memorial service for a just-departed classmate. I spoke to each of the half-dozen members of our class who attended. One of them went out of his way to tell me that he had never gotten over the rejection he had been subjected to by not being invited to join a fraternity sixty-nine years before.

During the rushing process, we had to go to the Garfield Club, which was composed of the men who had failed to make a fraternity. The student head of the Garfield Club was an outstanding man, a real campus leader, who had chosen not to enter a fraternity. I sought him out and told him that I had not joined a fraternity in high school and felt that the entire rushing system was bizarre, in its timing, method, and objective. I told him I intended to work for change and asked his advice as to whether I should work from outside the system, as he had, or join a fraternity and try to change it from within. He strongly advised me to take the latter course, which I did, joining Phi Delta Theta.

I majored in philosophy at Williams and am still very much

influenced by the thinking of Professor John William Miller, the head of the philosophy department, who taught at Williams from 1924 to 1960. I try to live by Miller's simple but profound definition of morality, "Never treat another human being as an object."

Miller was also interested in people taking action and being defined by, and held responsible for, the actions they took. "Man does not have a nature, he has a history," Miller often said. He urged his students to act upon what they believed in and to "cut behind appearance toward reality," which I tried to do all through my years as an intelligence officer. Williams was, and remains today, a great teaching college. And Professor Miller exemplified that tradition.

My athletic career was odd, to say the least. I was six feet two-and-a-half inches tall and weighed about 180 pounds. I tried out for football and soccer, but my inexperience doomed me to failure. I was a good badminton player and started an unofficial team that lost its only match to Columbia. I made the freshman baseball team and while sitting on the bench during a game entered the interfraternity track meet that was going on right next to the baseball field. My event was the javelin throw, which, to everyone's surprise, I won.

I was also on the informal polo team. I could ride and had a car with a ski rack to which we could attach our mallets. But I was left-handed, and there are no left-handed polo players. We would ride until October, when a local man took his polo ponies south for the winter. Then in February or March we would hear from places like Yale or Cornell asking us to come and play them. The results were one-sided, to say the least. The best I can say is that I never fell off my horse. That is the roster of my meager athletic achievements at Williams.

In 1951, the first college committee was formed to evaluate the need to change the fraternity system. The committee was named for its chairman, Professor Sterling, and I served on it, having been elected president of my fraternity. The year after I graduated, it pledged a Jewish student and was immediately kicked out of its national organization, which allowed only "Aryan" membership. Today, fraternities are long gone, women comprise half the student body, and Williams now has a far richer campus life than it did when I was there.

One of the other outstanding professors at Williams was Fred Schuman, a political scientist of some notoriety. He had been born in Europe and viewed the burgeoning tensions between the Soviet Union and the United States with great concern. In his freshman Political Science 101 course, Schuman pronounced solemnly: "I was born before World War I, survived World War II, and expect to be killed in World War III."

Schuman's words seemed ominously prophetic in 1948 with the imposition of the Berlin Blockade and the 1949 ascent to power of the Communist Chinese, and later with the opening of the Korean War in June 1950. President Truman's firing of General MacArthur in the spring of 1951 split the campus down the middle, and those of us about to graduate knew we were to become working parts of a tense and uncertain world.

In the middle of my senior year, the National Security Agency approached me to see if I would like to return to Washington to work at Fort Meade. The bespectacled NSA recruiter was a bookish man in his forties, who quickly saw that cryptanalysis was of no interest to me. After a few minutes of friendly conversation, he suggested I might think about joining CIA.

I had very little understanding of what that agency did and asked what its main purpose was. He replied unforgettably, and probably with some cynicism: "Oh, they jump out of airplanes and are going to save the world!"

That one sentence led to my serving with CIA for 31 years. I doubt that many men were recruited more easily than I.

But let me say something more about the influence of my father, which was at least as strong. Dad hated war. Having served in a hospital unit of the Colorado National Guard along the Mexican border in 1916 (chasing Pancho Villa), and having gone over to France in 1918 as an infantry private, Dad had had direct experience of war and wanted nothing more to do with it.

In 1939, the first trans-Atlantic air mail service was inaugurated by Pan American Airways. Dad got a first-day cover for that flight and wrote me a letter dated May 17, 1939, that had flown back and forth across the Atlantic. In it he wrote: "Your generation will have to devise the ways whereby nations plan together in friendly, increasingly unselfish ways, how all the nations of the world may be dealt with as members of a world community. . . . Maybe that will become your goal. Lovingly, your father hopes it may."

It is fair to say, that I have been deeply influenced by that thought and saw my work as an intelligence officer as a way of preventing greater conflicts among nations.

I was often asked, early in my career, how it was that I, the son of a YMCA officer, had joined CIA? My answer to that was that I did not see intelligence work as "a dirty business." The most effective relations between CIA case officers and foreign agents were based not on coercion but on trust—and produced intelligence that could keep us out of miscalculations that might well otherwise lead to war.

By the end of my final college semester, I had filled out the endless CIA forms, had been interviewed secretly, and had passed the polygraph. I was ordered to report to Washington a day or two after I took my last examination at Williams and was granted leave to return to campus for the graduation ceremony in June 1951.

I graduated cum laude, with no romantic interests whatsoever. My heart had been badly bruised at the end of my junior year, and I was then truly "fancy free."

PART TWO

INTELLIGENCE

4

Jumping Out of an Airplane for the CIA

There were about forty of us CIA recruits, freshly graduated, mostly from Eastern colleges. Many were from Yale. We first met in a safe house in Maryland, where we attended introductory classes and learned that we were to become paramilitary officers in the CIA Office of Policy Coordination.

I didn't make close friendships with other trainees, but one young man who impressed me a great deal was Jack Downey. He was right at the top of the group, as I think I was, too. But Jack was very smart, likeable, and he had a record that I couldn't touch as a collegiate athlete.

The training we received in our first several weeks was rudimentary and not terribly impressive. Our instructors would not talk about their own intelligence work, and we came to feel that they did not have much to tell. We learned about street surveillance, dead drops, safety and danger signals, the fundamentals of compartmentalization, and the "need to know" principle.

It was all very basic: chalk marks on post boxes to signal meetings; figuring out safe places to hide documents where they could be picked up by a supposed agent; counting the number of telephone rings coming at a certain time of night—three rings meant one thing, four rings meant another.

We were particularly inept at trying to follow people covertly. There was one rather jaunty man who always managed to spot us and then lose us, and we wondered if he was as good at following people as he was at losing those who sought to follow him.

It was embarrassing to meet with him after a training exercise and hear him tell us when he had picked us up as surveillants, and what he had done to throw us off the track. Most of us were rather large in stature, and he would often cite the value of "little grey men," which we obviously were not.

Our essential enemies were the Soviet Union and Communist China, whom we were fighting directly in Korea. "The spread of communism" was described as a sort of international virus that we had to combat wherever it erupted. The Soviets in particular were depicted as ruthless and violent, with an unshakable ideology that made them impossible to recruit as agents except through coercion. The operational examples we learned about came from American OSS and British MI6 activities in World War II.

After about six weeks training in Maryland, we were sent to Fort Benning, Georgia, and twelve weeks of training at the Infantry School. We were all put under alias, "to protect our identities." I took the name "Williams," which I felt I could remember under pressure. The training was superb. We learned from beribboned veterans with combat experience in Europe and Asia, who really knew what they were talking about.

Fort Benning was a sprawling base, with few trees, and sandy soil. We were there in August and September, and it was frequently over 90 degrees—and humid. For recreation, there was Phenix City, just across the Chattahoochee River in Alabama, where raunchy bars, hard-bitten women, and fist fights abounded.

The Korean War was not going at all well in those days, and lots of combat units were heading in that direction. A foul-mouthed comic in a particularly tough bar ended his act every night with the following warning: "There are three dread diseases you don't want to get: syphilis, gonorrhea, and 'gone to Korea.'" A lot of the Yale grads in our group seemed to drop out after the training, sensing either that they were not cut out for CIA or that the CIA was not what they'd expected it to be.

Our three weeks of jump school were unforgettable. For the parachute training, our group had been joined by a highly decorated Air Force Lt. Colonel, who had flown twenty-five combat missions as a bomber pilot over Germany. I got to know the man fairly well, and he spoke openly of his experiences as a wartime pilot. He remembered in particular several pilots who before taking off on a specific bombing mission expressed the feeling that they would be shot down that day. In most cases, they were. (It was referred to as "buying the farm.")

The colonel added that toward the end of his twenty-five-mission cycle, he awoke one morning with that same fateful feeling and expressed it to some of his comrades. Once in the air, the feeling of dreadful funk still oppressed him, and he grew less alert than usual. He said, "My co-pilot saved me. He saw some incoming German fighters that I should have spotted much earlier, and we had a truly narrow escape." Following that experience, he went out of his way to urge pilots who felt that they were going to "buy the farm," to be especially alert on that day, so that the feeling of dread would not become a self-fulfilling prophesy.

The most frightening moment of parachute training came when we trainees had to jump out of a 34-foot tower, hooked to a harness that caught us after a short fall and guided us to the ground on a sloping wire cable. Thirty-four feet may not sound high, but when you are up there, looking down, it feels like forever. After you jumped, the fall was short, and the jerk of the catching harness was most reassuring.

I was just behind the Air Force colonel when it became his turn to jump for the first time. He froze at the edge of the jumping platform and could not go off it. The training sergeant immediately saw the symptoms, pulled him back from the edge, and hurried him off of the tower. The trainers knew how contagious fear is, and by acting quickly, they kept it from spreading.

I will never forget the expression of shame on the colonel's face as he was led away. He looked liked a convict being led off to prison. We never saw him again. I was so afraid of freezing that I jumped before being given the signal to go, and had to do several sets of push-ups as punishment once I hit the ground.

In the third week, after endlessly practicing parachute landing falls, jumping out of the 34-foot tower and being hauled to the top of 250-foot towers, from which we were released under predeployed canopies, it was finally time to get in a plane and jump out of it. We were all sick with fear, not of the jump but of freezing in the open door of the plane and not jumping.

As we sat on the plane, stone-faced, I sought to loosen things up by telling my comrades about the wango-wango bird, which

I had learned about from a Canadian friend at Camp Ahmek. He had conjured up an entire mock zoo, including the "tight-skinned-utang" and the "red-assed kangaroo."

The wango-wango bird, I told my friends, flew to an immense height and then dove to earth, emitting the wild cry that gave the bird its name, and which meant to the bird "feel the fucking breeze!" This got a few laughs and I, for one, went out of the plane yelling "Wango-wango!" In that case, at least, humor trumped fear.

After finishing jump school, our parachutist wings were pinned on us by a colonel, who knew we were with CIA. Five minutes later, we had to hand them over to an administrative officer "to be put in our files." I have never seen my wings since that day.

In April 2011, I sat on a plane next to a young soldier who proudly told me he had just completed parachute training at Fort Benning. We compared notes and found, to our mutual surprise, that our experiences, sixty years apart, had been identical, down to the sequence of training events, the terminology used, and type of parachute employed. "If it ain't broke, don't fix it" certainly applies to U.S. Army parachute training.

5

The Stunning Young Woman in a Crowded Taxi

As I think back over my life, with all its choices made after agonizing deliberation, the careful weighing of options, and the consultations with respected elders, it is truly humbling to recognize with absolute certainty that, besides being born, the most important thing that ever happened to me was the result of error and random chance.

In October 1951, I had finished the training at Fort Benning and moved back to Washington, where I was living with my mother's younger sister, Charlotte Phinney, on a shady street in Georgetown. It was a tall, narrow house on 31st Street, divided into two condominium apartments. On the other side of the house, and enjoying warm and friendly relations with my aunt, were the Najeeb Halaby family. Najeeb later became the CEO of Pan Am and—much later—his daughter Lisa became the queen of Jordan. I met "Queen Noor" many years later in Amman, and we reminisced about life in Georgetown in the early '50s, including the very friendly black poodle they'd had in those days.

At any rate, one October weekend in 1951, while living in my aunt's condo, I went back to Hastings to visit my mother, who, as always, had been supportive of the career decisions I'd made. We had a good visit, and I was about to depart for my return trip to Washington, when my mother checked me out: "Do you have a clean handkerchief, do you have your wallet, do you have your train ticket?"

I had the handkerchief—but my wallet and ticket were missing. We searched the house for more than an hour and finally found my wallet under the fringe of a chair in a room that I did not remember having entered during my entire visit.

I was annoyed that I'd missed the New York-to-Washington train for which I had bought the ticket. The connecting train into New York was inconveniently timed, and I realized I was due for a very late arrival in Washington.

As I said good-bye to my mother, I speculated that I might meet a beautiful blonde on the train. No such luck, I sat next to a drunken man in a packed car, on a very unpleasant trip. I arrived at Washington's Union Station around midnight and headed for the station's west end, where taxis could be found.

A flood of people were competing for a few taxis, but after several minutes I heard a driver call out "Georgetown!" I rushed over and was told to get in the front seat. I stuck my head in the taxi to see three men stuffed in the back seat and the front seat, too, occupied—by a stunning young woman with bundles in her lap. I squeezed in beside her and was instantly smitten and terribly anxious to make a good impression.

My beauteous companion and I were crammed so close together that it was hard to get a good look at her without craning my neck and appearing to be some sort of goofball. But I saw she had shoulder-length chestnut brown hair, great cheekbones and sparkling brown eyes.

Small talk ensued, but the closest we came to identifying ourselves was to cite the colleges from which we had just graduated, Middlebury and Williams, and to assert that we both worked for "the government."

Luckily, my lovely seat companion was the first to be delivered to her door. I helped her and her bundles out of the car and carefully noted her address. I was impressed by how tall she was, almost 5 feet 11 inches. We smiled and said good-bye and, when I got to my aunt's house, I rushed to my room and wrote: "UNKNOWN! On Thomas Jefferson Street." I wanted very much to see her again, but had not wanted in any way to make our chance encounter seem like a pick-up, by blurting my name or by asking for hers.

I had a car, a pale yellow 1949 Chevy convertible, and I drove past her house every time I could. We had two brief encounters on the street and finally bumped into each other in a CIA library, where I asked: "May I introduce myself?"

"Please do," she replied. And thus began the defining relationship of my life, which continues joyously to this day.

Our first date was a drive out into the Virginia countryside, and we wound up eating at the Orient Restaurant, which was fitting since we later lived almost twenty years in Asia. It turned out that both Meg Curry and I worked for CIA, and that she outranked me, having studied Russian at Middlebury.

It also turned out that I had seen her picture in the *New York Times* when she was one of the six finalists for homecoming queen at a Middlebury Winter Carnival. I clearly remember looking at that picture during a socially desolate period in my undergraduate life and wondering why I never met such beautiful women.

Well, at last I had.

Meg and I dated over the next several months, in the course of which Meg met my mother. My arctic survival training interrupted the courtship.

Then my first overseas assignment suddenly arose, and I had to say a very difficult good-bye. There were four of us on that dismal night. Bill Everett, my college roommate and lifelong friend, was visiting Washington, and Meg had arranged a date for him with Sally, one of her Agency friends. Meg was staying that night at Sally's apartment on MacArthur Boulevard, and there on the sidewalk I had to say a sad and most unsatisfactory farewell.

I might have done better had there been just the two of us. As it was, I was stiff and inarticulate. On the way to my aunt's house, where Bill and I were staying, he tried to tell me that I had done all right—but I knew I hadn't.

I knew other men would pursue Meg—and, indeed, during the fourteen months I was away, Meg rejected proposals by a minister, a naval officer, a Southern aristocrat, and a man who wanted to make her into a nightclub singer.

I had no idea when or if I might return, and the night I said farewell to Meg was one of the low points of my life.

But my mother did me another great service by becoming friends with Meg when they met in Washington. I have a feeling that made it easier for Meg to wait for me.

Within two months of my departure for Asia, the dangerous operation in Vietnam to which I'd been assigned had been exposed as a fraud, and I was sent to Saipan for a two-year tour. With my future more secure, I began to write to Meg in a serious tone, and after a year on Saipan, in May 1953, I paid my way back to New York and immediately asked her to marry me, which involved going to live on Saipan.

Meg accepted, and we were married on July 4, 1953. I will never forget the dazzling smile Meg gave me as she entered St. Stephen's Church on our wedding day. She continues to light up my life, and ours is a relationship that grows deeper and richer with the passage of time. I am truly blessed, and somehow believe that our meeting "was meant to be."

A few weeks after our wedding, Meg and I returned to Saipan together, on a Pan Am Boeing 377 Stratocruiser. The Stratocruiser had double beds and a cocktail lounge downstairs. Ah, the good old days when everyone on a plane went First Class.

But in that pre-jet era, the flight to Saipan was a lengthy one. From San Francisco it took six hours to Honolulu, where we spent a night. The next day we flew to Wake Island, where we refueled, and then went on to Guam, where we were to change planes.

While landing on Guam, our Stratocruiser was misdirected onto a narrow taxi lane meant only for jet fighters. As a result, an intruding guy wire neatly clipped off our left wingtip. Meg and I were in the compartment directly behind the flight deck. I saw the wingtip drop to the ground, but the crew did not. I would think I am probably the only passenger in Pan Am's long history to have had the opportunity to tell a Pan Am pilot that his plane's left wingtip has been cut off.

The pilots were astonished, embarrassed, and furious with the control tower. The other passengers had to wait on Guam for several days until a spare wingtip could be flown out and attached. There was no proper hotel on Guam at the time, and we spent the night in cots, on a puddled concrete floor in a leaky airport hangar that had been drenched by a nearby typhoon.

Fortunately for us, we able to leave the next day on the short flight to Saipan, along with a number of local natives with their chickens and piglets, in the belly of a U.S. Navy patrol aircraft. Meg made a sensational entrance on Saipan, wearing a suit, hat, and gloves. I was so proud and happy to introduce her to my island friends, who had had to put up with me the previous year as a somewhat grumpy bachelor. Lucy Blanton, then married to a CIA officer, greeted us with particular warmth and remains a close family friend.

I'm not sure exactly how that clipped wingtip on the Stratocruiser shaped my views as an intelligence officer—but I'm sure that it did in some way. You learned in those days to keep your eyes open. The technology was cruder, the chance for human error always there.

Saipan is a beautiful island, and has the most northern coral reef in the world. A bloody battle in World War II had taken place there in 1944, and in 1953 the island and its environs were still littered with the detritus of war: half-sunken ships, rusting tanks, and, in the deep jungle, skeletons of fallen Japanese defenders. Unexploded ordnance was a danger, making some areas off-limits. We lived in a Quonset hut just off a beach where the Japanese had made one of the final "banzai charges" of the war. The sound of the surf was always with us, and we grew to love it.

During my first year on Saipan, I had lived in a Bachelor Officers Quarters (BOQ) right on the beach. I remember going to bed on my 25th birthday, December 5, 1952, and having my first intimations of mortality as I heard the surf pounding in, as it always had, and always would. I had not heard from Meg for a bit and was worried that I might lose her. I felt very small and ephemeral and lonely. It was totally different once Meg joined me.

6

A Glimpse of the Infinite from an Idaho Blue Jay

Earlier, during our paramilitary training, none of us had any clear idea of where we would be assigned, or what we would be given to do. Following our weeks at Fort Benning, we returned to the temporary buildings along the Reflecting Pool, ramshackle remnants from World War I and World War II, to find out what our futures might hold.

I ranked well in the training we had gone through and had stated, whenever possible, that I wanted to go to Asia, "where the action was." I was thus disappointed to learn that I was to study Bulgarian in preparation for taking over an undefined job in a large military warehouse in Europe. There followed a period of several weeks wherein I started to study Bulgarian, while making it clear that I wanted to be assigned to Asia.

My questioning of my future in Europe and my repeated expressions of hope for an Asian assignment had stirred my superiors. In early 1952, I was told that I was to attend arctic survival training in Idaho. I still am not sure whether this was a punishment for complaining or a reward for my performance at Fort Benning. In any case, off I went.

About twenty other trainees and I were flown into an air base at Mountain Home, Idaho, and introduced to our instructors, a very tough and capable-looking lot. We were issued snowshoes and sleeping bags, with which we were to become intimately acquainted over the next three weeks. Our first few days were spent in tepees made out of parachutes, placed by the side of one of the Payette lakes in northern Idaho. We cut pine and balsam boughs to lie on, and as soon as we learned to control the smoke vent at the apex of our tepees, we were quite comfortable.

Those days were quite idyllic, as we tried to learn how to make snares to catch rabbits, and how to fish through the ice on the lake. We also learned how to handle ourselves on snowshoes and were told that we would soon be living in snow way over our heads.

Within a week, about three or four of our instructors took us off into the mountains on snowshoes, carrying everything upon which we would depend to survive, including a semiedible substance that our instructors referred to as "pemmican."

One of our group was a socialite from Long Island named Irving. How or why he got into our group we never knew, but we all grew to like him immensely. He had a great sense of humor, was in terrible physical shape, and had a large towel from the Piping Rock Club, which he'd brought along to add "a touch of class" to what he'd predicted would be "a rather grubby" experience.

He was right.

One night around a campfire, Irving regaled us with stories of his mother's semiannual crisis, which came in the fall when she moved her family and staff to Florida from the Hamptons, with good reason, and back to Long Island in the spring. This involved the opening and shutting of large estates and the shipping of the staff to and fro, so that the family would not have to lift a finger. Apparently, she never got the sequencing quite right.

We were divided into groups of three or four. Each group had half a parachute to be used for shelter, and an axe with which to cut firewood. Soon after we left the lakeshore, our trail led steeply upwards, and snow began to fall. Irving fell far behind. As dusk approached, we were allowed to stop and were told to make shelters out of our half parachutes, to build fires, and to heat snow water in the large tin cans that we'd been provided.

We were in snow that was 15 to 20 feet deep, the wind was blowing, and visibility was slight. Before we could strike a match, we had to cut six logs and lay three of them east-to-west and three north-to-south. On these, we built our fires. These two-layered wooden bases kept our fires from melting the underlying snow and sinking deep below the surface.

After we had spread our parachutes over protecting pine branches, packed down the snow, cut logs for our fire bases, made fires, and heated water in our tin cans, Irving came staggering into camp, proclaiming in a loud voice: "I'm a surviving fuck!"

We sat him down and gave him hot water to drink, and later some pemmican. Pulling out his Piping Rock Club towel, with tears running down his cheeks, Irving pronounced his meal the best thing he had ever tasted. As he revived, even Irving began to laugh.

After another day of climbing, we reached the shore of a small lake, high up in the Payette Mountains. Here we tried to put into practice what we'd learned about building rabbit snares and fishing through the ice. The idea was to learn to ingeniously use material we had with us when we had to parachute from our falling plane, such as a safety pin for a fishhook and pieces of parachute cord for the snares. (I wasn't sure that grown men regularly carried safety pins with them but thought it best not to push the point.)

The rabbit snares were particularly frustrating. We made nooses at the end of long pieces of parachute cords, tied the upper ends of the cords to small trees that we bent over a trail, and then tried to design trigger mechanisms that would hold the open noose in place across the trail until a rabbit came hopping along, tripped the trigger mechanism, and got yanked into the air, with the noose around its neck.

Our instructors actually made snares and trigger mechanisms that seemed to work, but they involved smooth pieces of elaborately carved wood "made on earlier survival trips" that were far beyond our abilities to produce.

The instructors expertly showed us how to use our axes to cut holes in the lake ice, and how to dangle a safety pin at the end of thread down into the water, baited with a piece of fat from our pemmican, and wiggling seductively. But none of us ever caught anything—nor did we ever see an instructor catch anything, either.

They seemed, however, to be enjoying a more elaborate diet than we trainees were. We crunched away on our pemmican three times a day, and soon all reached the conclusion that to be parachuted into twenty feet of snow, without snowshoes, an axe, a knife, matches, and a lot of high-protein candy bars, was certain death.

We each had been given the latest thing in arctic sleeping bags and a rubberized ground sheet. At night we were instructed to strip naked, put our clothes on the ground sheet, get into our sleeping bags, and lie on top of our clothes.

This actually worked, and we slept well—except when having

to answer a call of nature in the frigid darkness, which involved getting out of the sleeping bags totally naked and putting on snow-shoes in order to get out of the tented area. In the mornings, our boots were frozen solid and had to be thawed out over fires we made while still half in our sleeping bags.

But morale was not bad, as the country was stunningly beauti-ful, a semi-humorous bond had developed between our instructors and us, and we were surviving. I even felt a certain regret as our training came to an end. We had learned something more of our-selves.

I remember climbing to the top of a ridge that opened up a view of lakes and mountains, all covered with fresh-fallen snow so beautiful that it overwhelmed my senses. I literally could not take it in until a single blue jay landed on a pine branch over my head, shaking snow down on my upturned face. Suddenly, I saw it all, through that one bird and that single branch.

In later years, in Asia, as I developed an appreciation of ink painting, I realized that what I had experienced on that Idaho ridge-top, was what has inspired Asian artists down through the centuries: to represent the infinite by a depiction of the finite. That alone was worth the entire arctic survival experience.

7

Jack Downey's Tragic Mission

On my first day back in Washington from idyllic Idaho, I felt a strong sense of claustrophobia as I walked into the rickety, two-story temporary office building along the Reflecting Pool. The corridors were narrow and windowless, the small offices were crowded with safes and desks, and the walls were covered with old maps.

I went directly to my superior and said that unless I was given a better assignment, preferably in Asia, I was going to resign. Things moved quickly after that, and I was sent to meet the Vietnam desk officer to discuss a new job.

The time was March 1952. The French still considered Vietnam part of their colonial empire, and they were fighting Ho Chi Minh's forces, the Viet Minh, in an attempt to maintain colonial control. It was two years before the French had their seminal defeat at Dien Bien Phu. The United States was being drawn into this conflict in support of the French.

My meeting with the desk officer was memorable. He rather sneeringly asked me: "Are you afraid to jump?"

Given my training at Fort Benning, I felt this was not only a rude question but a stupid one. I responded, "Are you going to give me a parachute?"

He told me not to be a "wise-ass." I told him I had jumped eight times and was ready to do so again.

He then told me my new assignment was to fly to Bangkok, Thailand, where I was to pick up a group of North Vietnamese, whom I would train in sabotage and small unit tactics at a secret base. Following completion of this training, we would be parachuted into North Vietnam.

I knew of no direct American interest in Vietnam, and so I asked what our mission was to be. I was coldly told that I would be informed of that just before jumping into the jungle. I accepted the assignment on the spot.

Looking back at that incident, it seems in many ways utterly ridiculous. I spoke neither French nor Vietnamese, I knew nothing of Vietnam or its history, and I was far from a veteran saboteur or guerilla leader. But having agitated for an assignment "where the action was," there was no way I could have backed out of what had been offered me. Beyond that, the desk officer had cleverly provoked me by his first question, so that if I had refused the job, he would have simply said, "So, you are afraid to jump after all."

And, finally, that was the way things were in those early days of CIA. An attractive post-debutante in her mid-thirties was the Vietnam plans officer, and I had heard her say, a day or so earlier, that her "Vietnam plan" had been accepted and that a cocktail party was being given to celebrate the occasion. I was not invited to the party but am sure that the plan's formulation and acceptance had caused me to be offered my new job.

So off I went, first to Japan, and then to Bangkok, where I picked up a group of very apprehensive and totally untrained Vietnamese, with whom I had no way of communicating. We were in an unheated C-46 transport plane, and they were wearing flimsy cotton clothes. As we gained altitude and flew north, it got very cold in the plane, and I gave them every bit of clothing I had in my luggage to try to keep them warm. They looked childlike, huddled in my shirts that were far too large for them.

They were appreciative, but still shivered and huddled together for warmth. They were all very young, and, we soon learned, were part of the Vietnamese ethnic community in Thailand, had never set foot in Vietnam, and had no idea of what lay ahead of them. I never learned how they had been motivated to get into that plane and fly north.

Those were wild and woolly days in CIA, and the Vietnam operation for which I'd been recruited was thus exposed as a fraud. It turned out that a corrupt principal agent had hoodwinked CIA officers in Bangkok and had "taken the money and run." The plan, whatever it had been, had to be canceled. I never learned any of its objectives: what targets were to be attacked, or how American interests would have been advanced by such a hare-brained scheme. But as a result of the plan's cancellation, my life expectancy increased, and I was sent to the agency's large training base on the island of Saipan.

I already had very mixed feelings about the CIA people I was encountering as a new recruit. I was comfortable with those who had a real track record, either with OSS or the U.S. military. I had been very much put off by some of our trainers, who did not seem to have done much actual intelligence work but acted as if they had. Then there was a group of men three or four years older than I, like the Vietnam desk officer, who were in mid-level positions of some influence, but showed no particular qualifications for being there.

We new employees were told not to ask questions about what senior people had done in previous assignments, as this would be in violation of the "need to know" principle. I came to feel that in many cases this was a camouflage for incompetence. I was also struck by how quickly many of my fellow paramilitary trainees left the Agency after finishing jump school at Fort Benning.

On Saipan, the same patterns seemed evident. On my very first night on the island, I took part in a poker game, where the senior man present got drunk, lost heavily on several hands to me, and angrily and unsteadily left the game. When the entire game broke up, an hour or so later, we found that the departed loser had left his wallet on the floor. All the remaining players, as a group, went to his house (a Quonset hut) to return the wallet to his rather suspicious wife. This man turned out to be my direct superior in the paramilitary training department, and I took care not to play poker with him again.

The two best senior men on Saipan were the late Joe Lazarsky, with a valorous OSS record fighting the Japanese in the jungles of Burma with the Kachins, and the late Colonel Gil Layton, with a variety of Army intelligence work that well suited his personality and his assignment to CIA. I learned positively from them. From a number of my other early CIA supervisors, I learned how not to do it.

We were training teams of agents who were to be infiltrated

one way or another, into hostile territories around the world. Most of the teams were Chinese or Korean, but we also had occasional groups from other areas, whom we treated with particular care and high degrees of security.

My favorites were the Koreans, mostly farm boys who regarded semi-tropical Saipan as a paradise. During the war, Korea was, with good reason, referred to as "frozen Chosen." The Koreans took well to their training, and had great senses of humor. I knew nothing of the missions on which they were to be sent, and could only hope that some of them survived.

During my bachelor year on Saipan, I had to make several trips to Japan. On one of those trips, in November 1952, I encountered Jack Downey, with whom I had gone through CIA training the year before.

Jack was full of excitement. The day after our meeting, he was to get on a plane that would drop supplies to an agent team, recently parachuted into Manchuria, that had sent an SOS message that its supplies had been lost in the snow. Besides dropping supplies, the plane would seek to withdraw a single agent by use of the "air snatch" technique, which involved yanking a man into the air by diving low and hooking a long rubberized rope attached to his back.

With another Agency friend, I had dinner that night with Downey at a Japanese restaurant near Tokyo and clearly remember his enthusiasm, and my muted sense of envy. I was also worried about him, knowing the dangers involved in the flight he was undertaking, but I tried not to show it.

The Japanese restaurant where we three ate was a colorful place, with spicy food and attractive waitresses. Jack was in high spirits, as he was at last "going to see some action." He was a big man, had played guard on the Yale football team, and had been a heavyweight wrestler. He was also highly intelligent, with a great sense of humor.

Our mutual friend, a Japanese-American (Nisei) was fluent in Japanese, and through him we engaged in earthy dialogue with our waitresses. It was a happy evening that all three of us clearly recall.

I returned to Saipan, and several days later learned that

Downey's flight had been lost, with all aboard presumed to have been killed. This news hit me hard , because of my admiration for Downey and because I knew and liked the pilot and co-pilot of the plane. Six months later, the Chinese announced that Downey's plane had been downed, that he was alive, and that he had been sentenced to life imprisonment. The Chinese also captured and imprisoned another young CIA officer, Richard Fecteau.

The dinner I'd had with Jack Downey in the Japanese restaurant would be his last meal in freedom for over twenty years.

The Chinese announcement made evident that the agent team had been captured immediately after being dropped in by parachute, that the SOS message requesting supplies had been sent under duress, and that the drop zone was a trap, ringed by heavy caliber guns where the resupply plane was shot down.

All agent teams had been trained in the use of "safety and danger signals" to indicate the presence or absence of duress when a clandestine message was sent. CIA launched some sort of investigation to determine the basis on which the decision had been made to send in the resupply flight. The results of this investigation were never made clear to me, and my assumption, widely held by others as well, was that signals within the SOS message had been ambiguous at best, and that the local decision had been to send the plane in, since it was so rare that anything was heard from agent teams after they had been dropped in.

As a result of this decision, several people on the plane, including its pilot and co-pilot, were killed. I knew the base chief responsible for making the decision to send in the resupply flight. I also knew that Jack Downey had been clamoring to get on the ill-fated flight. The base chief was never held responsible for making a bad decision, and his career meandered on to an undistinguished end

In 1973, after over twenty years in custody, Jack Downey was finally released. He is happily married to a Chinese woman, and they have a son. Jack serves as a judge in the State of Connecticut and has never expressed to me any resentment of the decision by his superiors that cost him so many years of his life, perhaps because he knows how much he wanted to be a part of the rescue effort. He has had a courthouse named for him and is universally respected.

On June 15, 2010, my wife and I were invited to CIA Headquarters in Langley to see a film that CIA had produced on the Downey/Fecteau mission, with actors recreating what had occurred. Both Downey and Fecteau were present and were cheered to the echo in a packed auditorium. Director Leon Panetta paid them tribute, and the film did a fine job of showing what they had been up against in solitary confinement in a Chinese prison. The film is not to be shown publicly, but will be used for training and orientation purposes.

I was glad to see this tribute being paid to two men who had suffered as a direct result of poor decision-making by their superiors. I hope that CIA will continue to make this kind of admission.

I should add that in 1958, I was named as a CIA agent in a broadcast out of East Germany. I was part of a large group, all accused of doing Agency work, some of whom had nothing to do with CIA. I suspected that this information resulted from Chinese interrogation of survivors of the Downey-Fecteau crash. I later learned that this was exactly what had happened.

When I was on active duty, there was a great deal of misplaced nostalgia for "the good old days" of the 1950s and '60s, when the Agency's image was far better than its actual capabilities. In the late 1970s, I had the job of orienting new CIA trainees headed for operational work on what the Agency's evolution had been. I used several of my own experiences to illustrate to them how much more professional the Agency had become since the early 1950s.

Today, CIA's image is at best a very mixed bag, but I believe it is accomplishing far more, under difficult and dangerous circumstances, than it did at any time in the past.

8

Happy Years in Japan

In late 1954, we learned that our next assignment was to be Japan. During our entire time in Japan I worked for CIA, which was an integral part of a massive American effort to help Japan rebuild after World War II and to become what it is today, a thriving, stable democracy that is a close and vital ally of the United States.

Our main opponent during my time in Japan was the Soviet Union. Moscow wanted desperately to pull Japan into its orbit, to help open up access to its remote eastern region, and, most probably, to gain revenge for its shattering defeat at the hands of Japan in the Russo-Japanese War of 1904–1905. The total failure of the Soviets to make an ally of Japan is a tribute to every American organization, military and civilian, that worked in Japan during its years as an emerging democracy. Equally important was Japan's emergence as a producer of world-class products, from automobiles to television sets to computers. And Japan's complete acceptance of American industrialist W. Edward Deming's emphasis on inspection and quality control was a key ingredient of its quick rise to economic prominence.

Meg and I arrived at Haneda Airport in Tokyo on a cold, gray day in early January 1955. We stayed at the Imperial Hotel, Frank Lloyd Wright's famous stone structure in downtown Tokyo—one of the few buildings to survive the 1923 Tokyo earthquake. It immediately cheered us. Its inner walls of rough stone somehow had warmth, and a sense of "friendly enclosure" was present everywhere in the hotel. I have not found that in any other building I have ever stayed in. Perhaps that was part of Frank Lloyd Wright's genius.

We located a small, western-style house at the edge of huge Aoyama Cemetery. We had a black Volkswagen "bug" with a red interior, small enough to navigate the narrow streets in our neighborhood. We loved our time in Aoyama. Our narrow house sat on a hillside. With one tatami room and many sliding doors, it was flexibly constructed, swaying and rattling noisily in the frequent small earthquakes that were a part of Tokyo lives. It had a lawn along one side, some flowering plants, but no trees to speak of.

The Japanese have a way of building seclusion and privacy into small places, and our house was an example of that Japanese talent. Our only "central heating" was a kerosene heater. When our first daughter Lucy arrived a year after our arrival, we had her crib in an upper hallway, outside our bedroom—the warmest place in the house.

Shortly after our arrival in Tokyo, I started my study of Japanese at the Naganuma School, up a hill in nearby Shibuya. The school was a three-story cement building in a walled compound, with a small parking lot. My classes were on Monday and Thursday evenings from 7:30 to 9 p.m. My teacher for the first two years was Tsuruko Asano, a small, bespectacled woman, who became a personal friend of the family and later became head of the school.

Miss Asano had a great sense of humor and made frequent references in Japanese to the large size of my feet. One of Ms. Asano's favorite teaching devices for beginners was a sentence in English that in Japanese clearly indicated the role of the important connective words *wa, ga, de, ni,* and *o*. Thus, one of the first phrases I learned to say fluently in Japanese was "John Booth shot President Lincoln in the head with a pistol." I was pleased to be able to say this correctly, but did not find many social occasions in which to use it.

I supplemented my education by strolling the streets of Tokyo and seeking out interesting bars. Particularly in the mid-1950s, the Japanese were delighted to encounter Americans interested enough in their country to try to learn to speak their language. A close friend, a burly Amherst graduate who was also studying at Naganuma, often accompanied me. We frequented certain bars, and the people working and drinking there helped us learn to speak colloquial Japanese.

In those days, job opportunities for young women were few and far between. Becoming an airline stewardess was perhaps the *ne plus ultra* of career opportunities. As a result, we often encountered graduates of Japan's best universities working as bar hostesses. Often their fathers had been killed in the war, and they claimed to be working to help their widowed mothers. In our encounters, we met Japanese men who admitted to having taken part in the war but never one who said he had fought against us.

In any case, the after-class discussions in a variety of bars were very helpful to me linguistically, historically, and politically. After four years of this, I was rated at the level of those who had studied Japanese full-time for two years. Being able to speak Japanese fairly fluently in Japan was one of my life's great pleasures, particularly on hikes in the mountains, on ski trips, in hot baths, and in countless bars and restaurants.

Shortly after our arrival in Japan we joined the Tokyo Lawn Tennis Club. The club, over half Japanese, had many foreign members from the embassies and business community and played a central role in our social lives.

As a child with TB, I had played no tennis at all until I was about sixteen, and then played infrequently until my years on Saipan. I was an inept player when we joined the TLTC, but its seven clay courts were easy to play on and the Japanese were friendly. I was tall, with an odd, left-handed serve, and I improved steadily. The club was nestled into a central area of Tokyo. Its simple, one-story clubhouse, with a partly shaded porch fronting the courts, was a dynamo of tennis activity, and we truly loved being members.

Every month or so, the club held intra-club tournaments that were a challenge and great fun. Crown Prince Akihito—now the emperor of Japan—sometimes took part in these tournaments, to the great pleasure of all the club's Japanese members. I was told that the Imperial Household Agency, a long-standing arm of the Japanese government, played a highly restrictive role, dictating what the crown prince could and could not do. At the TLTC, he was much freer.

In 1957, the crown prince met a lovely commoner, Michiko Shoda, on a tennis court in Karuizawa, a mountain resort in Japan. They began to appear together at the TLTC and, once or twice, I played with them. I had met Michiko previously when she was the friend and tennis partner of Saigo Takayoshi, with whom I often played. (Saigo was a direct descendent of Saigo Takamori, Japan's last and most famous samurai warrior, who had died in battle in 1877.)

In November 1957, Michiko's engagement to the crown prince was announced. It caused a great stir, as the crown prince had been expected to marry into one of the many families with a blood relationship to the emperor. Michiko appeared on the cover of *Time* magazine when the engagement was announced. I had a copy of that issue of the magazine in my hand one day at the TLTC to show to the members. Michiko unexpectedly came to the club, and I gave her my copy of the magazine. She thanked me very sweetly. I often wonder if she still has it.

I remember hearing from someone who knew Elizabeth Grey Vining, the crown prince's tutor in English from 1946 to 1950, that she had learned that Emperor Hirohito had for many years kept a Paris Metro ticket stub from a visit in the 1920s, because it reminded him of one of his freest days. Ms. Vining was the only foreigner invited to the crown prince's wedding.

The following spring, Shinzo Koizumi, a man I admired greatly, came to the TLTC to watch the crown prince play in a tournament. Koizumi, a noted scholar and former president of Keio University, had been the crown prince's academic tutor for many years. He had gruesome facial scars caused by burns he'd suffered trying to rescue books from his library after one of the American fire bombings of Tokyo. Those bombings, almost never discussed in America, caused many more deaths than the atomic bombings of Hiroshima and Nagasaki.

Koizumi invited me to sit with him as we watched the crown prince. After a long silence, he turned to me and said in English: "I think he'll be all right." I was surprised by this frank comment about the crown prince, and listened with great interest as Koizumi went on to say that since the imperial family needed to be less isolated from the Japanese populace, it would be a healthy thing to bring into the mix Michiko Shoda, who'd had no previous ties to the imperial household. I believe Koizumi was right, but the restrictive life under the sway of the Imperial Household Agency has been very hard on the empress.

In the spring of 1957, when we returned to Tokyo after taking home leave, we wound up in a large Japanese-style house in Yoyogi Hatsudai, where we lived happily for almost five years. It had a lovely garden, a large living room–dining room, and a Japanese wing with tatami floors, where my mother stayed during two of her four visits to Tokyo. During that period, we inherited from a departing friend an elderly dachshund named Bismarck. He and our children loved to play, both in and out of the house. In the garden, something was in bloom almost every month of the year. A particular joy was a plum tree that produced enough fruit, with the aid of our Japanese maid, for us to make plum wine.

Alison was born in May 1960, at Seiboin Hospital, with Dr. Eitel, a German refugee from China, and French nurses in attendance. Their procedures were much less regimented than those at the Army hospital, where Lucy had been born in January 1956, and Meg and Alison were quickly released. It was a particularly beautiful spring that year, and Alison was a joyous addition to our family, but her birth came at a tumultuous time in Japan and in the world.

I remember driving home from Seiboin Hospital after seeing newborn Alison and hearing on my car radio of the Soviet Union's shooting down of Gary Powers in his U-2 spy plane. Their fury at his penetration of their air space did not bode well for the future.

I thought: "What a dangerous world this child has been born into."

May and June of 1960 were marked by large demonstrations in Tokyo, protesting the negotiation of a new American security treaty with Japan. Douglas MacArthur 2nd was our ambassador. He was a nephew of General Douglas MacArthur, who had been in command of the U.S. occupation of Japan after its surrender in the summer of 1945. Ambassador MacArthur was instrumental in negotiating a new security treaty with Prime Minister Nobusuke Kishi. Though the U.S. Congress ratified the treaty, Japanese leftists in general, the Japan Socialist Party, and a trade union federation in particular strongly opposed ratification by the Japanese Diet.

A visit to Japan scheduled for summer 1960 by President Dwight Eisenhower had to be canceled. A huge demonstration near Haneda Airport had trapped his press secretary, James Hagerty, in his car. Sent to Tokyo to plan the president's visit, Hagerty had to be pulled out by helicopter.

Such demonstrations, which were largely peaceful, also brought down Prime Minister Nobusuke Kishi. Hayato Ikeda, a better man, replaced Kishi and served as prime minister for more than four years. Japan eventually ratified the security pact, and Prime Minister Ikeda pronounced it of great benefit to both countries.

One day during the protests, when Meg and I were in our Volkswagen on a shopping trip to a U.S. Army commissary, we came to a main street totally blocked by a marching demonstration made up of students, teachers, and trade union members, all carrying banners. But when the demonstrators noticed our car, with its American license plate, without our asking for any special treatment, they stopped the marchers, and courteously waved us across the street.

The central province of Nagano, with its beautiful Japanese Alps, frequently drew us out of Tokyo, for hiking in the summer and skiing in the winter. In the summer of 1958, we climbed Mt. Fuji, Japan's highest mountain at 12,388 feet, in neighboring Shizuoka province. Fuji is one of the world's most perfect volcanic cones, and the Japanese have been painting pictures of it ever since they were able to put ink to paper.

The mountain looks deceptively peaceful, but it is very dangerous, with a short climbing season of only two months in the summer. For the rest of the year, swirling winds, heavy rain, and sudden blizzards make any ascent of Mt. Fuji unpleasant at best and, often, extremely perilous.

In the early 1950s, several young CIA officers attempted a winter climb. One of them, a man I knew well, was wise enough to stop at a cabin on the slope halfway to the summit when gale force winds and blowing snow made it hard to see and difficult to stay erect. Others, not so wise, continued to climb.

My friend was huddled in the fireless cabin when he heard a heavy thump on its roof. Going outside to investigate, he found the broken body of one of his companions, who had been blown off his feet and slid with increasing speed down the icy slope, until a rock outcropping had thrown him fatally into the air. He had fallen several hundred feet.

The Japanese like to say that only a fool never climbs Fuji, and only a bigger fool climbs it twice. Meg and I would agree with that statement. The climb up, on a windy summer night, was marked by the rattle of tin cans blowing down the mountain's slope and by the pervasive smell of urine. Tens of thousands of Japanese ascend the mountain during its climbing season, and in 1958, there were no public toilets to speak of along the way.

Our climb did have one esthetic aspect. As we neared the summit, we heard the sweet tone of small bells. Looking down, we saw a long column of Buddhist pilgrims, clad all in white, each carrying a bell.

Our descent was great fun, as we were able to run and slide down long soft slopes of volcanic ash, where a fall was of no danger whatsoever. To this day, whenever I fly over Japan, I hope for a view of Fuji. And whenever I am able to see its beautiful cone, dark grey in summer or glistening white in winter, it gives me great pleasure to recall our climb and the satisfaction of reaching its summit.

I continued my study of Japanese through our first seven years in Japan. After four years of study, I graduated from the Naganuma School and thereafter switched to having tutors come to our house. By far the best of these tutors was a Mr. Honda, who had been a mountain climber in his youth and shared my love of Nagano prefecture. Under his tutelage, my Japanese was as good as it ever got.

One morning Honda *sensei* (teacher) gave me a lesson I never will forget. He said "Ask me a simple question and I will give you twenty different answers that will show you how I feel about you, how I feel about your question, whether I think you are superior or inferior to me in social stature, and whether our relationship has been harmed or strengthened by the asking of your question."

My question was: "Shall we go to Hakone?"

In response, Honda rattled off at least twenty answers. In so doing, he gave me a glimpse into the social intricacies of Japanese that make it such a subtle language, born of a rigid caste system, where the careful choice of a verb can make it clear whether a speaker feels he is superior or inferior to the person to whom he is speaking. To speak Japanese well as a foreigner is not hard to do, and the Japanese are forgiving of grammatical errors, which they attribute to the ignorance of *gaijin*, outside people. But to speak Japanese with a full knowledge of its social subtleties is something very few foreigners ever approach, much less achieve. I believe the intricacy of the Japanese language is a main reason the Japanese people are so hard for foreigners to fully understand.

As my time as Honda's pupil drew to a close, we invited him and his wife to dinner at our home. After some thought, he accepted. Mrs. Honda was an elegant, silver-haired lady dressed in a dove-gray kimono. She seemed to enjoy the occasion immensely. Honda later told me that it was the only time she'd ever been in a foreigner's home, and one of the few times she'd been out for dinner in the evening.

I was as close to Honda as to any Japanese I met during my Japanese years. In 1959, he and his wife came to see us off as we departed by ship from Yokoyama to return home for leave. He enriched my life deeply, through our shared love of the mountains in Nagano, and by the insights into the Japanese character that he gave me through his teaching.

In January 1962, I left Tokyo ahead of my family to visit South Vietnam in preparation for my next assignment in Washington. Meg, my mother who'd been visiting us, and Lucy and Alison joined me in Saigon, and we returned to America via India and Europe.

Highlights of the next two years were the purchase of our home on Keokuk Street in Bethesda and the birth of our son on July 4, 1963. Meg had had a tenuous pregnancy, and we were quietly celebrating our tenth wedding anniversary with a family gathering at the home of her uncle and aunt, Stanley and Mildred Fike. Meg suddenly went into labor and had to be rushed to the Columbia Hospital for Women in Washington, D.C. Our son quickly emerged, weighing in at two-and-a-half pounds. He was almost three months premature.

When I asked the doctor what our baby's chances were, he just shook his head. I immediately began thinking of a name and came up with John Phinney Gregg. There had been eight John Phinneys in a row on my mother's side of the family, including Captain John Phinney, the first settler of Gorham, Maine, in 1736. I felt strongly that the atavistic pull of that name would help John survive.

The next morning, Ted Eastman, our Episcopal minister, whom we had first met in Tokyo, came to the hospital to baptize John. He had to put on full surgical attire and a face mask to be allowed into the incubator area where John lay. Meg's father and I were watching through a large window, with tears streaming down our faces. Meg was there too, in a wheelchair, looking radiantly beautiful, with a smile on her face, and not a tear to be seen. She had a son!

John had to stay in the incubator for two months, until he had gained enough weight and strength to "come outside." He was greatly aided by a devoted German nurse named Zubenburber. She said she knew he would survive by the strength of his hand, which he would wrap around her little finger when she picked up a small bottle of milk and reached into the incubator.

After two years in Washington, and two in Burma, in the summer of 1966 we were suddenly ordered to return to Japan. A major operational embarrassment had taken place, which caused CIA to judge that it would be well to bring back to Tokyo a familiar figure. I had developed good relations with a wide spectrum of Japanese, official and unofficial from 1955 to 1962, and we were glad to return. We lived in an apartment near Roppongi in the center of Tokyo. Our friends at the TLTC warmly welcomed us back and were delighted to meet our son John.

In 1966, our patterns of life in Tokyo were different than they had been almost five years earlier. We were older, I was considerably more senior, our children were in school, and our Japanese friends had become more influential. I was elected to the board of governors at the TLTC shortly after our return. We continued to hike and ski in Nagano prefecture, but our circle of friends quickly broadened to include more of the diplomatic community.

Our fourth floor apartment was comfortable, with four bedrooms, a balcony, and a great view. On a clear day, when the wind had cleared away the smog, we could stand on the balcony and see Mt. Fuji in the distance.

I resumed my study of Japanese. During my time in Washington and Burma, I had entirely stopped reading Japanese and learning new kanji, and those skills had badly faded. In my final three years in Tokyo, I concentrated only on my spoken Japanese.

As a part of this process, I checked out some of the bars I had frequented as a Naganuma School student. Many had closed, but one in Shibuya, the Bullpen, was still functioning. Its senior hostess had been a strikingly beautiful Japanese woman with whom I very much enjoyed talking. When I returned to the bar, I was delighted to see that she was still there.

She remembered me and said in Japanese, "I haven't seen you lately; where have you been?"

I replied, "It's been more than four-and-a-half years since I was last here."

She shook her head, and her face grew sad. She said, "My life is always the same. I thought it had only been a month since I saw you." She suddenly appeared older, and we looked at each other in mute recognition of the fact that her life was monotonous and empty. I never returned to the Bullpen, as there no longer seemed to be anything to say.

In those years, the Australians still dominated tennis. Once a year, in the summer, they came to Tokyo to play in a tournament and always practiced at the TLTC, drawing a knowledgeable, enthusiastic crowd, which cheered and clapped.

One year, Roy Emerson, Ken Rosewall, and Lew Hoad all came. Emerson in particular was always jovial and approachable and on one day offered to "have a hit" with some of the watching TLTC members. To my delight, I was asked to play, and as the weakest member of our foursome, was partnered with Emerson.

Our opponents were Japan's Davis Cup coach and a young Japanese player who had just missed being selected for the Japanese Davis Cup team. He was very anxious to prove how good he was, which Emerson instantly sensed. As we changed ends, Emerson said to me in his wonderful Aussie accent: "I must say that bloke takes this all very seriously."

Emerson's skills as a doubles player were sublime, and whenever he could reach a ball he utterly defeated the young Japanese player's attempt to win even a point. After a few games "Emmo" suggested we change partners. My serve immediately came up, and on my first attempt, I managed to ace Emerson.

He dropped his racquet and clapped his hands, but thereafter I don't think I won a single point on my serve, as he paid me the compliment of taking me seriously. It was a great experience for me. I learned that day that the skills of the top players are at a level that we ordinary folk can hardly comprehend.

At the end of December 1967, I was invited to an all-male *sobetsu kai* (year-end party). One guest was a high-ranking member of Prime Minister Sato Eisaku's administration. As the evening progressed, and more drinks were consumed, the discussion shifted to American politics.

The Vietnam War was not going well for the United States, and President Lyndon Johnson was in trouble politically. I was asked whom I thought LBJ's Republican opponent for the presidency might be in the 1968 election. I suppose I predicted Richard Nixon would play that role. But what I remember saying was that I thought perhaps LBJ would choose not to run at all, given his awareness of the terrible impact of the Vietnam War on American society and his sense of responsibility for it.

A month later, on January 30, 1968, the Viet Cong launched their Tet offensive, which evolved into a large-scale military defeat for the North Vietnamese but was perceived in the United States as a repudiation of all of America's claims that victory was nearly at hand. On March 31, 1968, LBJ announced that he would not run for re-election. Late that night in our apartment, I received a telephone call from our ambassador, U. Alexis Johnson, asking me to come to his residence immediately.

The ambassador was a heavy hitter. He was one of the most senior serving Foreign Service officers in the world and had a distinguished record both in Asia and in Washington. His wife, a southerner, was hilarious—a great raconteur. The ambassador greeted me in his pajamas and said that he had received a stern call from Prime Minister Elsaku Sato asking why he had not been officially informed in advance of LBJ's decision not to run.

The ambassador said: "I told the prime minister I had been completely surprised by the president's decision." Sato responded that the embassy must have known what was coming as early as the end of December, because an American named Gregg had stated at that time that LBJ would not run. The ambassador now looked at me quizzically. I explained what had happened, what had been said, and who had been there.

Johnson laughed, patted me on the back, and said he understood completely. He was a sophisticated man, and we always got along well. Twenty-one years later, when he heard that I'd been nominated by President George H. W. Bush to be his ambassador to South Korea, Johnson's friendly note of congratulation said: "You were obviously tailor-designed for the promising but tortuous road that lies ahead there."

In the spring of 1968, Meg and I were invited to a garden party featuring the odd sport of duck-netting, held on the grounds of the Imperial Palace. This was an annual function, sponsored by the Imperial Household Agency. Swarms of people were there, wandering around the huge gardens or standing in line to shake the hand of our official host, a very senior Japanese official.

We were standing in line when a heavily accented voice spoke from behind us, saying, "Hello, Mr. and Mrs. Gregg." We turned and faced a Russian named Yuri Totrov, known to be with the KGB. He carried a camera and quickly took our picture, saying as he did so: "Such a lovely couple." As he scuttled away, we knew our picture was headed for KGB headquarters in Moscow.

About that time, I had another, completely different encounter with a Russian in Tokyo. We had learned through a third country that a young Russian diplomat wanted to defect to the United States. Our check of the diplomat's background did not show him to be of intrinsic intelligence value, but he was from a distinguished Russian family. So I was authorized to "check him out" and judge whether he should be accepted as a defector.

We had a long and increasingly friendly conversation. I asked the young man why he wanted to defect. He said he was fed up with the ineffective (and collective) leadership of Alexei Kosygin and Leonid Brezhnev and that he felt "Russia is going nowhere." He was clearly of no intelligence interest and was too idealistic to be recruited as an agent, so I spent a couple of hours persuading him to stay where he was and to work for change in Moscow. We parted as friends, and twenty years later, when the Berlin Wall came down, I thought of him with real satisfaction.

In 1994, while working at the Korea Society in New York, I received a letter from Mikio Haruna, the Kyodo News bureau chief in Washington, sending along two pictures Totrov had taken of us. Haruna said Totrov had been in Washington, had come to his office, and had asked him to send me the pictures as a signal that the Cold War was over. A few months later, I received a friendly phone call from Totrov, who was again in the United States as a security consultant. I told him how glad I was to have received his pictures and expressed the hope that our two countries could work constructively in the post–Cold War era. Totrov agreed and invited me to visit him when next I was in Moscow.

In June 1969, as our time in Tokyo approached its end, the TLTC gave us a farewell party, which was both delightful and nostalgic. We received an engraved silver plate, urging us to return to Japan. In many ways, we hated to leave. But it was time to move on, and we said good-bye to a decade that remains in the minds of the Gregg family as a happy and powerful period in our lives.

My most memorable farewell was much smaller and far less formal. I was invited by a prominent and influential Japanese friend to attend a farewell geisha party. I accepted his invitation, with no idea what would be involved. My prior experience had been entirely with Japanese hostesses in Western dress, who drank, danced, and sang with their guests. I had never been to a true geisha party.

My host picked me up in his large black car, and we were driven into the depths of the Yoshiwara district, a neighborhood of narrow alleys and traditional wooden buildings that since the days of ancient Edo had been the center of geisha life. When we got out of our car, a dark, covered rickshaw passed us, pulled by a loping man taking a geisha to her work or her assignation.

We entered an old, Japanese-style building, took off our shoes, and went upstairs to a large room on the second floor. There to greet us were four ladies in dark kimonos, seated on the tatami floor, smiling and friendly, not at all heavily made up, and all appearing to me to be at least sixty years old.

My host, seeing my surprise, laughed and said, "Relax, I think you are going to enjoy this."

Indeed, I did.

The ladies did not rise to greet us, but invited us to sit intimately among them on the floor. Sake was quickly served, and we began to converse in Japanese. The sake was top class, and it flowed. I was asked the usual questions about how long I had been in Japan, where I had learned to speak Japanese, and whether I had a wife and family.

I learned, as the evening progressed, that the ladies were all retired geisha, some quite famous. They had been forced back to work by a newly imposed antiprostitution law that had brought to an end the generous pensions on which they had depended. They must have resented this development, but gave no hint of that to me, and threw themselves into a highly successful effort to tease and entertain me.

As we conversed, the ladies' ages became completely irrelevant, banished by wit and charm honed for decades. They all were handsome, and I could see that, in youth, one or two of them had been radiantly beautiful. All had a great, risqué sense of humor and wickedly applied them to me. (Japanese humor is always at the expense of others, never directed at oneself.)

When the ladies realized that my Japanese was quite good, they began to ask each other questions about me in stage whispers, which they knew I could hear and understand. "Do you think that the size of his feet and the length of his nose have anything to do with the length of anything else?" one would ask another, with a slight rolling of her eyes.

A perfect response would have been for me to say, "I'm sorry, but I'm afraid it's more than any of you can handle." This would have evoked shrieks of laughter, but I did not have the wit or courage to say anything so appropriate, and probably mumbled something about the size of one part of my anatomy being unrelated to the size of any other part. One might then have said in response: "How unusual. I wonder if all foreigners are like that."

We later moved to a low table, where beautifully prepared food, sushi and sashimi, red, white, and yellow with fragrant, steaming broth were presented. The ladies continued to direct their fusillade of fun at me, as they speculated that the rather awkward manner in which I sat on the floor might have been caused by an erection. Nothing was sacred or off limits that evening.

At one point, two of the ladies read my palm, which allowed them to speculate colorfully to each other about my past and future, particularly as it related to the opposite sex. They were also very good at card tricks and sleight of hand, often leaving me quite befuddled. I felt like a plaything in their hands.

As I write these words, a Japanese phrase I have not thought of for many years has floated to the surface of my memory. It is, in phonetic Japanese, *"hana no shita ga nagai hito,"* a person with a long upper lip. For a Japanese woman to say that about a man means that she thinks he is highly active sexually, with a lascivious nature. That phrase was applied to me rather early in that long-ago evening, and my denials only aroused more hilarity among my delightful tormentors. Even the way they laughed was erotic, with delicate hands over their mouths and their heads turning away in humorous ecstasy.

A great deal of sake was consumed, and all of the ladies held their liquor far better than I did. At the end of the evening, the ladies whispered something to my host, and he told me: "They have enjoyed teasing you, and only wish that you were a bit younger, as you are a little too old for their taste." (I was then 41.)

So the night ended, gracefully and humorously, but with a tinge of regret about what might have happened had we met at an earlier time. It had been an unforgettable experience, giving me a glimpse into a way of life that has entertained and fascinated Japanese men for centuries.

We left Japan in June 1969. Thirty-four years later, on the occasion of our 50th wedding anniversary in 2003, Meg and I took our children, their spouses, and our grandchildren to Japan. We wanted to renew our feelings about a country where we had lived so happily and to introduce Japan to our grandchildren. Sad to say, our Japanese-style houses in Tokyo had been obliterated by apartment buildings. Even the apartment we'd occupied in 1966–1969, was gone.

But there was still one strong connection remaining to the Tokyo that Meg and I so fondly remembered: the Tokyo Lawn Tennis Club, where Meg and I had played constantly and where I'd taught Lucy, Alison, and John to play.

I arranged to have the family visit the TLTC. An old friend of mine was president of the club, and he kindly arranged to have the International Doubles trophy, which I had won three times, shined up and put on a table, where my family could see it and take pictures of it. A very happy memory was brought back to life, as I saw again, inscribed on the trophy, the name of my former tennis partner, the late Saigo Takayoshi.

Our family traveled to Kyoto as well, which will forever retain its unique charm and where we visited timeless temples and gardens. The rest of the family flew home from Kyoto, but Meg and I returned to mountainous Nagano prefecture, where we'd hiked and skied so many times. Though things in the prefecture were more crowded and "developed" than they'd been in days gone by, the people remained the same: simple, friendly, and welcoming.

My rusty Japanese made a remarkable comeback, especially after a drink of sake. The smell of fresh tatami evoked for us nights spent in simple mountain inns, and the sight of Mt. Fuji's symmetrical cone was the strongest symbol of the Japan that remains such a powerful part of our past.

PHOTO GALLERY I

Roughhousing with my father, Abel Jones Gregg, on the lawn of our home in Hastings-on-Hudson, New York, summer 1931. *Family photo*

Coping with TB in Colorado, with my mother, Lucy Phinney Gregg, 1935. *Family photo*

Williams College graduation, 1951, with roommate and close friend Bill Everett. (L to R:) Mrs. Everett, my aunt Charlotte Phinney, Bill, another aunt of mine Catharine Gregg, me, and my mother, Lucy P. Gregg. I was already signed with CIA. *Family photo*

Joyous marriage to Meg Curry at St. Stephen's Episcopal Church, Armonk, New York, July 4, 1953. *Photo courtesy Bill Everett*

Tokyo International Doubles—won three times with Saigo Takayoshi. *Family photo*

Tennis with Crown Prince Akihito (standing at left), circa 1960. (We lost the match.) *Family photo*

Meg's parents, Margery and Gene Curry, on their 1965 visit to Rangoon, with Meg, me, and our children Alison, John (in Meg's lap), and Lucy. *Family photo*

Three generations of Greggs—my uncle Renick Gregg, with my son John and me, up in the Ute Pass near Colorado Springs, 1966. John has just fallen and bloodied his nose, but posing for the picture cheered him up. *Family photo*

Back to Japan—Greggs at Yu-
kata party at Tokyo Lawn Tennis
Club, 1969. *Family photo*

Photo of Meg and me
surreptitiously taken
by KGB officer Yuri
Totrov in Tokyo, 1969,
as we posed for some-
one else. Totrov re-
turned the picture to me
in 1994, via a friend in
Kyodo News, as a signal
that "the Cold War is
over." *KGB photo*

9

JFK and Vietnam

My direct, physical involvement in the Vietnam War came in two sections: first from February 1962 to June 1964, when I was head of the Vietnam desk at CIA in Washington; and second, from September 1970 through June 1972, when I was regional officer in charge (ROIC) of the ten provinces surrounding Saigon, then called Military Region III by the U.S. Army.

My mental involvement in Vietnam will never end. It was in Vietnam that I was shot at for the first times, though only in helicopters. It was there that I was most fully used as a CIA officer and supervisor. And I found my involvement in the misbegotten Vietnam War a time to test all my theories about how to deal with other human beings—whether friends or enemies, subordinates or superiors.

I'd had a sense of guilt about not having been old enough to serve in World War II, and having escaped the Korean War by dint of my Army enlistment in 1945-47. When I returned home from Vietnam at the end of June 1972, that feeling of guilt had been completely assuaged.

In January 1962, after seven very happy years in Japan, I was routed home via Saigon, where my family joined me after I'd been there several days.

My first important meeting was in late February 1962 with General Paul D. Harkins, a rigid, grim-faced man with four glittering stars on each shoulder, who was commander of the Military Assistance Command, Vietnam (MACV).

Harkins was a recent arrival in Saigon, as MACV had been established only a couple of weeks before. We met in the General's large, drab office—which had not yet accumulated any of the usual clutter of plaques, photos, and weapons with which generals show who they've met and what they've done.

Harkins briskly assured me: "I don't care what you hear from other people, I tell you we will be out of here with a military victory in six months." I was not certain what that meant, but Harkins was very confident in his assertion.

Others I talked with seemed far less confident. Harkins had the nickname "Ramrod" and, where our involvement in Vietnam was concerned, seemed uninterested in any shades of gray. The emptiness of his office made his sure pronouncements of victory ring all the more hollow.

CIA was then involved in working with the Montagnards, tribal hill dwellers with a strong antipathy to outsiders. We were developing what were called Civilian Irregular Defense Groups (CIDG), designed to attack Viet Cong units operating in their areas.

I visited one of these areas and was impressed with the toughness and enthusiasm of the CIA officers involved. I also visited a fortified Vietnamese village near Saigon, led by a strong-willed Vietnamese Catholic priest noted for having fought off several Viet Cong attacks on his parishioners. The central government armed and supported him.

The U.S. military presence was limited to small district- and province-level advisory teams of three or four men. Even in my short visit, it became clear that those sitting in Saigon were a lot more confident about the future of our involvement in Vietnam than were the men working in rural areas.

After my family and I reconnected in Saigon, we had a joyous trip home, with stops in India, Italy, France, Switzerland, and London. My mother had come to visit us in Tokyo for Christmas and had stayed on to make the return with us. The trip ended with one of the roughest Atlantic crossings on record, with the dining room virtually empty, the ship constantly heaving, and passengers either prostrate in their bunks or vomiting over the side. Except for that, the trip had been a great experience for us all.

Once in Washington, after we moved into the home we'd bought on Keokuk Street in Bethesda, I settled in for my first period of work at CIA headquarters. I had many people looking over my shoulder as Vietnam desk chief. CIA's commitment of personnel to Vietnam was growing rapidly. The person most interested was William "Bill" Colby, then chief of the Far East division.

Colby had had a great career in OSS. He was known as "the warrior priest" because of his demonstrated valor and his devout Catholic faith. He was lightly built, smoothly handsome, wore glasses, and had perfectly combed hair. He looked more like an investment banker than a man who had been parachuted into France and Norway during World War II and who struck effective blows against Nazi occupation in both countries. He had risen quickly within CIA and had recently served as station chief in Saigon. He was thus an extremely knowledgeable supervisor.

Colby was always willing to do "the extra thing," and expected his subordinates to do the same. He wanted to know where I was at all times. He called me off a tennis court at Georgetown University one Saturday afternoon, and an hour later I was on my hands and knees on his office floor, having taken his *National Geographic* map of Vietnam off his wall and marking it to show the DCI where CIA was dropping agent teams into North Vietnam. This involved a lot of cutting and pasting, and I was creating quite a mess.

Colby saw I was grinning as I worked and asked me what I found amusing. I was still in my tennis clothes and remarked that I was not appropriately dressed for what I was doing. He laughed and said that I was doing the right thing at the right time. We got on very well, and I quite often represented CIA at senior interagency meetings on Vietnam, when Colby could not attend.

In June 1962, I was selected to attend the first "counterinsurgency course" for both civilian and military officials. An excellent course lasting several weeks, it had been pulled together by Walt Rostow, an economic historian and senior advisor to President Kennedy. Rostow was interested in the economic stages of growth in countries under guerrilla attack and how hostile insurgencies could best be defeated by a mixture of good intelligence, economic assistance, and limited, highly specialized military force. The driving goal of the course was to learn how to "win the hearts and minds of the people" under attack.

Upon completion of the course we were all taken to the White House and got to shake President Kennedy's hand. The president came outside to greet us in the Rose Garden, and we all stood in line. I was just behind a brigadier general, the son of "Vinegar Joe" Stilwell of World War II fame. The president instantly picked up on the name "Stilwell," and left my classmate, a very nice officer, glowing with pride.

I was immensely impressed by the president's physical presence, his intensity, his intelligence, and his strong belief that counterinsurgency was the way forward in a difficult situation in Vietnam.

The Cuban Missile Crisis of October 1962 remains one of my most vivid memories. Knowledge of the crisis slowly spread at CIA headquarters, as more and more people had to be told about it. As it became clear that nuclear war was a real possibility, I found each day to be more and more like waking up *to* a nightmare, rather than waking up from one. I particularly recall one sad night when we and our next-door neighbors explored our cellars to determine the best place to hide in despair if Washington was hit by a nuclear bomb.

When President Kennedy announced the crisis to the American people, virtually all CIA employees knew of it and were fully aware that our headquarters building would be a prime Soviet missile target. I was given directions to a secret file repository deep in Virginia and was told to go out and familiarize myself with it, so that "if I survived" I would know where to go, to try to start over.

I drove back from that grim assignment after dark, and as I topped a rise and looked down at the city of Washington, there was a sudden bright flash from the downtown area, probably an electric train hitting a third rail. My heart beat wildly, as I truly felt that I had seen the start of a nuclear attack. I had to pull off to the side of the road, to calm down. I was drenched with sweat.

The following day at headquarters there was a general announcement that any survivors of a nuclear attack were to assemble at the Charles Town Race Track in West Virginia. That was the extent of emergency planning at that time. President Kennedy's announcement that the two-week crisis had safely ended brought a sweet sense of relief to me that I can only equate with my feelings later in Vietnam, after having narrowly avoided what would have been a fatal crash in a small helicopter.

My admiration for President Kennedy grew as the inside story of how brilliantly he had handled the crisis slowly emerged. I later had to deal directly with two of the senior military figures whose lethal advice he had so wisely rejected, Generals Maxwell Taylor and Curtis LeMay. Seeing them in action in a war game, with all the strength of their misguided convictions fully displayed, greatly increased my respect for Kennedy's strength of character and his wisdom.

The period of May through November 1963 was an unrelievedly bad period for the United States and for South Vietnam. It started in the central Vietnamese city of Hue with Buddhist protests against the policies of President Ngo Dinh Diem, an unpopular Catholic in a predominantly Buddhist country. As the central government cracked down hard, the protests rapidly escalated and spread south to Saigon.

I was with Colby in his office in June 1963 when news came that an elderly Buddhist monk, with great composure, had burned himself to death at a major intersection in Saigon. We immediately watched it on television. It was the first self-immolation I had seen, and it was ghastly. Even Colby, a very cool customer, was shaken by it and correctly saw it as a tragic harbinger of worse things to come. Diem and his family were all stiff-necked Catholics, and his brutal mishandling of the Buddhist protests had an immediate, negative impact on the Washington view of him and his relatives.

Roger Hilsman, a West Point graduate who had served with distinction in Burma, first with Merrill's Marauders and later with OSS, was a deep believer in counterinsurgency and the need to keep psychologically in tune with the Vietnamese people. Hilsman was head of the Bureau of Intelligence and Research (INR) at the State Department at that time, and he, along with most senior State Department officials, was increasingly cynical and negative about Diem and his policies.

In mid-1963, the U.S. ambassador to Vietnam, Frederick Nolting, was called back from Saigon to Washington to assess the situation. I represented CIA at a meeting chaired by Hilsman at State, which directly raised the question of whether or not to continue our strong support of Diem. Hilsman clearly saw the situation in Vietnam through the prism of his experience in Burma, as a guerilla fighter with Merrill and with OSS. He went on at length about the need to find better South Vietnamese leaders, if we hoped to "win the hearts and minds of the people."

Ambassador Nolting sat silently through this tirade. Finally, Hilsman turned to him and said, "Well, Fritz, you were sent to Saigon specifically to work with Diem and his family. What do you have to say?"

Nolting rose and spoke quietly, indicating his full awareness of how hard it was to influence Diem. He closed by saying "There is no one else in Vietnam with the guts and *sangfroid* of Diem and Nhu (his brother). If we let go of them, we will be saddled with an endless cycle of mediocre generals." He sat down and did not speak again.

Frederick Nolting was right, but that was not what Hilsman wanted to hear. Planning for a coup began, and late in August 1963, Ambassador Henry Cabot Lodge replaced Nolting.

I find it astonishing how research and declassification of highly sensitive information have laid bare the bones of the skeletons in the Vietnam closet. Most vivid of the evidence I found was an actual recording of President Kennedy on the 4th of November 1963. He was dictating a memo into a Dictaphone, dealing with the U.S.-supported coup in Saigon that had resulted in the assassination of President Diem and his brother only a day or two previously. JFK's voice was grave and regretful, as he noted who had favored and who had opposed a coup, the results of which had shocked him.

Suddenly, his dictation was interrupted by the voices of his small children, Caroline and John, running into his office and claiming his amused and loving attention. I was deeply moved by this strong aural evidence of what kind of a man JFK was, coming less than three weeks before his own assassination.

On November 22, 1963, I was in the parking lot of CIA headquarters when I heard of the president's death. The entire building was in a state of silent shock and immense sadness. Everyone recognized that Kennedy's sagacious handling of the Cuban Missile Crisis the year before had probably saved the Agency building from atomic attack, and so the collective feelings of grief and loss were staggering. My heart still aches every time I think of John F. Kennedy.

As I walked back to my office on the day of his murder, I saw many employees openly weeping in the halls. It was a truly sad day for the country—and a tragic day, one with dark implications for many years to come.

Four days later, on the 26th of November, I sent a letter to my mother, describing what we had done that day. She kept it and made copies for the family, one of which I found as I prepared this book.

Mother dear,

It has been a strange and awful time. We can accept the fact of the President's death now, but the ramifications of it will be unfolding for years. In a way, I feel this event grew out of the assassination of Lincoln, because had Lincoln lived to carry out his policies in the South, the nation would be better united today and, a century later, President Kennedy's racial policies would not have aroused such passions. There is a great remorse now, and a chance to exorcise much of the violence which has grown into our national life—but whether we will take this chance, or spiral down to greater unease, suspicion and hatred, remains to be seen.

We watched television for hours but wanting to participate more directly, on November 25th, we rose before 6 a.m. and drove into the city of Washington on the day of JFK's burial. Traffic was light but people were on the sidewalk opposite the White House, lying under blankets. The House itself looked gaunt in the flat light of dawn. Around the Capitol, pink light was touching the marble, and the people moved about in gentle masses. The line stretched endlessly away. We drove over to Arlington, and saw the fresh-dug grave just below the old mansion of Robert E. Lee.

That afternoon, I took Lucy, age seven, to Arlington Cemetery. It was a long climb, but I carried Lucy on my shoulders. We stood by the winding road and watched the procession pass. Then came the horse-drawn funeral caisson, led by a single dark horse with the boots turned backwards in the stirrups—sad beyond belief.

The black caisson rumbled hollowly past—stark with

its tragic burden. Then came the Kennedy family, stiff and courageous in great black cars. After them, a solemn Who's Who of the world: Charles de Gaulle, of France, a heavy face with a great beak; Emperor Haile Selassie of Ethiopia, small features and flashing eyes over his beard; and Prince Philip of England, in a white naval cap, visually the most impressive of all....Lyndon Johnson, the new President, was surrounded by huge panther-like Secret Service men, who stared about constantly.

There were countless more world figures there, all just momentary flashes, but I hoped Lucy would remember. We walked up the hill and I held her on my shoulders over the crowd. The sun was slanting down through the bare limbs on a windless, hushed day—a noble setting for a tragedy of immense proportions. As we walked in, we saw tiny groups of mourners, around other graves, and heard the pop of rifles. Others had died, but their passing was dwarfed, by human standards at least.

As I write these words, I think of my grandfather, as a boy of twelve, watching Lincoln's funeral train pass through his home-town in Ohio in 1865, and I wonder how many times we are fated to go through such tragedies.

10

Lurching Toward Catastrophe

In December 1963, I accompanied Secretary of Defense Robert Mc-Namara on a quick trip to Saigon. President Johnson was just settling into office and wanted an expert evaluation of the situation in Vietnam in the wake of the assassinations of the presidents of both South Vietnam and the United States.

General Harkins was still in command of MACV, and the U.S. military presence remained small, consisting of advisory teams, headed by captains or majors, at the district and province level. I sat several rows in back of McNamara and could see the back of his neck gradually redden as he heard a constant repetition of the Harkins mantra: "We will be out of here with a military victory in six months." It was no truer then than it had been when I'd first heard it early in 1962.

At the end of his first MACV briefing, McNamara made clear that he was greatly dissatisfied with what he'd heard. He said angrily: "I'm totally dissatisfied with this reporting. It is unsatisfactory to have all of you say the same thing. I'm going into the field tomorrow to see things for myself and expect better analysis when I return."

The lights at MACV burned far into that night, but to no avail. Upon his return, McNamara heard essentially the same optimistic estimate, except that the time frame had been extended to twelve months before a "military victory" would be achieved. Much later, I read McNamara's report to President Johnson. He said that he was "disturbed" by the unrealistic reporting he had heard and that things were not nearly as good as Harkins's people seemed to think they were.

Harkins left Vietnam in mid-1964 and was replaced by Gen. William Westmoreland. Upon Westmoreland's arrival, there were fewer than twenty thousand U.S. troops in Vietnam. When he left four years later, more than half a million were in place, and the fighting continued.

In the spring of 1964, a war game was held at the Pentagon to judge the efficacy of bombing North Vietnam, as a way of getting Hanoi and the Viet Cong to stop their attacks on the South. These attacks were fueled by a steady stream of supplies down the Ho Chi Minh Trail, through Laos and Cambodia, into South Vietnam. I was CIA's representative on the Blue (U.S.) Team, at the working level. We met in a large, windowless room in the basement of the Pentagon.

An Air Force brigadier general named John Vogt led the working-level group. He told us that we were to decide what to do about the idea of bombing, prepare an analysis of how we planned to implement our decision, and what the impact of our planning would be. We would then present this plan to the senior Blue group, led by General Maxwell Taylor, chairman of the Joint Chiefs of Staff, and other luminaries, including Director John McCone of CIA, General Curtis LeMay of the Air Force, the director of USAID, and a senior State Department official.

General Earl ("Buzz") Wheeler, Army chief of staff, headed the Red Team, essentially representing China and North Vietnam. His team would be informed of our planned move by the war game's Control Group and would plan its response. The Control Group would evaluate our plan and the Red Team response and construct a resulting situation to which the two teams would react.

The game would end with the two teams meeting to discuss what had taken place. I noted with satisfaction that the CIA representative (working level) on the Red Team was a very intelligent operations officer named Harry.

To Brigadier General Vogt's surprise, the Blue Team's working group was divided on the issue of bombing. We were presented with a plan worked out by the U.S. Air Force that would start with the bombing of military targets at the southern end of North Vietnam and gradually work its way north, unless Hanoi called off its attacks on the South. The plan left no doubts about its successful impact in North Vietnam.

The State Department representative and I felt that this bombing plan would achieve nothing but hardening Hanoi's determination and bring down heavy international condemnation on the United States, as civilian casualties increased.

After an extended discussion, General Vogt called for a team vote, which went against State and CIA by something like 8 to 2. The team's military members then turned to planning how the bombing attacks would be implemented. Vogt asked me to write an intelligence estimate of the impact of the U.S. attacks.

Shortly thereafter, we were joined by the senior Blue Team, as eminent a group as I'd ever seen up close. National security advisor McGeorge Bundy came into the room. I was not sure whether he was with the Red Team or on the Control Group.

Brigadier General Vogt gave a fair account of the split on the junior Blue Team but said we had voted to proceed with bombing attacks. An outline of the attack plan was presented and seemed to meet with general approval.

General Vogt then turned to me and asked for CIA's analysis of the effectiveness of the plan. I started with a short description of the rationale for the plan and what its objectives were. I then began to explain why I believed the plan would fail.

I was stopped in a peremptory fashion by General Taylor, who had bright blue eyes and an icy glare. He asked General Vogt how it could be that the Blue Team was launched on a plan that its own CIA representative thought would not work.

At this point, CIA Director McCone looked at me intently and turned to his senior aide, Hal Ford, obviously asking, "What's going on?" It was a very vivid moment for me.

Vogt, an honest man, said that he had not asked me to write an analysis supporting the Blue Team plan; he had just asked me to write what I thought. After a very brief discussion, it was decided to completely ignore my analysis and to proceed with the bombing. I wondered if my opposition to bombing North Vietnam had just blown up my own career.

In the discussion that ensued, it became clear that General LeMay felt that one of the plan's great virtues would be to draw China more openly into the conflict. LeMay felt that Hanoi would immediately want to respond to our bombing attack by striking at targets in the south. Lacking the capability to do this, they would turn to China.

LeMay thought that China would then covertly fly missions into the south, just as the Soviet Union had done in the Korean War. These Chinese missions, which we would discover and publicize, would then open up the possibility of launching U.S. air attacks against China's emerging nuclear weapons facilities, targets LeMay was itching to attack.

The Red Team's response to our bombing attacks was, I thought, sagacious. There were no retaliatory air attacks, only loud protests over the deaths of innocent civilians, a formal protest launched from the United Nations, an increased flow of men and materiel down the Ho Chi Minh trail, and stepped up attacks in South Vietnam.

The war game did not go at all well from the point of view of the Pentagon's planners, who wanted their bombing plan validated in advance. At the final meeting of the game, involving all its participants, LeMay furiously attacked Red Team leader General Wheeler. LeMay, a florid, heavyset man, leaned forward and glared at Wheeler, saying: "Buzz, you know goddamn well that if I attack your capital, you are going to attack mine."

General Wheeler responded mildly, "Curt, I know that is what you want me to do, and it is the last thing in the world I would consider." I noted my CIA friend Harry smiling quietly at Wheeler's reply.

LeMay famously retorted: "I think we have lost track of the fact that we can bomb North Vietnam back into the Stone Age in twenty-four hours."

A long silence ensued, until McGeorge Bundy laconically commented, "I guess our problem may be that North Vietnam is too close to the Stone Age already."

The war game ended in disarray, but U.S. bombing of North Vietnamese targets started soon thereafter. My standing in CIA was not damaged by my war game participation. Director McCone, a very astute man, was never a full-blown supporter of the Vietnam War.

Not too long after this, Meg and I saw the film *Dr. Strangelove*, in which Sterling Hayden brilliantly caricatured LeMay. I recall clearly the scene in which LeMay, portrayed by Hayden, advises the president to preemptively attack the Soviet Union with nuclear weapons. LeMay's live performance in the war game came back to me with a rush.

In 1965, President Johnson and Secretary McNamara forced General LeMay to retire. Perhaps the most haunting quotation ever by any American war planner belongs to Curtis LeMay: "I do not believe there are any innocent civilians."

We are lucky to have survived that man.

11

Burmese Days

"Burma is as far away from New York as you can get." In late June 1964, I had that thought as the Gregg family climbed aboard a Pan Am jet flying to Rangoon. Our son John was not yet one year old when we departed for Burma. Lucy recalls her younger brother looking like "an angry plucked chicken" when she saw him shortly after his birth. He was still small and did not weigh much, but his determination was strong, and off we went.

Though neither of them had complained about going to Burma, I had stressed to eight-year-old Lucy and four-year-old Alison how quickly we were going to get there, as that was our first jet flight. I was trying to play down how far away from home we were going to be. John always seemed content in Meg's arms.

As a small boy, I had first became aware there was a country named Burma via roadside advertisements touting a brushless shaving cream called Burma-Shave. I remember them as series of small, horizontal white signs, spaced a few hundred feet apart, along rural roads, particularly out west. Each sign had only a few words. For example:

(First sign) A WOMAN WILL LEAP
(Second sign) FROM A FIRE ESCAPE
(Third sign) TO TRY TO AVOID
(Fourth sign) A HAIRY APE
(Fifth sign) BURMA-SHAVE

or

GRANDPA'S BEARD
WAS STIFF AND COARSE
AND THAT'S WHAT CAUSED
HIS FIFTH DIVORCE
BURMA-SHAVE

or

HE HAD THE RING
HE HAD THE FLAT
BUT SHE FELT HIS CHIN
AND THAT WAS THAT
BURMA-SHAVE

During World War II, I read about the Burma Road, over which supplies were laboriously driven from India into China for use in the fight against Japan. Later, I learned that the Japanese attempt to drive through Burma into India in 1944 was stopped by a British General named William Slim, in desperate fighting at a place called Imphal, near the Indian border. Until we moved to Burma, that was about all I knew of that truly extraordinary place.

Burma (its formal name is Myanmar, but the British colonialists found "Burma" easier to pronounce) is larger than France, Denmark, Holland, and Belgium combined. North to south it stretches more than 1,200 miles, and it has over 1,000 miles of coastline along the Bay of Bengal and the Andaman Sea.

Burma was once the world's largest exporter of rice. It has vast mineral and wood resources. At its northernmost tip stands "Burma's Icy Mountain," Hkakabo Razi, which is over 19,000 feet and was not climbed to the summit until 1996. Burma's mighty rivers, the Irrawaddy and the Salween, carry with them tremendous loads of silt and are rapidly extending Burma's delta to the south. Pegu, the ancient capital of southern Burma, a seaport until about 1700, is now more than 50 miles from the coast.

The British moved into Burma in 1855. Rangoon became known as "The Pearl of the Orient" for its pleasant climate, its architecture, and ambiance. The British administered Burma as part of India until it gained its independence after World War II.

Burma had long been riven by hostilities between the dominant Burmese and the more than a hundred ethnic minorities that ringed its fertile central plains. Of these minorities, some were Muslim, some Christian, some animists, and some Buddhists. The Burmese were especially hostile toward the Karen, a powerful hill tribe that lived along the Burma-Thai border.

An ancient Burmese saying that typified the ethnic hostilities concerned the Muslim Arakanese, who lived along the coast of the Bay of Bengal northwest of Rangoon. It was: "If you meet a cobra and an Arakanese, kill the Arakanese."

Once in Rangoon, we quickly located, on Wingaba Road, a large, British-built concrete house, with a garden and a tennis court. We inherited a fine staff, except for the Pakistani cook, who grumbled constantly and soon left us. The key staff were two lovely "nannies,' Bibi and Nona, both Christians and members of the Karen tribe.

The Karen, who are resisting the central government in Rangoon even today, are similar to the Montagnard in Vietnam, having been driven from the fertile river plains into the mountains by the dominant Burmans. Driven off they may have been, but the Karen have had significant armed units ever since the end of World War II, and the Burmese Army has never been able to end their insurgency.

Bibi and Nona absolutely dedicated themselves to the care of our children. Lucy, Alison, and John never had more devoted care. There was an international school, and the diplomatic corps and American embassy staff were all friendly, so we adapted quickly and happily.

Once we settled in Rangoon, we came to enjoy the writings of Maurice Collis, an Irishman who had a long career in Burma as part of the British colonial administration. Collis's books, published in the 1940s, could still be found in Rangoon's moldering bookshops. Collis's first posting, in the 1920s, was to a remote village on the Bay of Bengal, where he was the lone Westerner.

Collis found that his Burmese servants, longtime local residents, were always aware of approaching visitors from another place long before they arrived. When he asked his servants how they could have sensed the approach of strangers two hours before their arrival, they only wondered why he could not. Collis came to believe that noisy modern life deafens us to what is conveyed to those who are comfortable with silence and remain attuned to it.

He lived in Burma for many years, and as he became fully attuned to its silences and pace of life, he had several experiences that were truly occult. Most vivid were Collis's encounters with an apparition, a male figure dressed in old-style Burmese clothes, which woke him at night when he slept in a deserted old British commissioner's house high on a bluff overlooking the southern port of Mergui. In the late seventeenth century, Samuel "Siamese" White, an enterprising British trader, operated profitably out of Mergui. In 1687, local mandarins massacred many of White's associates.

Collis assumed that the apparition he encountered was related to that tragedy, as the British house and White's building had both been located on the same bluff in an attempt to escape malarial mosquitoes. Cliff and Nancy Forster, who served with USIA in Burma in the 1950s, had a similar ghostly encounter while staying in the same old house during a visit to Mergui. Unaware of Collis's experiences, in 1968 they were amazed to read about them in our apartment in Tokyo. Collis deals extensively with these matters in two of his fine books, *Into Hidden Burma* and *Siamese White*.

The closest we came to such an experience occurred in Rangoon. Our British colonial house was surrounded by a large garden that petered out in swampy ground in back of the house. We had a gardener from the Mon tribe who lived with his family in a rude structure in the back yard. We had palm trees of various kinds and a variety of exotic blossoming plants, so that something was always ready to be picked. Our gardener had a vegetable garden of his own, the products of which he generously shared with us.

One day the gardener told us that dangerous snakes had moved into our compound. We called the Rangoon Zoo, which had a huge collection of poisonous reptiles, and they promised to help us. I expected a truckload of men with long poles, rakes, and machetes to arrive. Instead, just at dusk, one young soldier showed up with a big gunnysack. I thought he had lost the way and had come too late to do his job, but he assured me that he worked best in the darkness. He asked me to turn out all the garden lights. I did so, and the silent tropic darkness closed in.

A couple of hours later, the soldier knocked on our door and proudly lifted his wildly heaving gunnysack. "I think I got them all," he said. I asked how he located the snakes, and he said simply, "I listen for them, and then I catch them." As Simon and Garfunkel sang in the "The Sounds of Silence": "Hello darkness, my old friend. I've come to talk to you again…"

Having rid the place of snakes, I decided that I should learn to say "There's a snake in the garden" in Burmese, as our gardener spoke no English whatsoever. That came in handy at the end of our tour. My replacement was another tennis player, liked our house and tennis court very much, and was interested in moving in. But he did have a concern about snakes as he, too, had small children. I told him that since we'd had our garden cleaned out by the young soldier, I had not seen a snake on our property. He was much assured, and we drove off to a diplomatic reception, with Tun Sein, our driver at the wheel.

We immediately encountered a large green tree viper coiled ominously in the middle of our driveway. "Run over that snake!" I ordered in a loud voice. With sweat popping out all over his shaven head, Tun Sein, devout Buddhist that he was, carefully avoided running over the viper, which turned its head to watch us as we passed. My replacement, sitting in front, missed none of this, and was in a frenzy of concern, saying that he could not possibly move into our house. At the reception that followed, I introduced my replacement to a number of friends, several of whom commented later that he did not seem particularly happy to be in Rangoon.

At the end of the evening, Meg and I returned home, having dropped my replacement at his hotel, and Tun Sein near his house. I had looked into the various reptiles we might encounter, living as we did at the edge of a swamp. Cobras were most active and fast moving. The vipers were slower and not as far ranging.

I was looking for the viper as we headed up our driveway, and sure enough, there it was, about four feet long, draped in a thick hedge, several feet off the ground. I left the car with its lights focused on the snake, escorted Meg into the house, and went around back to the gardener's hut. He instantly responded to my carefully rehearsed Burmese phrase, and appeared holding a machete in one hand and an iron rod in the other.

He gave me the rod, and ran toward the car. I followed him and was in time to see him pull the snake out of the hedge with his machete and quickly end its furious writhing by cutting off its head.

The gardener bent over and carefully examined the dead snake. He then turned to me, and in a vivid pantomime, made one hand into a snake's head, and struck his other arm with it. He then turned slack-jawed, rolled his eyes, and dropped his head to his chest. I got the message. The gardener proudly trotted off, with the snake draped over the blade of his machete. I suspect he ate it for breakfast.

I told my replacement the next day that the viper had been killed and that the gardener, a non-Buddhist, was a skilled and valiant ally. He decided to move into our house, and I heard he had a successful and happy tour.

Tennis played a large part in our lives. The court at our house was always busy, and we all played regularly. I entered the Burmese tournaments, and, since there was not a lot going on, these received considerable coverage in the daily English-language paper. The tennis writer was an amiable man with a sense of humor, who referred to me, at age thirty-five, as "the grizzled American veteran."

The tournaments were tough. From the quarterfinals on they became best-of-five-set matches, which, in Rangoon's heat, were an ordeal. I never won one of the big tournaments, usually getting worn out in the quarterfinals or semi-finals.

In one tournament, I had the bad luck to draw the Burmese national champion as my opponent in an early round, which was a best-of-three-set match. I played well and, after losing a close first set, won the second set. I had nothing to lose and was playing confidently, with my serve producing lots of winners. The third set was extremely tense, with a large crowd gathered around our court. My opponent was grim-faced and raised his game, rushing the net behind his good serve. He broke my serve in the tenth game of the set, and won 6-4.

I was pleased with my showing and wondered how the local press would cover the fact that the "grizzled veteran" had taken a set from Burma's number one player. In the paper next day, there was no written commentary on the match, and the score of the second set had been reversed, so that it appeared I had lost in three straight sets. I was both amused and annoyed, and noted that the tennis writer avoided me for the next tournament or two.

Another time, I was playing one of the best young players in Burma and thought I had beaten him, but the umpire called my winning shot out. I argued briefly, blew my cool, and eventually lost the match. Late that night, our Burmese telephone rang, a very rare occurrence. I stumbled downstairs and found that it was the umpire from my match, calling to apologize for his bad call. "I never thought you would lose," he said, only making me feel worse about the whole thing.

Another vivid memory resulted from our taking John to the Rangoon Zoo, shortly after our arrival. He was about thirteen months old and still very small. The zoo had a magnificent array of tigers and, as we approached the cage of one huge male, it stopped pacing, turned, sat down, and stared balefully at John in his stroller. Feeling unsettled, I moved on to the next cage, where three young tigers were playfully wrestling with each other. As soon as we stood in front of the cage, they stopped their play, came to the bars of their cage, and all looked intently at John.

One of the zookeepers hurried over and whispered in my ear, "They all want to eat him." I left the tiger cages immediately and went to the monkey area, where the simians paid not the slightest attention to us. Several months later the Rangoon press reported that the three young tigers had attacked and killed a careless keeper.

John loved going to the zoo, and several months later we took him back. This time, the tigers were totally indifferent to him. Whatever he had exuded before was no longer there. Perhaps very young animals give off a scent that makes them both attractive and totally vulnerable to the big cats. It was all part of the exotic Burmese scene that we sensed but couldn't fully grasp.

In September 1964, we took our first major trip within Burma, going by train north to Mandalay, where we stayed for two or three days. We left late in the afternoon and rode quietly through lush green rice paddies, watched villagers gathering at their wells, saw cooking fires being lighted and golden pagoda domes gleaming through the fading light. We slept well in a Japanese version of our Pullman cars, and arrived refreshed in Mandalay the next morning.

After checking into our hotel, we headed west in a Jeep station wagon, through bustling streets, past countless pagodas, where stonecutters work all their lives making images of Buddha, through the town of Amarapura, where the old capital of Burma was briefly located, and out into the broad valley of the Irrawaddy River.

The river was high at that time of year and flooded widely but not dangerously. After driving some miles through paddy fields, we came to the nine-span Ava Bridge, opened by the British in 1934, blown up during World War II and later restored. It carried both cars and trains and was then the only bridge across the Irrawaddy, which flows for over nine hundred miles, from its source in the northern mountains to the delta south of Rangoon.

To say merely that the Irrawaddy flows through Burma would be like saying elephants are gray. In America, many of our rivers have become something to be merely observed or endured during seasonal flooding. The Hudson River, beside which I grew up, was something to be looked at, something that sometimes froze, and something on which big boats traveled. But we did not swim in it, wash in it, drink from it or use it to water our gardens.

The immense Irrawaddy is to Burma in many ways what the Nile is to Egypt. It is cyclical and vital to the growing of crops, and it does not turn savage and drown thousands of people, as do the rivers of China. I think of it as a great animal that carries much of Burma on its back.

After a stop at a silver shop, we drove past countless crumbling pagodas set in fields where cacti flourished, and turbaned Indians, striding along with heavy burdens, were timeless reminders that Burma has been a crossroads for centuries, where India and Southeast Asia blend. I felt at a corner of the world, looking west to the brown sweep of India and the Middle East, and east through green Asia to the blue Pacific.

On the next morning we rose at 5:30 to climb Mandalay Hill, which rises 700 feet above the flat valley floor. The moon shone brightly as we started up, and noises from the valley rose to our ears: train whistles, dog fights, the shout of soldiers at morning calisthenics, and gongs striking the hour of six.

The view from the hilltop was wonderful. We looked west to the distant Irrawaddy and could dimly make out the Ava Bridge.

Below us, early morning golfers marched up and down, and tiny shafts of light from their swinging clubs winked up at us. To the east, the mountains rose sharply, and a cool breeze gave a touch of freshness, which we had not felt since arriving in Rangoon.

Later that morning we drove 42 miles up to Maymyo. At a height of about 2,700 feet, Maymyo is one of the "hill stations" for which the British were famous. It was the summer capital of Burma in British times, and it still bore the stamp of colonialism. Old British school and office buildings abounded, and Maymyo taxis were four-wheel horse-drawn carriages, copied from those the British used. We stayed at a missionary guesthouse that reminded us of Colonial America warm brick, white pillars, fireplaces, and double staircases.

In the afternoon, we played the Maymyo golf course with a gentleman of Persian descent who had once been the best golfer in Northern Burma. He'd been in the brewery business all his life and was semiretired. He had a charming English wife, and besides golf enjoyed making wines, jams, and jellies from the fruits that abound in the area.

That evening we had dinner with the part-Shan principal of an Episcopal school. His son was in the Burmese army and spoke of fighting Karen insurgents in southern Burma. It was a warm family evening, of which we quickly became a part. That night we slept under blankets and awoke to the sound of horses' hooves outside the guesthouse. We returned to Rangoon that evening by train.

The only really charming thing in Burma was its people. We saw no inns in Burma that Duncan Hines would recommend, nor did we encounter much in the way of food we would take home with us. We were in a country with a strong, simple, and friendly people who worked hard. Largely cut off from contact with the West, they were eager to see us. We felt that Burma was going through a stage ("The Burmese way to Socialism") that was intended to change it completely but which would not succeed in doing so.

Burma was not ready for a metamorphosis such as Japan had gone through. Its rural life was then and remains still deeply patterned and tied to land and water and trees and pagodas built to gain eternal merit. While we had no wish to become part of that pattern, we hoped we could come to understand it better.

Burmese life was punctuated by a series of yearly Buddhist festivals, based on the life of Buddha. In April, a very hot period near the end of the long dry season, came the four-day Thingyan—a water festival. During those four days, throwing water on another, friend or stranger alike, was encouraged. Powerful plastic water pistols, locally made, were sold from stalls all over Rangoon. They could soak a person from twenty feet away.

In April 1966, our second April in Rangoon, we decided to give a water-throwing party, to which we invited a large number of our Burmese friends and selected diplomats whom we knew to possess a sense of humor. The party was a huge, drenching success, from which two events stand out. The first was the arrival of a lovely young American wife from the embassy staff, who was very new to Burma. She showed up with a bouffant coiffure, wearing a frilly frock and looking fresh and alluring. She had just gotten out of her car and was standing with a smile of greeting, when a grinning Burmese on top of our porte-cochere hit her squarely with a full bucket of water.

I am still laughing as I type these words, almost half a century later, thinking of her instant transformation from a demure damsel on delightful display to a drowned rat, with her long hair plastered over her face. I should add that she immediately got into the spirit of things and furiously pursued her assailant until she had fully retaliated.

My second memory concerns my good friend Narendra Singh, India's ambassador to Burma. Narendra was a tall, handsome man from a thoroughly Westernized Sikh family of great wealth. He was a powerful tennis player, and we often competed. I remember him returning from leave in India with several old muskets, heavily adorned with silver, which he had taken from what he called "the family armory" to decorate his residence in Rangoon.

Narendra was an enthusiastic participant in our water-throwing party. He also consumed a great deal of a powerful wine punch we had specially concocted for the occasion. The vinous party continued on well into dusk, at which point Narendra asked if he could lie down for a few minutes. He was led into our study, lay down on a couch, put a wet cloth over his eyes, and was almost instantly asleep.

A bit later came an inquiry from the British embassy, asking politely: "Is Ambassador Singh still with you?" I asked the caller to hold the line, and roused Narendra.

He quickly recalled, with considerable profanity, that he was due to attend a black tie dinner at the British Embassy. He said there was no way he was going to make it.

I regretted for him ("Ambassador Singh regrets that he has been unavoidably detained"), and our friendship was strengthened by the general hilarity of the occasion.

Our tennis court was used for all sorts of activities. Games of catch, bike riding, hopscotch, and Girl Scout meetings. Large evening dinners took place there. Once on a Sunday we had a game day for our staff, involving informal contests we made up for the occasion. I challenged our gardener, our nannies, and our house manager to a contest of blowing Ping-Pong balls across the court. The gardener in particular was flabbergasted to see me on my hands and knees blowing my assigned ball. He laughed so hard he literally could not get up off the ground. One of the nannies won that contest rather easily. It was great fun for all.

The Burmese loved to dance, and parties were frequently held that featured dinner, drinks, and dance music. Those were the days of 33 rpm LPs. We had brought Chubby Checker's famous twist record with us, and it was an instant hit and widely copied. So I think it's fair to say that we brought the Twist to Burma. On a trip to Singapore, I was able to buy an early Herb Alpert and the Tijuana Brass LP that was equally popular.

Astronaut John Glenn made a short visit to Burma, about three years after his famous Earth orbits. He was still in uniform, and his facial pallor matched the greenish tones of his Marine uniform, as he made the mistake of brushing his teeth with the tap water at his downtown hotel, the Strand. I got to know Glenn when he became a senator, and he said he had never felt worse in his life than during his Rangoon visit. Sick as he was, Glenn made every appointment and had a powerful impact on the people of Rangoon.

The U.S. Davis Cup team, led by Herb Fitzgibbon, Marty Riessen, and Clark Graebner, also came to Rangoon and played exhibition matches. With the aid of USIA, I made a tennis training film with Fitzgibbon, which the Burmese Davis Cup coach was happy to receive. For all I know, they may still be using it.

One day while Meg was playing golf in Burma, she spontaneously bought a baby goat from a family tethering the herd nearby. The goat was very cute, and Meg insisted on paying the enormous sum of five dollars for it, then rode home via Alison's nursery school to pick her up.

Back at home, our gardener's father, a stooped and frail-looking gentleman, hadn't had quite enough to do. He quickly assumed care of the goat, leading it around the compound on a leash, and very happy to have some further purpose in life. Eventually the kid became Billy Goat and smelled like a goat. We also added a Nanny goat to the family. When we left Rangoon we urged the staff to continue the good care of these goats, but I'm sure they had a great goat roast to celebrate our departure!

Those were two vivid, happy years in Rangoon. They were saddened by Burma's long domination by a military dictatorship, marked by corruption, cruelty (Meg had many Burmese friends who had high-ranking husbands in jail without trials), and indifference to the aspirations of its people. We saw the beginnings of that oppressive regime in the 1960s, led by a general named Ne Win.

Now in 2014 there is hope for change for the better in Burma, embodied in the person of Aung San Suu Kyi, the tenacious daughter of General Aung San, Burma's national liberation hero and founding father, who was tragically murdered in 1947 by a political rival named U Saw. Suu Kyi was kept under house arrest for more than a decade, following a 1999 election in which she won great prominence. The Rangoon government cracked down brutally, killing and imprisoning hundreds of students and protestors. Suu Kyi was encouraged by Burma's military leaders to leave Burma, which she was free to do. She refused, knowing that once she left, she would not be allowed to return.

In late September 2011, she spoke directly from Rangoon via Skype to Charlie Rose and Bishop Desmond Tutu of South Africa. In a deeply moving exchange, she spoke about never losing hope, being encouraged by talking to Burma's leaders, of working for "value change, not regime change" and the need for common people to live free of fear. She has demonstrated, as powerfully as anyone I know, the power of one person to make a difference—and today she leads her country toward greater political freedom.

Suu Kyi has been elected to Burma's parliament and now plans to visit her sons in England, leaving Burma for the first time in over twenty years. Would that there were more people like her in the world!

12

Searching for a Crippled Boy

While living in Tokyo in the 1950s and '60s, I saw Korea and Koreans largely through the distorting prism of Japanese prejudice. Unsolved crimes were often blamed on Koreans. They had low-class jobs and no social contacts with the Japanese, who treated Koreans with a hostility that was as pernicious as it was pervasive.

In the anger and confusion right after the disastrous earthquake of 1923, the Japanese scapegoated Koreans and killed as many as 6,000 Koreans then living in Japan, as if the Koreans were somehow responsible for that epic natural disaster and the fires that raged in its aftermath. During World War II, the Japanese brought thousands of Koreans to Japan against their will, as essentially a slave labor pool.

One day in my final tour in Japan, a friend and I had to drive through Shinjuku, an area of Tokyo well known for its bathhouses, brothels and criminal activity. A delivery truck held us up on a narrow street, and, as we waited, a group of small boys came skittering out of an alley, happily calling out to each other, perhaps on their way to a playground.

Then behind them came another boy, perhaps eight or nine years old, limping grotesquely as he strained to keep up. As he struggled past us, he lost his balance and fell against our car. His face was inches from mine as he grasped the car door handle to keep from collapsing. He never looked at me—his eyes were on his disappearing playmates—but his determination was, in its way, magnificent.

My friend and I were both moved by this incident, as all of our children were in good health. A few weeks later, on the U.S. Armed

Forces radio network, I began to hear a series of announcements by the Shriners, promising to fully pay for surgery on any child crippled by polio. Their announcements made clear that the offer was not limited to Americans, but literally included any child.

I suggested to my friend that we try to find the crippled boy who'd made such an impression on us. He readily agreed, and so back we went to Shinjuku. My friend was a Nisei whose Japanese was fluent. My Japanese was good enough to ask storekeepers in the neighborhood if they knew of a crippled boy. Our questions achieved nothing but to stir up bits of suspicious curiosity.

We were about to give up when, in a dingy drugstore, an old woman heard our questions and the questions the pharmacist asked in response about why we wanted to locate this child. When she heard us explain that we might be able to give medical assistance to the boy, she burst out, "But he's a Korean!" implying that he didn't deserve any help.

We persisted with our questions, and the old woman said she thought the boy's father worked in a bathhouse nearby. We went to the sleazy bathhouse, were told that they had a man on their night shift who had a crippled son, and were given an address.

We knocked on the door of a very small apartment in the dank basement of a tenement. We awakened the father, who at first was both fearful and suspicious. He calmed down as he learned what we were about. Yes, he was ethnic Korean (with a Japanese name). Yes, he had a crippled son who was at school, and yes, he would be glad to take his son to see the Shriners.

We gave him the essential information, he thanked us, and we left. I later heard that surgery was performed and that the boy's condition had been partially alleviated. That's all I know about that one case, but it brought to life for me what so many Koreans living in Japan over the years have been up against.

13

Fort Apache

I woke up early on the morning I was to leave for Vietnam. Meg was still sleeping beside me. I found myself thinking of the untold millions of men down through history who'd had a similar sad moment, leaving family and familiarity behind to face the deep uncertainties of war. I felt confident I would return, but was not sure how well I would cope with what lay ahead.

"Well, it's my turn," I thought, as I sat up and put my feet on the floor.

My return to Vietnam took place in September 1970, almost seven years after my visit to Saigon with Secretary McNamara in December 1963. It had been hard to keep track of the war while we were in Burma. CNN had not been invented, we had no television, and the war was of little interest to the local Burmese news editors. I sensed that the war was not going well and that we were getting dragged deeper and deeper into a jungle morass.

When we returned to Japan in mid-1966, things became clearer. We had television there, and a good daily paper, the *Japan Times*.

My first meeting with George H.W. Bush took place in Tokyo in December 1967. He was then a Texas congressman, en route to Saigon on a "fact-finding" mission. An ex-CIA friend with whom I had gone through arctic survival training in Idaho accompanied Bush and introduced us.

Bush was tall, youthful, and friendly. He was charming toward Meg and made a highly positive impression on us both. Bush asked for my views on how we were doing in Vietnam. I said something like: "Unless the South Vietnamese build a solid foundation for our efforts, we are going to sink into the sand." I did not then think of

Bush as a presidential possibility, nor did my friend, who had gotten to know Bush in Texas, where they were both in the oil business.

The North Vietnamese Tet offensive at the end of January 1968––a military defeat for them, a catastrophic psychological defeat for us—brought on Vietnamization, a process of U.S. withdrawal that was well underway when I arrived in Saigon.

My home would be in Bien Hoa, a river town about twenty miles northeast of Saigon. It was between a sprawling Army base at Long Binh and a U.S. Air Force base just outside Bien Hoa. I was in charge (for CIA) of the ten provinces surrounding Saigon.

My main military mission was to stop rocket attacks into the crowded port area of Saigon, where a steady flow of vulnerable cargo ships brought arms and ammunition into the war, and to disrupt attacks on the bases themselves. I was also ordered to penetrate the remaining Viet Cong structure and to develop a reliable, validated agent network. I would find that the second mission was much harder than the first. My CIA title was Regional Officer in Charge (ROIC) of Military Region 3.

A CIA officer who would be working for me drove me to Bien Hoa. I remember thinking that it was one of the ugliest places I'd ever seen. Barbed wire was strung haphazardly along the sides of the road, festooned with rags flapping in a hot, dusty wind. My office was in a fort-like walled compound beside the muddy Dong Nai River. We called it "Fort Apache."

I lived alone, two blocks up from the river, in a concrete Vietnamese house with ceiling fans, parquet floors, and plastic windows. My bedroom was upstairs. Laid out for me were a flak jacket, a steel helmet, and an Uzi submachine gun.

Fort Apache was where I ate all my meals. Several CIA officers lived and worked there, and dozens of Vietnamese employees shared the working space, serving as translators, interpreters, cooks, maids, and liaison personnel. It had a large and comfortable recreation room upstairs with a pool table and shuffleboard.

Best of all was a large open porch opening to the west and overlooking the river, which was about 300 yards wide. Seen by day it was always muddy, but with sunset's reflections on its surface, it became beautiful, filled with small ferries and narrow fishing boats, from which standing men, wondrously balanced, threw their circular nets into the water.

I quickly decided that the only things of beauty in Bien Hoa were the river and the sky, and one could see them both from our porch. Sunsets were often spectacular, with wild clouds and a fierce coloration I had never seen before, not even in Burma.

One evening in October 1970, sitting alone on the porch, I wrote the following lines, seeking to record the faint sense of menace that I felt, particularly as night came on:

> Misshapen clouds
> Lurked on the skyline
> Writhing witches
> Feeding fire and chaos,
> Far to the west.

Our Vietnamese support staffers were friendly, well informed, and eager to help. I asked what I should be reading to learn about Vietnamese history and character, and a copy of *Kim Van Kieu* was quickly produced. First published in Vietnamese in 1804 and in print ever since, it's a legendary epic poem about a beautiful, virtuous daughter who allowed herself to be sold into a house of prostitution in order to save her revered father from bankruptcy and prison.

In its portrayal of a decaying family, vulnerable to misfortune, *Kim Van Kieu* resembled stories from the great Chinese novel, *Dream of the Red Chamber*. It spoke of "pale fate" awaiting us, of "walls having ears," and of the need to avoid chance encounters with old friends who might be dangerous. The tale was full of adventures, but the tone was one of sadness, loss, and regret, in keeping with Vietnam's tragic history.

About a month after my arrival, an abrupt announcement came over the public address system near the close of business, sternly stating that the compound gates would be closed, and no one would be allowed to leave the compound. I called the administrative officer to ask what had happened and was told: "Some money is missing." He suspected that one of the Vietnamese staff had taken it. I asked why he thought so, and he had no good answer.

I immediately went on the PA system, the first time I'd ever done so. I said that the gates would not be closed, but asked all employees, before they went home, to look for an envelope of money that had been mislaid. Two minutes later, a smiling Vietnamese secretary came in with the money, saying she had seen it lying on a desk in a training room.

I thanked her, announced over the PA system that the money had been found and waited. Within minutes an embarrassed CIA officer came into my office, saying he had put the money down inadvertently and could not remember what he'd done with it. The administrative officer's tour ended shortly thereafter, and my stock went up with the Vietnamese employees.

In Saigon, I was briefed in some detail on the Hamlet Evaluation System, a computerized portrait of all of South Vietnam, based on carefully constructed questions that each U.S. officer serving as province- or district-level advisors had to answer on a frequent, scheduled basis. Does the Vietnamese hamlet chief sleep in his bed at home or in a bunker? Is the school open regularly? Are crop prices going up or down? Were there any firefights? If so, who was killed, and how many?

Based on answers to such questions, each hamlet was assigned a rating of red (bad), yellow (cautionary), or green (good). MACV headquarters had a giant screen on which all these judgmental lights flashed dramatically. I carefully looked at the ten provinces for which I was to be responsible and was gratified to see a vast majority of green lights, some yellows, and very few reds.

Upon my arrival in Bien Hoa, I scheduled visits to each of the provinces in which CIA had small outposts of two or three officers and planned to drive around to all of them. I was told that it would be utterly foolish to drive to some of the local offices, due to the danger of ambush along the roads.

My comment that this advice seemed overly cautious in light of what I'd seen on the giant screen in Saigon was greeted with snorts of contempt. Hau Nghia province, just west of Saigon, was considered highly dangerous, due to large tunnel complexes used by the Viet Cong as hiding places, storage facilities, and launch points for attack.

When I asked why these complexes were not attacked directly, I was told that the Army of the Republic of Vietnam (ARVN) was reluctant to go after these bunkered areas, as they were heavily mined and cleverly defended. U.S. forces were scheduled for departure, and no one wanted to be associated with "the last men killed in Vietnam."

The huge tunnel complex in Cu Chi, just northwest of Saigon, is now a major tourist attraction and has been found to extend all the way to the Cambodian border. Only small elements of it had been located when I was there. The computerized system in Saigon had major shortcomings.

I drove whenever I could and, in so doing, became acquainted, at least superficially, with the attitude of U.S. Army units still deployed in the area. One small base east of Bien Hoa contained an armored unit with several large tanks, which I frequently saw parked along the main road—on patrol, no doubt. One tank was manned by a crew of men badly needing haircuts, wearing headbands, smoking (probably pot), and flashing the peace sign. On the side of their tank's turret were painted the words HEAVEN HELP US ALL.

Another time, I followed an Army diesel truck driven at high speed that repeatedly ran Vietnamese civilian pedestrians off the road. When pedestrians were spotted, the truck would accelerate, spouting a gust of black smoke, and drive right at the walking people. Several times, I saw pedestrians have to jump into ditches to avoid being hit.

I was disgusted by this and passed the truck. Three men were in the front seat, all laughing. I was told later that the transportation unit to which that truck belonged was notorious for its drug consumption. I reported what I'd seen to the unit commander but got no feedback and was probably regarded as a rear echelon pain in the ass to whom no attention need be paid.

All CIA communications from Bien Hoa went to Saigon, where my boss was the chief of station. In Bien Hoa, I was also attached to the Civil Operations and Revolutionary Development Support (CORDS) structure, led by Ambassador William Funkhouser, a Foreign Service officer who had been our ambassador to Gabon and had requested an assignment in Vietnam. The CORDS structure had been established in 1967 and was an effort to win "hearts and minds."

Bill Colby had returned to Vietnam to ensure that Viet Cong

prisoners were well treated and not tortured. He also had designed and implemented the Phoenix Program, which sought to improve coordination and targeting among military and civilian units in fighting the Viet Cong.

By the time of my arrival, the Phoenix Program seemed essentially somnolent. It never played a role in any of the operations run out of Bien Hoa in my time there. I respected Colby greatly and approved of what he had done, but the inescapable fact was that, despite all his fine efforts, we were still losing the war.

Some of the personnel who worked for me were career CIA officers; others were ex-military and ex-law enforcement. We also had three females assigned to Fort Apache: two reports officers and my secretary, a wonderfully feisty woman named Sheila, who was as tough as any man in the region.

I was also in close liaison with two senior Vietnamese officers, Colonel Cong of ARVN intelligence and Colonel Hien of the National Police. Both were men of high quality. I drew on my good relationships with these men to try to present a monthly report to Saigon about how the war was going in all ten provinces in MR 3. We also had isolated and sporadic agent reports to draw upon, but the observations of the small CIA outposts in several of the provinces were far more informative.

It had quickly become clear to me that the collective, highly skeptical view in Bien Hoa of how the war was progressing differed greatly from Saigon's pervasive optimism. In my initial Saigon briefings I'd been told things were going well and that the decision by Congress to cut major funding was the greatest obstacle to "winning the war."

Two other features on the local landscape were a squadron of A-37 fighter-bombers, based in Bien Hoa, and a large Vietnamese hospital, staffed in part by doctors and nurses from Australia. I mention these two entities in the same sentence, as there was strong symbiosis between the fighter pilots and the Australian nurses.

The pilot's lounge at Bien Hoa was notable for its bar, over which hung a large glittering sign saying simply "FUCK COMMUNISM!" Local wags commented, largely in envy, that the sign's exhortation was being applied to the nurses as well.

Such was the strange agglomeration of organizations and people that six years of war and bureaucracy had created in Bien Hoa. I soon became accustomed to its varied demands and obligations and, within a month or two, was thankful to be in Bien Hoa and not Saigon, where the atmosphere of forced optimism on the war was both cloying and suffocating.

Next to Fort Apache, on the edge of the Dong Nai River, was a helicopter-landing place called Echo Pad. The thump-thump-thump of incoming Huey choppers was a daily occurrence, and I did a great deal of flying in that manner to close-by provinces. For longer distances, Air America was available, with Pilatus Porter single-engine, piston planes, which had an amazingly short takeoff and landing (STOL) capability.

The countryside, viewed from the air was quite beautiful, except for the mud-filled pockmarks—ugly reminders of the constant U.S. bombing attacks of the past six years. Other scabrous areas had been deforested by Agent Orange applied, *a la* crop dusters, in an effort to cut down jungle growth that the Viet Cong expertly used as camouflage.

There was fighting across the border in Cambodia during most of my tour, much of it staged out of Tay Ninh province right on the border. I went up there to watch the mounting of a large-scale helicopter attack on targets in Cambodia. It was something straight out of the film *Apocalypse Now*, with helicopter pilots wearing old-time Seventh Cavalry hats and six-shooters strapped cowboy-style low on their hips.

Every month, CIA representatives of the four military regions went to Saigon for a meeting with Ted Shackley, the chief of station, a man with whom I had developed an uneasy relationship. This perhaps resulted from my effort, soon after arriving, to put together an intelligence report, based on prisoner debriefings and defector reports, which showed that MR 3 was far less secure, and much more dangerous, than its depiction on the giant screen in Saigon indicated.

Shackley refused to disseminate this report to Washington. I protested and was told that my data were "outdated." I put together another version, based on newer and better data, but that one also never saw the light of day.

I came to dread the monthly meetings because MR 3 always

ranked last in the number of validated penetrations of the Viet Cong we'd developed. Shackley put unrelenting pressure on us to produce more validated reports and sometimes mocked MR 3's low production. I had inherited one excellent VC penetration in an outlying province, but I was hard-pressed to even approach its quality with the operational efforts under my direction.

We were constantly dealing with chimerical operations with neither substance nor validity, many of them proposed to us by corrupt or incompetent Vietnamese officials, and sometimes the result of torture. As I read today of efforts to penetrate the Taliban organization in Afghanistan, I am deeply sympathetic.

A major milestone in my tour came on 26 March 1971, when the 1st Cavalry Division (Airmobile) went home, after six years of action. Its headquarters had been just north of Bien Hoa, and the "First Cav," with elements scattered all over South Vietnam, had been one of the largest American military units "in country." A total of 145,000 men had served in the division, mostly on one-year tours, and approximately 4,300 of those men had been killed.

I still have the folded program that was handed out at the departure ceremony. On its front is the statement "Homeward Bound—Mission Completed." On the front I wrote: "I attended this ceremony. Very mixed feelings—officers glum, enlisted men cheerful."

General Creighton Abrams, the overall American commander in Vietnam, was there and gave a stirring speech of commendation and farewell. I do not believe that anyone who was to remain in Vietnam, as I was, felt that the First Cav's mission had been completed.

By the end of 1971, the Australian and New Zealand forces had left, the Thais were on their way out, and Cambodian units, created as part of our invasion of the border area, were ineffective. U.S. forces in MR 3 amounted to only four combat battalions.

As I became more fully attuned to the tempo of the war in MR 3, I'd come to realize that our best chance to damage the Viet Cong structure was to attack it directly. This we could still do, based on intelligence gained from POWs and defectors, and because even as Vietnamization progressed, there were still U.S. helicopter units ready to fight if they were given solid targets to attack and CIA elements to guide and fight beside them. We had Provincial Reconnaissance Units (PRU) under our control, made up largely of Montagnards with whom CIA had had relations for almost a decade under the CIDG (Civilian Irregular Defense Groups) program that I had first encountered in 1962.

The most vital ingredient enabling Bien Hoa to move into an "attack not penetrate" mode was the presence of Felix Rodriguez and two or three former Special Forces officers now under contract to CIA. Felix was a Cuban recruited by CIA for its ill-fated Bay of Pigs operation. Felix had gone ashore in Cuba before the attacking force, which, lacking any air support, had quickly been surrounded and captured. He escaped capture, got out of Cuba, and rejoined CIA.

He then was sent to Bolivia and led the group of local forces that captured Che Guevara. Felix strove mightily to keep Che alive, but the Bolivians were determined to kill him, which they did. Felix and Che, in the few days of his captivity, grew to admire each other, and Felix to this day is proud to possess Guevara's Rolex watch, given to him just at the end.

Handsome, stocky, and dark haired, Felix was and is a warrior, utterly fearless and determined, who worked well with PRU groups and with American helicopter pilots still eager to carry the fight to the Viet Cong. Once we had developed intelligence on the location of a Viet Cong bunker, supply point, or rest area, we'd mount an operation, with Felix in a small, two-seater helicopter called a Loche in the lead, and heavier craft following.

Felix would fly at treetop level until he'd located the hostile target, often engaging it directly himself. It would then be attacked by following Huey helicopters with heavy machine gun fire, and follow-up ground attacks by the PRU. Felix had several crash landings as a result of his small helicopter being hit by ground fire, but he survived them all.

Through POW debriefing we learned of a Viet Cong unit whose specific mission was to attack with rocket fire incoming supply and ammunition ships in Saigon's port area. Felix pursued this unit doggedly, even learning the name of its commander. One evening, he came to my house, in full battle regalia, to proudly report that the Viet Cong unit had been successfully attacked and disrupted and that he had personally shot and killed its leader.

For this work, and for his capture of Che Guevara, Felix was later deservedly awarded CIA's Intelligence Star, an award rarely given in those days, and only to those who had demonstrated valor under fire and/or in extreme operational conditions. Felix still calls me two or three times a year to say "hello." He still hates the Castro regime in Cuba, which for years placed a price on his head.

In the summer of 1971, chief of station Shackley had all four of the regional officers in charge (ROIC's) come to Saigon to brief Ambassador Ellsworth Bunker on the status of the war. It was the only time in my entire tour that all four senior field officers of the large CIA station met together. I met two of the other ROICS for the first time on the day we briefed Bunker. Our four presentations were utterly uncoordinated, but they were all deeply pessimistic about the war.

(My now-declassified report to Saigon for the month of June 1971 started out as follows: "MR 3 at midyear is a somber-toned mosaic. The largely completed American withdrawal from the area has created something of a power vacuum, which South Vietnamese forces have yet to fill. Viet Cong and North Vietnamese forces, long engaged in regearing and reorganization, have been able to exploit this situation in some parts of the region.")

As all four of us spoke in the same pessimistic tone, Bunker sat in Olympian silence. The last man to speak was a retired American major general, kept on as a sort of embassy liaison to the U.S. and Vietnamese military. This officer, a charming, upbeat individual, spoke optimistically about bridges reopened, new weapons delivered, and positive changes in Vietnamese commanders. At last Bunker spoke, saying, "Thank you, gentlemen. I find all of this very encouraging."

Robert Komer, a senior embassy official who'd been the first head of the CORDS organization, had attended the briefing. I angrily asked him what I should make of the ambassador's characterizing our pessimistic reports as "encouraging."

Komer replied, "Oh, don't worry, Ellsworth heard you. He just didn't want to make negative remarks that might be leaked to the press." This seemed to me to be more unrealistic thinking, right at the top.

Unrealistic thinking and general sloppiness were not limited to

Saigon. There were many such things to be found in Bien Hoa itself. Richard Funkhouser's weekly staff meetings for CORDS personnel often witnessed people talking past each other and raising contentious issues for which no solutions seemed possible. This sort of thing was maddening to Funkhouser, a Phi Beta Kappa graduate of Princeton who'd been a pilot in World War II, flying dangerous missions "over the hump" from India into Burma. Funkhouser did not suffer fools easily but often found himself surrounded by them.

At one of my early CORDS staff meetings, held in a large, drab room where movies were shown in the evening, Funkhouser put a series of pertinent questions on the war to his staff, which numbered about forty men, mostly mid-grade officers and Army civilian employees. Funkhouser sensed that Vietnamization was taking its toll on American morale and that a lot of people were "going through the motions," as they waited for their paycheck or for their tours to end.

Funkhouser got no decent answers to his questions and grew angry. "Has anybody here read a book recently?" he shouted.

No answer came.

He turned to me, and I knew instantly I was in trouble. He said, "Well, Gregg, you're supposed to be my intelligence advisor, you must have read something."

As a matter of fact, I had just finished reading *Kim Van Kieu*, the Vietnamese epic poem referred to above. I was caught out and had to tell "an inconvenient truth." I described *Kim* as an interesting tale that shed light on the Vietnamese psyche.

Funkhouser jumped on this, and said to his staff, "That sounds like an important thing for us to read. How many of you have read it?"

Not a single hand went up, and no one mentioned any other thing he had read on Vietnam. Funkhouser then turned to his U.S. Information Agency advisor and said, "Surely, you have read it?" The poor man had not.

I counted heads in the room and estimated that there was at least a collective two hundred years of U.S. experience in Vietnam in the room. But it seemed that no one had bothered to try to learn much about the country in which he was serving.

I was not very popular with the CORDS staff from that day

onward. I had "rocked the boat" in a situation wherein a lot of people had found a comfortable, nonthreatening way to serve in a war—even while drawing hazardous duty pay—often involving live-in Vietnamese mistresses and, in some cases, marriage.

My own CIA crew included ex-servicemen who had stayed in Bien Hoa, based on familiarity with Vietnam and hopes for its future. I judged most of them to be competent and fully engaged in their work.

This was particularly true of Rudy, a gifted and committed paramilitary officer, with several tough tours under his belt. He had met and married a lovely Vietnamese war widow with children and lived with her in a Bien Hoa apartment.

Early one evening, I had a frantic call from Rudy. He said he had just returned from a mission to find one of his children "desperately ill." He asked me to come over with medical help. I rounded up one of the Australian nurses and rushed to Rudy's home, where we found a tragic scene: a beautiful little girl lying silent and still, frightened siblings, an anguished mother, and Rudy trying to comfort her.

The nurse quickly confirmed that the child was dead. We later learned that she was eight years old and had suffered a massive heart attack. Rudy asked me to take the child away, and I did so, leaving the nurse to try to console the mother and the other weeping children.

And so I found myself carrying the still warm body of a lovely child whose name I did not know down the stairs and out to my car. I laid her gently on the back seat, trying not to let my tears fall on her tranquil face. I drove to my house, and not wishing to leave her alone, carried her onto a couch in the living room. I was reminded vividly of carrying my own small daughters, Lucy and Alison, to bed after they had fallen asleep.

It took a while for me to settle myself enough to make the necessary phone calls. No one knew what I should do, and so I decided to drive to the emergency room of the U.S. Army hospital at Long Binh.

Back to the car we went. I had brought some sort of blanket to wrap about her, but did not want to cover her face. I guess I hoped somehow she would magically awaken.

I did not know exactly where to go, but spotted U.S. Military Police in a jeep and asked for their help. They expertly guided me onto the base and to the hospital. What I had thought of as the emergency room was in fact a combat surgery ward, to which battlefield wounded were flown by helicopter. A helicopter landing pad was just outside the hospital.

Carrying the child, I walked to large doors with red crosses on them, which flew open as I approached. An American Army nurse ran toward me, with an almost hostile expression on her face, as if she was thinking: 'What is he doing here, bringing a kind of death we do not deal with?'

The nurse expertly took the child in her arms, and the inevitable administrative questions began, almost none of which I could answer. As I was struggling to establish who I was, who the child was, and who her parents were, I heard the pounding noise of an incoming helicopter landing just outside.

A bell rang, the big doors burst open, and in rushed medics carrying a muddy, bloody figure on a stretcher. I was pushed aside and leaned up against a wall, trying to sort out what I was seeing and feeling.

The figure from the stretcher was placed on an operating table and was almost instantly surrounded by a large medical crew who seemed to know exactly what they were doing. There was a mutter of conversation between nurses and doctors, then a short silence.

Suddenly someone laughed. I saw the figure on the operating table with his head up, looking around dazedly. He had been stripped bare, and it had become apparent that he was basically in good shape except for superficial cuts that had bled profusely. An incoming artillery shell had blown him into a deep mud puddle, leaving him unconscious but basically uninjured.

The nurse came over to me, patted me on the cheek and said, "Life goes on." After I signed some papers, I was allowed to leave, and walked into the night, utterly spent. That was only the first of three visits I would pay to that hospital. Worse was to come.

David Konzelman was a bright, confident, and engaging young CIA officer working in one of the more troubled provinces in MR 3. I had met him only a few times but had been impressed each time by his energy and the clarity of his reporting. Each province in MR

3 presented its own pattern of war-related events, depending on geography, topography, and the quality of leadership shown by both sides. Dave's province was complicated and dangerous, with local leaders whose allegiances appeared tenuous and shifting.

I heard one day that one of our local operations had gone awry, that a helicopter had been forced to make an emergency landing, hurting someone in the process. It turned out to be much worse than that. Dave had been horribly burned by a white phosphorous grenade. It was a windy day, the helicopter pilot had apparently requested that a smoke grenade be thrown to show him wind direction as he landed in a small area, and that a white phosphorous grenade had been used by mistake.

Dave was immediately flown to the Long Binh hospital. I could not get there for several hours. I would not have recognized him, his burns were so horrific. But he saw and knew me and spoke almost jauntily of being in a cool place, with his clothes off, surrounded by lovely women. "Just what I've been looking for," he said. That remains by far the most courageous statement I have ever heard made, particularly by someone at death's door, and suffering terrible pain.

The doctors told me Dave had almost no chance of survival, but he lived on to be flown to Japan, and later to the Army's burn treatment center in Texas. There he died, weeks later. Each interim report we received on his condition referred to his amazing courage and his repeated expressions of gratitude to those seeking to ease his pain. Dave was twenty-seven years old.

Those of us left in Bien Hoa who had known him gathered to talk about his life and death. One man said it would have been better had he died immediately, thus avoiding weeks of suffering. As we mulled that over, another man disagreed: "Living is the name of the game, and in these last weeks Dave showed us what kind of man he truly was. If he had died right away, we might never have known."

That was the theme I used when I wrote Dave's parents in the state of Washington. I told them what courage he had displayed, and how much those caring for him admired him. I drew a parallel with a little apple tree that was planted in our yard when I was a very small boy. It never flowered until finally one spring it was resplendent with blossoms, then died soon afterward.

Dave's name is one of those displayed on the Wall of Honor in the front hall of CIA headquarters. Each time I go there, I find his name and remember.

This tragic triptych was completed when, later in my tour I learned that Colonel Hien of the national police, with whom I worked closely, had been ambushed and severely wounded. As the horrific details emerged, it became clear that Hien had been specifically targeted by the Viet Cong. Deadly Claymore mines, captured by the Viet Cong, had been placed along a road regularly used by Hien and were set off as his jeep passed by.

Incredibly, Hien had been hit by only one fragment of a mine, but that one deadly piece had blinded him. On the day after he was attacked, I went to Long Binh to pay my respects to him as a colleague and close friend. I had to stand in line to do so, behind a shuffling procession of sad Vietnamese, many of them weeping. There was Hien, sitting up in his hospital bed, his freshly bandaged eyes still oozing, thanking his friends and subordinates for coming to visit him. Some Vietnamese expressed the hope that American medical expertise could save his sight, but nothing could be done.

I stayed in touch with Hien as doctors performed some reconstructive surgery on him and as he was released from the hospital. Just before I left Vietnam, I went to see him in his home. He was beginning to adjust to his blindness, blundering about with a cane. His beautiful wife looked devastated. Hien was fluent in English and we talked about what we had worked together to try to achieve: a free and secure South Vietnam. Neither of us was at all optimistic about the future.

As I rose to go, I had a final question to ask him. He asked what it was. I said, "Think of the fragment that took out your eyes; if it had been an inch to the front, it would have missed you, if it had been an inch to the rear, it would have killed you. Are you lucky or unlucky?"

He dropped his head and said: "Why do you ask me such a question?"

I replied, "That is a question you will be dealing with for the rest of your life, and you might as well answer it now."

He reached out to his wife, who stood next to him. She took his hand, and he replied, "I guess I'm lucky."

I said "I agree with you." We embraced, and I left Vietnam the next day.

Seventeen years later, I got a letter from Hien. It was neatly typed and carried an American stamp. I was in Seoul as U.S. ambassador to South Korea, and a few days earlier our residence had been broken into by students protesting our pressure on opening up the Korean beef market. We'd gone on international television after the incident, and Hien in his letter said he had heard and recognized my voice.

His letter went on to say that he had spent four hard years in a North Vietnamese reindoctrination center but that he "had been remembered by American friends," who had helped him and his family get to the United States He was proud of having learned to type in Braille and sounded content. I responded, and we've kept in touch ever since.

In 2000, the Hiens invited Meg and me to the marriage of their daughter, a nurse, to a physics professor. The family lives in Falls Church, Virginia. At the wedding service, Hien asked me to speak, and I told the story of his wounding, his courage, and the question I had asked him. Hien and his family are very lucky, they know it, and rejoice in that fact.

On July 1, 1971, a day that would have been my late father's 81st birthday, I wrote a family letter that summed up the way I felt about the war.

> We have not succeeded in nearly all that we have attempted. Most U.S. forces are out of the part of Vietnam in which I work. The Vietnamese army has not yet moved to fully fill the gap that our pullout leaves. We have pretty well run our race and are passing the baton to the Vietnamese. We have tried so hard and so long that it will be hard for many here to "let go." But "let go" we must, and whatever happens it is their country, not ours. The domino theory, which brought us here has been debunked, at least to my satisfaction if not to Walt Rostow's. So I do all I can to give the South Vietnamese the best start possible, and also try to learn from what I see. It is a very interesting place to be, but it is an unhappy place.

Early in the fall of 1971, I was summoned to the chief of station's office in Saigon, with no agenda being announced. I was tense as I drove into Saigon. Ted Shackley and I had had an uneasy relationship almost since the time of my arrival a year earlier, as my view of how the war was going differed greatly from his. Shackley, probably taking his cue from Ambassador Bunker, was conveying optimism about the war in what he reported, and what he allowed others to report. My view, sent officially to Saigon in monthly reports on MR-3 activities, was not optimistic, as reflected in the family letter quoted above. I do not think my official views were ever sent to Washington—at least not while I was still in Bien Hoa.

I walked into Shackley's office, and he got right to the point. He cited our differing views on how the war was going, reminded me that he was chief of station, and that I was not, and then accused me of undercutting him "via the ten-cent pouch," by which he meant private letters sent by me to senior officials in CIA headquarters. As evidence for his suspicions, Shackley said, "I have been hearing from Washington some of the same things you have been saying here."

I told him I had never gone out of channels to Washington, that I was angered by his accusation, and wondered if he wanted me to leave my position in Bien Hoa since he seemed not to trust me.

Shackley backed off by saying that he did not want me to leave and that he'd just wanted to make certain his station was speaking with one voice. The meeting ended awkwardly for us both, as the tensions between us had been raised to a personal level.

I seethed as I drove back to Bien Hoa and thought briefly of resigning. But I quickly realized that would be a cop-out on my part. So I stayed in place and told no one of my meeting.

I last saw Shackley when he made his only visit to Bien Hoa, accompanying Director Richard Helms, who was on an inspection trip. Shackley's attention was focused entirely on Helms, with whom he had a long-standing relationship. Our chief of station knew little of who we were, or what we did on a daily basis, and his introductions of us to Helms were perfunctory. Shackley and his immediate subordinates rarely left Saigon, and I think that this accounted, at least in some part, for their overoptimism regarding the war.

Around Thanksgiving 1971, Meg paid a short visit to Bien Hoa. That visit, deeply welcomed by me and all who met her, tided me through the year-end holidays. I put Sheila, my secretary, in charge of a cocktail party I gave at my house to celebrate Meg's visit. Sheila's invitation cited "coat and tie" as the dress code. This was unheard of in Bien Hoa and caused Dave Wilson, a man with a waggish sense of humor, to call up and ask if coats should be tucked into trousers or left to hang outside.

Ambassador Funkhouser arrived in a pristine seersucker suit and black knit tie, in stark contrast to Felix, who "came clanking in"—Meg's phrase—carrying a machine gun, sweating profusely in a flak jacket, with hand grenades attached to his belt. He apologized for having been delayed by a mission but said he "did not want to miss the party." He added greatly to it, and Funkhouser was delighted to meet him.

After Meg's departure, I chose to spend my second straight Christmas in Bien Hoa, allowing as many personnel as possible to go on leave. I found this Christmas easier to deal with than the first had been. I knew the routines, had a leave to look forward to, and my tour was slowly moving toward completion.

My January 1972 leave flew by, but it was a very happy time. Meg and I drove north to Hanover, New Hampshire, to visit my mother and got a refreshing taste of real winter. My mother, then 81, was as courageous as ever. She had kept all of my Bien Hoa letters, many of which I have drawn on to write this memoir.

I returned to Bien Hoa in good spirits, but the last five months of my tour proved to be its most tumultuous. I fully anticipated a main-unit attack by the North Vietnamese designed to test ARVN's fighting qualities and had annoyed some in Saigon by predicting this just before I went on home leave.

All was quiet upon my return, but Felix said some of his Montagnard PRU units operating well north of Saigon sensed something ominous in the wind.

Fort Apache had become something of a social center for Americans and Australians in Bien Hoa. We were on the DOD movie circuit, and two or three nights a week we showed films to which all were invited. The films were not necessarily new; I remember enjoying *Gone with the Wind* on one particularly rainy night.

One evening we were surprised and delighted when one of the senior Australian nurses suddenly appeared, by herself, at Fort Apache. Tall, dark-haired, with strong features and dancer's legs, she made an evocative impression on the half-dozen of us in the large recreation room.

She knew who I was, seemed to want to talk, and so we went out on the porch. It was a humid night, with no moon and a faint breeze blowing in off the river. The click of pool balls punctuated our conversation.

This particular nurse was in a close relationship with an American colonel, on leave at the moment, whom I found overbearing and prone to throwing his weight around. I asked her how she was enjoying her tour. She spoke emotionally of how she and the other nurses had to cope with an experience that was far more intense and stressful than any of them had expected.

She said: "We all came here hoping to be friends with everybody, but the different pressures here are such that that is impossible." She explained that work at the civilian hospital, often dealing with war's carnage, was difficult, that they all got tired, and the relentless social pressures and general intensities of living in the midst of war were overwhelming.

Most nurses had found that the only way to cope was either to not go out at all, or to develop a close relationship with one person that could provide both personal fulfillment and a refuge from other pressures. She seemed both regretful and apologetic as she spoke to me, and I was impressed by her willingness to speak of such a sensitive issue.

I said that I fully understood what she'd said, that we all appreciated what the Australians, male and female, were contributing through their work at the hospital, and that just having them around was a great pleasure for all of us.

We had a beer together, I walked down with her to her jeep, and she drove off into the darkness. That was the last conversation I had with that particular nurse, but I appreciated her words, admired her, and envied her friend the colonel.

One night in Bien Hoa in early 1972, I was invited to dinner by the only ethnic Montagnard to have achieved flag officer rank in the Vietnamese Army. (Think of Geronimo as a brigadier general.)

I was accompanied by friends who told me that, however much I drank, I'd be free of hangover in the morning by virtue of a magic potion dispensed at evening's end.

Our host was a noted drinker and the evening was truly uproarious. Martel Cognac flowed like water. Whoever in Paris had the Martel account was living high off the hog.

As we rose unsteadily to leave, our host produced a bottle of dark brown liquid, of vile appearance. He said, "I won't tell you what is in this, or you would never drink it. But my advice, particularly to you M. Gregg, is that you take a small cup, for the sake of your health."

I gulped a shot glass full of the awful stuff, expecting it not to stay down. Stay down it did. I slept deeply and well, and arose in the morning full of *joie de vivre*. War is not always hell.

Major General James Hollingsworth had become the senior American officer in MR 3 in early 1972. He was the most colorfully profane man I've ever known. Other military friends told me later that the only thing that kept him from becoming a four-star general was his language. A 1940 graduate of Texas A & M, Hollingsworth is that famed school's most decorated graduate, with an endless array of medals for valor and six Purple Hearts for combat wounds. He fought in seven major campaigns during World War II and was a senior commander under General George Patton, of whom he often spoke with great admiration.

Hollingsworth was famous, in some quarters infamous, for an incident in divided Berlin in the late 1940s, where he commanded an Army battalion designed to be "the pane of glass" the Soviets would have to shatter if they intended to directly attack West Germany. Apparently, venereal disease had become an issue in Berlin, and a senior medical officer addressed Hollingsworth's battalion directly on this subject. Upon the conclusion of these remarks Hollingsworth was asked if he had anything to add. He said simply, "Soldiers who don't fuck, won't fight."

Hollingsworth, whose helicopter call sign was "Danger 79er," spent much of his time flying around MR 3, visiting both Vietnamese and U.S. units. He quickly became aware of the CIA's paramilitary operations being run out of Bien Hoa and thoroughly approved of them. He was most appreciative of tactical military information we provided to him, as he was increasingly apprehensive about a possible main unit attack by North Vietnamese divisions designed to capture Saigon.

In early 1972, I began to meet with Hollingsworth every morning at 7 a.m. He was tall, muscular, and leathery-faced, and his glare was like a fist in your face. His smile, rare as it was, seemed almost a benediction.

Some of those early morning meetings were colorful. One day I reported intelligence out of Cambodia that significant enemy supplies were moving west from the Ho Chi Minh trail to Angkor Wat. Someone asked where Angkor Wat was, and I pointed it out on the wall map. Hollingsworth, scowling at the map, growled: "I remember that goddamn place, a bat shit on my hat."

General hilarity ensued, and the MR 3 G-2, a corpulent colonel known as King Arthur, said, "Well general, everyone to his own thing, I went there to get some stone rubbings." Hollingsworth's remark was memorable—a thousand years of cultural history pushed aside by a bit of bat droppings falling on his hat.

Hollingsworth's Vietnamese counterpart was General Nguyen Van Minh. The two men could not have been more different. General Minh's energetic and aggressive predecessor, General Do Cao Tri, had been killed in 1971 in an aircraft accident connected with fighting in Cambodia. Minh was intelligent but cautious. I had gradually gotten to know him. In June 1971, Minh's father died at 88, there had been a funeral in Saigon, and I had been the only American to attend.

Hollingsworth urged me to see as much of him as I could. Minh spoke English well, and we met more and more frequently. Minh was interested in what I told him about the American point of view, and Hollingsworth and senior people in Saigon were glad to get a feel for Minh's morale and view of the future.

When I returned to Bien Hoa from leave in early February 1972, Ambassador Funkhouser asked to see me. Our relationship, somewhat prickly at first, had developed into one of mutual respect. Both Meg and Felix had made a great impression on him when he met them at our Thanksgiving party, and that may have contributed to his telling me that during my absence a senior Foreign Service inspector had come to Bien Hoa to evaluate the overall performance of CORDS, which Funkhouser headed.

The inspector went to see General Minh and asked what it was that the Americans were doing for him that he found most helpful. Minh replied that it was the work done by CIA in MR 3 that he valued most. It was very nice of Funkhouser to tell me this, and he seemed pleased to do it. I was delighted to pass this news on to Felix, Rudy, and the others who were personally carrying the fight to the Viet Cong.

The pace of events seemed to pick up during February and March of 1972: Rudy and Felix, in helicopters, were helping coordinate air strikes on a VC bunker area when a 500-pound bomb was dropped in the wrong place, landing in the midst of Vietnamese Rangers. Several were blown through the air.

Felix landed and picked up an inert, mud-covered form lying at the edge of the bomb crater, whom he assumed was dead. On the helicopter, the man awoke, was shocked to find himself flying, then felt himself to see that all arms and legs were present and functioning. They were—he was unhurt except for a roaring headache. No one was killed by the mistake. The bomb had a time-delayed fuse and burrowed in before exploding. In Vietnam, such things were funny.

In late February, the Australians held a memorable party. The occasion was the arrival of a new team of nurses, which attracted many of the pilots from the Bien Hoa air base. The Australians had hired an excellent band, and some exuberant dancing featured Dave Wilson, sporting a beard and longish hair. Some Koreans asked him where he had learned to do some of their dances. He was flattered by this attention.

A hulking Special Forces major, in full battle array, with hair about a half-inch long, confronted Wilson, after watching him dance and demanded: "Who the hell are you and what do you do?"

Wilson replied: "Oh, I'm a New Zealand dentist," and carried it off.

In the same humorous vein, two other "only in Bien Hoa" incidents bear repeating: One night in February 1972, I was in my house doing my 1971 income tax return. My phone rang, and it was Sheila, my secretary, telling me that an American helicopter pilot had fallen out of the window of Ann's fourth floor apartment. Ann was one of our two reports officers. She was very smart, attractive, and rather heroically endowed—think of Elizabeth Taylor around the time of husband number three.

I rushed to the apartment building. All seemed quiet outside. Upstairs I went, to find a weeping Ann, shaken but relieved to know that her guest had survived. She had last seen him, "drunk as a skunk," take a lurching step backward, trip on a low settee, and disappear out her window, tearing out its screen in the process.

Others told me that the pilot's fall had been broken by a series of awnings on lower floors, and a large metal drain cover on the ground, which bent accommodatingly under the impact of his final landing. The pilot returned to flying duty within a week, none the worse for wear. Apparently, the pilot's alcoholic intake had helped him survive, by keeping him relaxed during his fall.

Wilson, the dancer, had become smitten by a very pretty, newly arrived Australian nurse. He felt that his pursuit of her might be enhanced by a boat ride on the Dong Nai River at dusk. Wilson asked me if I would like to join him and the nurse on a "sunset tour." I accepted, but took a gun with me. The river made me nervous.

We got the outboard motor started, and I became the designated driver as Wilson and the nurse sat in the bow. Their words were blown back to me by the breeze, partially obscured by the motor's burbling.

Wilson pointed out objects of local interest as we went upstream. The nurse's replies were unintelligible to me. She had the thickest Australian accent I'd ever heard. Wilson asked her out for dinner, but he did not understand her response.

"What did you say?" he asked, over the heavy sound of the motor. Her response was repeated.

"I'm sorry, I just didn't get that," said Wilson. Her reply to that was a booming: "I'm all booked up, for Christ's sake!" Wilson and I returned, crestfallen, to Fort Apache.

Shortly after that upriver jaunt, I wrote "The Water Skier":

White wake on brown water,
an arching figure
scythes curving patterns
through a sullen river.

In jungle shadow,
eyes slit open
at motor's throb,
and a gaunt head rises.
Gunsights fork the pale chest
and a shot's ripping echo
drowns cry and collapse
in midstream.

Staring eyes and slack mouths
turn astern
and then ashore,
toward hidden menace.

Tow rope
skips errantly.
Skis float
criss cross.

Red wake on brown water
An indistinct figure
face down,
drifts toward the sea.

As indications of an upcoming main-force attack by North Vietnamese divisions accumulated, the need for better tactical intelligence grew acute. For months I had been in an intense debate with the ARVN Corps Interrogation officer, a colonel appropriately named Sinh, on the issue of torture. Sinh routinely abused his prisoners, thereby producing a heavy flow of intelligence that was largely unreliable, coming from men who would say anything to stop the pain.

In early 1972, we knew Sinh had captured a well-known Viet Cong leader, who had fought famously in MR 3 for several years. I immediately asked Sinh for control of this prisoner. He refused. I remember him shaking his head and smiling ruefully, as if to say: "You Americans will never learn the nature of this war."

Several days later, to my great surprise, Sinh turned the battered prisoner over to me, saying: "He knows a lot, but will not talk to me."

I gave charge of the prisoner to a talented CIA officer who had been a schoolteacher and spoke some French. My directions were to heal the man's wounds and to find out what was on his mind and what it might take to get him to talk to us. We quickly learned that he was worried about his family, which had gone into hiding following his capture. He knew exactly where they would be hiding, and we used this information to mount a PRU operation designed to bring them safely to Bien Hoa. This we were able to do, and the prisoner was grateful to be reunited with his loved ones.

The prisoner's next request was to be taken into Saigon, a city he hadn't seen for many years. He and his case officer went together to Saigon, traveled freely about town, and had a meal together. The case officer then came to me and said that the prisoner would tell us anything we wanted to know, as what he'd seen in bustling, prosperous Saigon had convinced him that he had been on the wrong side of the war.

We put him in a helicopter, without a map, and flew him around a large, hotly contested area in MR 3 (War Zone D), which he knew intimately. He pointed out several small potential targets, which we noted on our map, but did not show him. He was then taken back to Bien Hoa, given a different map and told to locate on the map the targets he had located from the air. This he was able to do easily, thereby confirming the accuracy of what he had told us from the air. Several of these targets were quickly attacked, all produced either explosions, indicating storage of ammunition, or firefights with VC units that had been in hiding.

The most important intelligence we gained from our prisoner was that North Vietnamese units were planning large-scale ground attacks. In this context, he knew of a significant bunker/tunnel complex near Bien Hoa, from which a large rocket attack on the Bien Hoa air base was being planned, perhaps in conjunction with the upcoming ground attacks. He could not specifically locate that complex, but knew its general location, and that it was large and important. This information was analyzed by General Abrams in Saigon and General Hollingsworth in MR 3, and a B-52 strategic air attack was planned to obliterate the targeted area.

On the night of the B-52 attack I was awakened by a noisy rattling. I got up and looked outside. I could hear nothing, but I saw faint flashes on the horizon to the north. I realized that the plastic windows in my bedroom were vibrating from concussive effects of the B-52 bombing.

I returned to my bed with mixed emotions. Information gained from a prisoner who would not talk under torture but responded to kindness was resulting in the deaths of some of his former comrades in arms. I felt only deep sadness at the tragedies of war.

Ironically, my friend Colonel Hien had a female agent working for the National Police, posing as a courier for local Viet Cong units, who was in the bunker complex when it was hit by the B-52 attack. She somehow survived and reported that a high-ranking North Vietnamese officer was also in the bunker.

When the bunker's clay walls partially collapsed and the lights went out, there was general panic and confusion in the dusty, choking darkness. Survivors produced flashlights and began looking for their leader. They were able to dig him out, and his first words were, "That was the Americans. They are leaving, and that was their last chance to kill us. We are going to win this war!" He was right, in the long run.

In late March 1972, there was a Davis Cup tennis match in Saigon between Japan and South Vietnam. I drove into the city to attend, as I knew the Japanese Davis Cup captain, Isao Watanabe, from my years in Tokyo. The occasion was quite festive. Ambassador Bunker was in the audience, and there was a rare glimpse of what South Vietnam might have become if the fighting had ever stopped.

The sun was shining when the matches began, but dark clouds gathered, and thunder began to rumble to the north. I left before the second singles match ended (Japan won both) and drove back toward Bien Hoa, toward an ominous wall of clouds, almost black, with constant flashes of hectic lightning.

On April 1, 1972, just a day or so later, six North Vietnamese divisions came crashing into MR 3, led by tanks, driving south toward Saigon. At his early morning staff meeting, on the day of the attack, Hollingsworth started proceedings by stating: "The shit has hit the fan."

The North Vietnamese drive was stopped at a small, crossroads town called An Loc, fifty miles north of Saigon, where a heavily dug-in South Vietnamese unit fought well. Hollingsworth was galvanized by the attack and marshaled everything he could lay his hands on in the way of American air assets to help the Vietnamese on the ground.

All available U.S. ground forces were gone. He added to his already illustrious reputation by the way the coordinated and directed B-52 strikes, involving bombers flying in from thousands of miles away, with tactical attacks by A-37 fighter-bombers launched from Bien Hoa, less than fifteen minutes flying time away.

One day during the An Loc siege, Hollingsworth asked me to check out an entrenched Vietnamese unit in a village near An Loc that was also under heavy attack. Its fall would have freed other North Vietnamese units to put pressure on An Loc, and Hollingsworth was worried about it. I agreed to go, and a very friendly colonel named Johnson offered to go along with me. We flew in a small, four-seat helicopter, Johnson in front with the pilot, and me in the rear.

When we got over the besieged village, the pilot did a corkscrew landing, descending directly on the landing pad, to lessen the chance of our being hit by ground fire. I knew the local commander. He seemed in good spirits, was optimistic about his chances. We had a friendly talk in his bunker, augmented by shots of Martel brandy, which the Vietnamese liked immensely.

Our departure was unlike our arrival. Heavy fire had erupted to the east and south of the village. When we took off, the helicopter pilot kept us as close to ground level as possible, hurtling west at full speed. He was looking to the left, where some of the firing was coming from, and I saw we were heading directly for a huge, dead tree, probably a eucalyptus, that towered over the tall grass.

I fumbled for the radio button that would have allowed me to warn the pilot, but Colonel Johnson saved us by tapping the pilot's shoulder. He reacted instantly, and the helicopter seemed to rise vertically. Its landing skids tore through the top branches of the tree, we lurched, the chopper blades fought for air, and we broke free.

"Sorry about that," said the pilot laconically. Fortunately, it was an apology, not an epitaph, as it so often was in those days. That was the closest I ever came to "buying the farm" in Vietnam.

I found it hard to get to sleep at night during that period. So I wrote a lot of letters home to Meg and my mother. Reading those letters today ignites many memories that are helpful to this writing.

I also wrote a few poems for Meg, such as this:

Tonight
I find no shelter in memory
Where my thoughts can rest.

Blind birds —
They bump and thrash
Among rocks and thistles of past disasters
Or flap weakly
Lost in future's fogs.

At last
They alight in the palms of your hands.
As you draw them closer,
Blowing gently on their sightless eyes
They subside into sleep.

When you write intelligence reports and political analysis, how you feel is beside the point. When you write poetry, it is everything.

The siege of An Loc ground on. Hollingsworth's carefully coordinated air strikes had inflicted heavy casualties on tank-led North Vietnamese attacks. Supplies and ammunition were airdropped to the South Vietnamese defending the town. Two American officers were in An Loc, in underground bunkers but with full radio contact. They gave invaluable information about the tactical situation and helped direct the timing and targeting of air strikes.

Forward Air Controllers (FACs), American pilots in slow-flying single-engine monoplanes (think of Piper Cubs) also made their daring contributions by directing both artillery and airborne attacks. Brigadier General McGiffert was Hollingsworth's deputy, and I did a lot of flying with him around An Loc, where we could hear the interplay between the FACs and the two underground officers

On one particularly memorable afternoon McGiffert's helicopter picked me up at Echo Pad, and we went over to ARVN Headquarters at Lai Khe, where I briefly met with General Minh. From there, we flew north past the struggling Vietnamese infantry units, slowly fighting their way toward An Loc. Except for the flash and smoke of incoming air strikes, and the dust of impacting artillery, the besieged town looked quiet.

But the constant interplay of radio conversations made it clear that An Loc was still under heavy attack. The three-dimensional aspect of this war came through clearly as we listened to air-to-ground, ground-to-air, and air-to-air conversations, clearing fire and drop areas, marking targets, and warning other aircraft away. The voices were distinctive. One major in An Loc called everybody "Babe," and had a slight stutter. ("OK B-babe, drop your hard stuff right down their g-goddamn throats.") A FAC whose call sign was "Skillet Hotel" had a faint British accent and changed his r's to w's. ("All wight, Chico Six, you are fwee to dwop your awdnance near the candy-stwiped woad.")

We flew farther north to Loc Ninh, over blasted vehicles in the road, and one convoy of ARVN trucks and tanks lying shattered at an intersection. Loc Ninh, in North Vietnamese hands, appeared deserted except for one motorcyclist, spotted by our door gunner. His machine gun swung downward, its muzzle sight pricked like a wolf ear. Unexpectedly, the gunner smiled, shook his head, and swung his weapon upward, sparing the lucky soldier below. He turned, looked at me, and shrugged. Such are the vagaries of war.

We then swung northeast, and located some roads and trails that McGiffert felt were being used to resupply the hostile invasion. We followed one trail with fresh tire tracks to the Song Be River and a grove of bamboo on the river's southern edge. Faint trails could be seen on the northern side of the river.

Like some sort of aerial Daniel Boone on a scout, this meant to McGiffert that the trails were supply routes leading to the river from Cambodia, and that the bamboo grove on the southern shore was a place where trucks loaded incoming supplies and took them south. He immediately called in a C-130 Spectre gunship to hit the bamboo grove with cannon fire. This was immediately done, and the Spectre pilot reported hostile reactions and secondary explosions. So McGiffert's guess had been an accurate one.

We then flew back to Lai Khe, where I had about ninety minutes with General Minh. He appeared to be in reviving spirits after a recent success in Tay Ninh province, but he still looked to me like a conductor leading a symphony orchestra slightly too large for him. He had the woodwinds and violins going well, but the brass and percussion did not quite keep time.

Then back to An Loc, just at dusk. Two choppers were to take in supplies, and three new officers to replace those two officers in the bunker. What was happening on the ground was obscured by the gathering darkness, but again the radio voices in the air told the story: ("Pop your smoke, the friendlies are coming in! They're down!" A pause. "We're being swamped by fucking wounded. Get those bastards off the skids! Are they airborne? Jesus, where is that fire coming from? Both birds are away—they're overloaded! Leave me alone, I'm busy!")

So it went. McGiffert grimaced as he listened and struggled to see. At last it became clear that the two craft had gotten in and out, that the wounded ARVN soldiers who had climbed on board had overloaded both choppers, but that the two U.S. officers had been brought out.

We swung south again, relief easing our faces. Hollingsworth had been there too, and his Texas tones came through the dark, saying he was heading home. So the day ended.

I remember having breakfast the next day with the two officers who had been extracted from An Loc. They'd had their first baths in a month, were headed for two weeks of leave, and were "glad to be back in the world," as they put it. The major who called everybody "Babe" over the radio seemed to have lost his stutter.

May 11th was a particularly bad day at An Loc. Four A-37s were downed by ground fire. The crews of three of the planes survived, but one crashed in flames deep in the jungle. The lost pilot was Michael Blassie, 24, a highly decorated first lieutenant, whose death left one of the Australian nurses utterly grief-stricken. I never met Blassie, but knew the nurse he had captivated. She spoke of him with deep sadness and great affection.

Blassie's remains were located by a South Vietnamese patrol in October 1972 but were not properly identified. They were later placed in the Tomb of the Unknowns in Arlington Cemetery. On

Memorial Day 1984, his remains were honored by the Reagan administration as the Vietnam War's "unknown soldier." President Reagan gave the dedication, and according to the *New York Times* grew emotional as he said: "About him we may well wonder, as others have, did he play on the street of some great American city? Did he work beside his father on a farm?"

Improved forensic techniques, notably DNA, later revealed that the remains were those of Lieutenant Blassie. In 1998, his remains were returned to his family, and he is now buried, with full honors and identification, in St. Louis. As his mother, Pat Blassie, once put it, "He's frozen in time. He's very fortunate."

In late May, the North Vietnamese divisions drew back into the jungle, ground down by Hollingsworth's ferocious air defense and finally facing heavy South Vietnamese reinforcements from Saigon.

Vice President Spiro Agnew arrived in Saigon about that time and was told by General Abrams that it had been General Hollingsworth's bravery and resourcefulness that had kept the North Vietnamese from besieging Saigon, thus allowing the vice president's visit to take place.

I fully agreed with that assessment. Hollingsworth's energy and aggressiveness became legendary. One early morning, unable to sleep, he arrived at his office in darkness. Finding the door locked, he ripped it off its hinges to get to his maps and charts. He spent hours each day aloft in his helicopter, and his call sign, Danger 79'er, became synonymous with the courageous defense of An Loc.

Hollingsworth also placed maximum pressure on General Minh to reinforce An Loc by bringing up heavy Vietnamese units along the main road from Saigon. The South Vietnamese response was slow, and Hollingsworth grew furious about it. As he put it, "Every time those guys get hit by a rocket-propelled grenade, they want a B-52 strike."

Late in the siege, at one of his early morning staff meetings, Hollingsworth started proceedings by growling loudly: "I've figured out what's wrong with these fuckin' Vietnamese. They suffer from optimorectitis, where their optic nerve gets tangled with their sphincter and gives them a shitty outlook."

Crude as he could be, Hollingsworth was also a shrewd military diplomat. When Minh's forces finally broke through to An Loc, Hollingsworth was lavish in his praise of them, and of their leader.

Ted Shackley had left as Saigon chief of station and been replaced by Tom Polgar, who seemed to have a more realistic view of what was going on in the countryside. Polgar was generous in his appraisal of the work being done in Bien Hoa and, as the end of my tour approached, he offered me an interesting-sounding job in Saigon—a new position he had created. But this would mean at least another year in Vietnam.

I wrote a careful letter home to Meg, who had stayed in Bethesda with our three school-age children, sounding her out on this idea. She had been functioning as a virtual single parent during my time in Vietnam. It was hard enough having me away, anywhere —but having me off *in Vietnam* made things much more difficult, particularly for Lucy, our eldest. She was by then in her mid-teens, and her peer group had decisively turned against the war. Vietnam War protests were rampant on high school and college campuses.

So Meg's return letter to me was short and to the point: "No way. FUCK YOU!"

This profane reply, so totally unlike Meg, was an entirely appropriate, and indeed sagacious response. I left Vietnam on schedule.

At the very end of my tour, General Abrams hosted a lunch for me at MACV headquarters in Saigon, undoubtedly at the suggestion of Hollingsworth. It felt odd to be going into MACV to receive praise, when so often in the past I had been excoriated. I was flattered and glad to have the chance to talk to Abrams, who was by far the best of the three commanders we'd had in Vietnam.

I sat next to Abrams at lunch with six or eight of his subordinates in attendance. We had plain food, served by Vietnamese orderlies. I knew Abrams had been in Vietnam for some time and asked him how long it had been. "Six years," he replied proudly. I asked him how he kept going. "Well, I keep learning things," he said.

I asked him, politely, what he had learned recently, and he said that he had just finished reading Bernard Fall's book *Hell in a Very Small Place*, a vivid account of the French defeat at Dien Bien Phu in

1954. Abrams went on to say that he now understood Fall's reasoning as to why the French had failed to reestablish their colonial rule in Vietnam.

"How did Fall explain it?" I asked.

Abrams replied, "Fall said that the French lost because they failed to politically organize the terrain. I think I understand that now, but I would not have understood it a year or so ago."

I did not know what to say in response to this, but when I see pictures of our heavy battle tanks, named for General Abrams, crashing around in Iraq and Afghanistan, I think of his answer.

I took off from Saigon a day or so later, in late June 1972, on a Pan Am flight home. As the jet swung northeast after takeoff, I knew it would pass over Bien Hoa, and I pressed my face to the window, hoping for a last glimpse of that dusty town beside a muddy river, where so many unforgettable things had happened to me. Clouds obscured my view.

A year later, CIA asked me to pay a short visit to Saigon, to evaluate changes that had occurred since the complete withdrawal of U.S. forces. Tom Polgar, the station chief, was guardedly optimistic. I went back to Bien Hoa, which still had a few CIA officers in place. It seemed ominously quiet.

I had hoped to meet with General Minh, still the MR 3 commander, and now a four-star general. I was told that he was water skiing on the Dong Nai River, so I did not see him.

I went back to my house, which now stood empty. In a closet upstairs in my old bedroom, I found a drawing my daughter Alison, at age ten, had sent me as a Christmas present in 1970. I sat on my bed with the drawing in my hand, as my thoughts ranged back. I was so glad to have found something of my time in Bien Hoa still there. I left the next day and have not returned to Vietnam since.

When CIA finally closed Fort Apache, one of the departing case officers took the eightball from the pool table and threw it into the Dong Nai River.

PHOTO GALLERY II

My 43rd birthday, in the jungle north of Bien Hoa, Vietnam, December 5, 1970. *Personal photo*

Colonel Cong, ARVN intelligence officer, second from left, with fellow officers, Bien Hoa, 1971. *Personal photo*

On the porch at Fort Apache, by the Dong Nai River, 1971.
Personal photo

Three close friends (L to R): Lt. General James Hollingsworth, Brigadier Roh Tae Woo (president of South Korea when I was ambassador), and Major General Jangnai Sohn (Korean division commander), Binh Long Province, Vietnam, 1972.
Photo gift of General Sohn

Meg's visit to Vietnam, November 1971, near Cham temple, Nha Trang. *Family photo*

Showing off—four trophies from the 8th Army tennis tournament in Korea—two wins, two runners-up, 1975. *Family photo*

14

The Abduction of Kim Dae-jung

Following my tour in Vietnam, I went to Seoul as CIA chief of station. In mid-1973, as I was preparing to leave for Seoul, President Park Chung-hee, South Korea's brilliant but dictatorial leader, was rethinking his relationship with Washington. He had committed two full South Korean army divisions to the war in Vietnam, having troops in place from 1965 to 1971–72. In all, 312,000 South Koreans were sent to fight in Vietnam.

By 1973, the United States had withdrawn all of its troops from South Vietnam, and it was clear that despite South Korea's large-scale assistance, we had lost the war. That did not sit at all well with President Park, who had seen Vietnam strictly in Cold War terms. He began to have real doubts about the strength and reliability of the United States as an ally.

In 1972, Park sent the head of the Korean Central Intelligence Agency, Lee Hu-Rak, to meet with Kim Il-sung in Pyongyang. He also started a secret nuclear weapons development program and began to covertly purchase weapons systems that the United States did not want him to have. We thought they could destabilize the peninsula. KCIA's use of torture was also egregious and widely feared in South Korea.

I knew little of those things as I prepared to leave for Seoul. What did come to my attention was that Kim Dae-jung, a liberal politician who had narrowly lost a 1971 presidential election to President Park, was in the United States and being harassed by suspected KCIA operatives as he criticized various political measures taken by President Park. These measures put control of future presidential elections in the hands of the incumbent and meant that

Kim, if he ran again, would stand no chance of winning the presidency.

I arrived in Seoul at night and felt good about it. I liked the feeling of being on the mainland, and was reminded of how I had felt in Burma, another country close to the huge bulk of China. The city was not well lighted, and red neon crosses in dark neighborhoods spoke of the strength of Christianity. I knew the house where I was to live. I'd had dinner there in 1968, and it was comfortable. I went right to bed and rose early to look at the mountains looming to the north of Seoul. I was glad to be there.

My first duty was to call on our ambassador, Philip Habib, a man for whom I developed tremendous respect. Brooklyn-born of Lebanese-American parents, Habib was gruff and outspoken. By his looks and demeanor, he could have been a haberdasher, but he went on to win the Medal of Freedom from Ronald Reagan for his diplomatic legerdemain in the Middle East.

Habib spoke to me as follows: "I don't know what you CIA guys do, and I couldn't care less, as long as you don't screw up. But there is one rule for you, and you had better follow it. I don't want you to have anything to do with Tongsun Park. He's a corrupt son of a bitch who tries to buy off congressmen. Keep away from him, he'll try to climb in your pocket." Habib was right about Tongsun Park, on all counts.

My second courtesy call was upon KCIA Director Lee, a man for whom I developed an instant aversion. Lee had a huge office on the top floor of a building right across from the American Embassy. A movie cameraman filmed my entrance, and I realized I had goofed sartorially by wearing a turtleneck sweater under my coat. Lee sat at a huge desk, with several flunkies in attendance, all in black suits, shimmering white shirts, and ties.

CIA was getting virtually nowhere in collecting information on North Korea, and one of my major jobs was to see if, by working closely with KCIA, we could improve the quality of the intelligence we collected. After an exchange of pleasantries, I asked Director Lee how it had felt to sit across from his lifelong enemy Kim Il-sung, whom he had visited the previous year.

Lee's answer surprised me. He broke into English and said with gruff enthusiasm: "Quite a guy, one-man rule, very strong, quite a guy!" Lee made it clear to me that his talk with Kim had led him to believe that if South Korea was going to seek better relations with the North, it would need to tighten up on political and security issues, so as not to be undermined by subversion from Pyongyang.

My subsequent efforts to improve intelligence gathering on North Korea in cooperation with KCIA got nowhere. They had one or two excellent North Korean analysts, but their main emphasis was to keep South Korea quiet politically. In that light, KCIA saw Kim Dae-jung as a major nuisance and threat. Kim had traveled to Japan, where he was continuing his powerful criticisms of President Park's "Yushin" system, which ruled out direct popular voting for presidential candidates.

One day in early August 1973, I was at a reception with Meg at an Army officers' club several miles from the Embassy. A military officer rushed up to our table and said that Ambassador Habib wanted to see me on an emergency basis. On my way to the Embassy I called my office and asked what was going on. My secretary said she did not know.

Habib was furious. He told me that Kim Dae-jung had been abducted from his hotel room in Tokyo and that his current whereabouts and fate were unknown. Habib made it clear that he suspected KCIA of kidnapping Kim.

He went on to make the comment I've quoted in this book's Preface: "I know how things work around here, they're going to kill him, but they may wait to see what I have to say. If you're able to tell me tomorrow morning who has him and where he is, we may be able to keep him alive."

The following morning, I was able to tell Habib that KCIA had kidnapped Kim. He was on a small boat somewhere in the straits of Tsushima, between Japan and Korea.

Habib didn't ask how I had learned this. He believed me instantly—perhaps because it had confirmed his own suspicions. He thanked me for the information but we did not talk long. He asked me to keep him informed of developments in the case. Then, knowing that time was of the essence, Habib moved quickly to send a message to President Park, trying to keep Kim alive.

As we talked in Seoul, Kim at sea had been blindfolded by his captors, chained hand and foot, taunted and roughly handled. He fully expected to be thrown into the sea. He had resigned himself to dying and was praying for his family.

Sometime after mid-day, an airplane flew low over the boat on which Kim was held. Soon thereafter, he was unchained, treated humanely, and given water to drink. The boat returned to Korea. Later that night, a dazed Kim was released on the streets of Seoul near his home. All this I learned from Kim after he had become president. He was convinced that the plane that had flown over his boat was from CIA, and that it was CIA that had ordered his release. I told him that it had not been a CIA plane, and that most probably it was a South Korean plane, carrying word from Seoul that Kim was to be released, not killed.

I never asked Habib directly what he had done with the information I'd given him. I erroneously assumed that he had jumped in his car, rushed to Blue House, the presidential manse, confronted President Park with what he knew, and demanded Kim's immediate release.

Habib was much smarter than that. He knew Park had a temper and an ego and that the kidnapping involved Lee Hu-Rak, the second most powerful man in South Korea and Park's closest confidante. A personal confrontation on this issue would have been explosive, with uncertain results. Habib wisely sent an emergency message to Park, telling him that he knew of Kim's kidnapping and that Kim's death would have a shattering effect on U. S. relations with Seoul. He urged Park to do everything possible to keep Kim alive.

This approach gave Park time to think and to construct a scenario that saved him direct embarrassment. He allowed the story to emerge that rogue elements of the Korean government, acting on their own, had attempted a dastardly act that he, as president, had prevented by his swift intervention. This explanation "saved the president's face," always a major concern in Asia.

Habib wisely allowed this story to play out, knowing that for Washington's relations with Seoul to improve, good relations with President Park were imperative. It was only a year or so before his death in 2009 that President Kim told me he had evidence that President Park himself had ordered KCIA to kidnap and kill him. Only Habib's astute intervention had kept him alive.

My other main liaison relationship was with Park Jong Kyu, head of the Presidential Protective Force, their equivalent of our Secret Service. PPF Park, as I shall refer to him, was a man I rather liked. He reminded me of a Japanese samurai, absolutely dedicated to the protection of his master. It had quickly become clear to me that PPF Park did not like KCIA's Lee, whom he told me was overly ambitious and rather uncontrollable.

As the story emerged publicly that Kim Dae-jung had been kidnapped by an element of KCIA, protests and riots broke out on various South Korean university campuses, most notably that of Seoul National University, the "Harvard" of South Korea. South Korea security services, primarily the National Police, cracked down severely on these demonstrations.

It was widely known that KCIA had become involved in seeking to quell the SNU riots. They had arrested an American-trained Korean professor, whom they accused of having stirred up the rioting on his campus. The professor was taken away to a dreaded KCIA interrogation center, where he was either tortured to death or to the point that he jumped out a window to avoid further agony, as he continued to deny the false accusations concocted by KCIA.

His wife reportedly was a doctor and for some time was kept from seeing his tortured body. These facts were widely known, and I duly reported them to Washington. I soon followed up that report with a request that I be allowed to protest this brutal action on KCIA's part. My boss in Washington, a man who died over a decade ago, rejected my proposal. He told me to "stop trying to save the Koreans from themselves" and to focus only on reporting the facts.

I brooded over this oral directive for several days, as this was a major moral crisis for me. Then, for the first and only time in my career, I deliberately disobeyed an instruction. I went to PPF Park, told him I was speaking personally, and not with Washington's approval. I said that I found it very difficult to work with an organization that tortured its own citizens for their political views and paid so little attention to the North Korean threat. Park listened to me very soberly, took notes, asked no questions, and thanked me for coming to see him.

Within ten days, it was announced that Lee Hu-Rak had been

fired as KCIA director. He had fled the country and was being sought abroad. His replacement, the former minister of justice Shin Chick Soo, immediately asked me to come to see him. Gone were the movie photographer and the stuffy assistants. There was just one very concerned official, alone in his office.

Director Shin told me that he would be as much against those who broke the law on behalf of his government, as he would be against those who broke the law in opposing his government. His first internal directive was the prohibition of torture. Things at KCIA changed greatly, and we worked effectively with them for the remainder of my tour, though I regret to say we made very little progress against the extremely tough North Korean target.

I never reported a word of my disobedience to CIA headquarters. My boss was a real "hard case," and I was certain that he knew I had acted contrary to his orders. But since it had turned out well, he had decided not to call me to account.

Over the past dozen years, I have spoken to several groups of CIA officers. In each case, I have told them of my disobedience and urged them to do likewise if they ever found themselves in a position like mine, where they believed they had to do something or else lose faith in CIA, and eventually in themselves.

After one of my talks to such a group, I received a nice letter of thanks from George Tenet, who was DCI at the time. I'd like to think that Tenet's letter was more than a perfunctory gesture on his part, but I cannot be certain of that. For a DCI to specifically endorse rule-breaking would be a dangerous position to take, as the risks involved are very high.

I was reminded of that in April 2013, when I spoke to an impressive group of West Point cadets on the verge of graduation. I told them my Korean story. After my talk had ended, a cadet with a warrior's face approached me and said, "I don't think I'd have the guts to do what you did. You risked everything."

I replied, "Yes, I did risk a lot, but I had come to the conclusion that how I felt about myself was more important than how the CIA leadership felt about me."

The cadet looked hard at me. We shook hands, and he walked away smiling and shaking his head. It was a powerful moment for both of us, and I wish him well.

15

President Park Chung-hee:
Too Long in Power

Lt. General Jim Hollingsworth, with whom I had worked so closely in Vietnam, was in command of the joint ROK-U.S. Corps, located between Seoul and the DMZ. It was then one of the largest ground commands in the world. Hollingsworth had worked closely with the two South Korean divisions in Vietnam and was known and respected by his Korean counterparts north of Seoul.

In the year since I'd last seen him, Hollingsworth had neither aged nor mellowed. He was still the leathery epitome of a Texas gunfighter. In his frequent meetings with top Korean commanders, Hollingsworth was profanely confident that any attack from North Korea would be quickly turned back.

"We'll kill every son of a bitch at the northern edge of the battle line!" he shouted one day to a large and enthusiastic group of South Koreans sitting on the southern bank of the Naktong River just south of the DMZ.

In private talks with me, Hollingsworth was much less confident, not at all certain that an invading North Korean army could be kept out of Seoul, due to the North's great advantage in heavy artillery and the South's lack of counter-battery fire, a problem that continues to this day.

The fear of an attack by North Korea was still very strong in the South, and memories of the January 1968 Blue House raid by thirty North Korean commandos remained vivid. In Seoul, there was a midnight curfew seven nights a week, and serious air-raid drills once a month. On South Korean golf courses, flat fairways where a North Korean AN-2, radar-evading aircraft might land had holes bored in them, and at dusk South Koreans inserted long poles in them to deter airborne infiltration by night.

During my tour, the South Koreans discovered and blocked several North Korean tunnels, laboriously dug under the DMZ. When I recently asked Alison what she remembered about our years in Seoul, she recalled, "Tracer bullets in the sky," as they fired at a suspected air infiltration near Blue House.

A rather entertaining incident resulted from the U.S. Navy's discovery that South Korea had secretly ordered a midget submarine and its "mother ship" from Germany. With the American admiral in charge of our naval forces in Korea, I discussed how to get the Koreans to admit they had a submarine, something the United States had strongly discouraged.

The Navy knew the date and time that the mini-sub was to be "exercised" off the west coast of Korea. So, at just the right moment, the admiral notified his Korean navy counterparts that he was scrambling U.S. jets to "attack" a hostile submarine that had just been spotted. The Koreans then had to admit that the ship was theirs. The "attack" was canceled and the submarine quickly placed under close joint control. This ended South Korea's secret weapons purchases, so far as we knew.

In August 1974, President Park was making a speech at the National Theater, commemorating the twenty-ninth anniversary of the ending of Japan's occupation of Korea. Suddenly a North Korean agent in the audience leapt to his feet, pulled out a pistol, and fired at him. The president ducked to safety behind his armored speaking podium. But, tragically, one of the assassin's bullets struck Yuk Young-soo, the president's wife, fatally wounding her. There was an infamous picture taken of the assassination attempt showing everyone who'd been sitting on stage diving for cover, except PPF Park, who had drawn his gun, run to the front of the stage, and fired at the assassin.

Park's shots missed their intended target, but killed a young girl, a choir member in the audience. The assassin was subdued, Madame Park was carried out of the theater, and the president finished his speech. His wife died later that day.

PPF Park had to "take responsibility" for the tragedy and resigned as head of the Presidential Protective Force. The assassin, an ethnic Korean living in Japan had smuggled a pistol stolen from a Japanese policeman into Korea. He was tried, found guilty, and executed.

In South Korea, this bloody incident created tremendously bad feeling toward Japan. The fact that the assassin lived in Japan and had used a stolen Japanese policeman's weapon to kill the Korean president's wife raised all kinds of hostile feelings in Seoul toward anything Japanese. Irate South Koreans surrounded the Japanese Embassy and, screaming insults, cut off tips of their fingers to show the depths of their outrage. (My daughter Alison recalls it as "mass hysteria and protests against Japan, with people cutting their thumbs off across the street.")

Richard Ericson was chargé d'affaires at the time, as Phil Habib's tour had ended. Ericson did a sterling job in calming things down. He reminded both U.S. allies that the assassination had been committed by North Korea, not anyone else, and that to create friction between Tokyo and Seoul played into Pyongyang's hands.

President Park had been devoted to his wife and went into semi-seclusion after her death. A November 1974 visit to Seoul by President Gerald Ford, en route to a meeting with the Soviets in Vladivostok, made Park feel a lot better about his relations with Washington. Ford stressed America's continued interest in Asia and our view of South Korea as a valued ally.

Shortly after the Ford visit, to my great surprise I was invited to play golf with President Park, along with Ambassador Dick Sneider and U.S. Forces commander General Richard Stilwell. In the eighteen months I had been in Seoul, I had attended several meetings with President Park, but this game was my first social contact with him.

President Park knew I had spoken out against KCIA director Lee Hu-Rak to PPF Park, and he probably knew it was I who had told Ambassador Habib who had kidnapped Kim Dae-jung. He also knew I had suggested to PPF Park that the president needed a "Minister of Bad News" to tell him the unpleasant things he needed to know.

I was thus very interested to see how Park reacted to me. He was not a particularly good golfer and, on an occasion early in the golf game when we both hit our balls into the rough, I spoke to him in Japanese.

He gave me the standard response: "You're very good at Japanese. Where did you learn to speak so well?"

"I lived in Tokyo for ten years, so I had to have learned something."

We continued to converse in a friendly way, measuring each other. Park had a very good sense of humor and said, "If you worked less hard, you'd play better golf."

Over dinner after the game, I was struck by how reluctant the other senior Koreans in the golfing party were to even speak to their president. The minister of defense and the Army chief of staff sat stiffly in their seats, almost like plebes at West Point. At the end of a long silence, I asked the president if he ever compared himself to Kemal Ataturk, the founder of modern Turkey.

The president shifted his heavy gaze to me, contemplating me as a rattlesnake might look upon a mouse. After a pause, he replied, "I do not know much about Kemal Pasha, but I would like to do for Korea what he did for Turkey—make it economically strong and militarily secure." Park added that he did not intend to serve indefinitely as president, and had he not chosen to stand for another term in 1971, his wife might still be alive.

Sneider, Stilwell, and I all took Park's remark to mean that he would not run again for president, but we were mistaken. Five years later, when the KCIA director who had replaced Shin Chick Soo assassinated Park, he had been at South Korea's helm for eighteen years.

My two colorful years in Seoul went very quickly. Tongsun Park did try to "get into my pocket," as Habib had predicted, luring me into a hotel meeting with a totally false social invitation. I broke off the meeting rather scathingly, and Habib was as pleased by hearing that as by anything else I ever told him.

Shortly before my tour ended, Representative Lester Wolff, chairman of the Asia and Pacific Subcommittee of the House Committee on Foreign Affairs, came to Seoul with another congressman. He asked me to accompany him and his colleague as they called on Director Shin of KCIA.

Shin greeted Wolff with these words: "I sometimes dread my meetings with Mr. Gregg, because he often tells me things that I don't want to hear but that I need to hear. I am very grateful to him for that." A few days later, Shin called me back to his office, gave me a fancy pink decoration, and thanked me for improving relations between our organizations.

Our family had enjoyed our time in Seoul and left South Korea with no idea that we would ever return.

16

The Pike Committee and the Carter White House

In the early autumn of 1975 I returned to Washington from Seoul and learned, to my surprise, that I was being assigned to the CIA Review Staff, headed by the late Seymour Bolten. The Agency had established the Review Staff to deal with the double-barreled congressional investigation of CIA conducted by the Church Committee in the U.S. Senate and by the Pike Committee in the House. My job was to deal with the Pike Committee. I replaced a CIA officer who had quit in disgust less than three months into the job. I soon learned why.

As I once told the CIA's historian Gerald K. Haines, the months I spent with the Pike Committee made my tour in Vietnam seem like a picnic. I would have vastly preferred to fight the Viet Cong than to deal with a polemical investigation by a congressional committee.

In a 1979 article in *Studies in Intelligence*, Haines wrote, "The investigations of the Pike Committee, headed by Democratic Representative Otis Pike of New York, paralleled those of the Church Committee, led by Idaho Senator Frank Church, also a Democrat. While the Church Committee centered its attention on the more sensational charges of illegal activities by the CIA, the Pike Committee set about examining the CIA's effectiveness and its cost to taxpayers. Unfortunately, Representative Pike, the committee, and its staff never developed a cooperative working relationship with CIA or the Ford administration."

You can say that again.

Haines continued: "The committee soon was at odds with the CIA and the White House over questions of access to documents

and information and the declassification of materials. Relations between the Agency and the Pike Committee became confrontational.
CIA officials came to detest the committee and its efforts at investigation."

My first encounter with one of Pike's young staffers set the tone
for the trying months to come. Glaring at me over her granny glasses, a young woman named Emily said firmly: "What I want from
you is a list of every gift worth more than $200 that CIA has ever
given to a foreigner."

The request was preposterous, and I was both amused and
disgusted by it. I explained that the Agency had files on people,
not gifts, and that to answer her request we would have to search
through all of CIA's files, many of which had been retired to locations outside Washington. I said that to answer her question would
require hundreds of man-years and would be a colossal waste of
time.

Her response to me was succinct: "Bullshit."

A long argument followed as to how to deal with Emily's question in a realistic fashion that would not tie up the operational desks
indefinitely with meaningless work.

I learned later that Emily and a number of her fellow staffers
had been influenced by the 1975 Robert Redford film *Three Days
of the Condor*, which had CIA conducting draconian operations on
the basis of information contained in a huge, virtually omnipotent
computer. Perhaps Emily imagined that I could have gone to such
a computer, pushed three buttons titled "Gifts," "$200," and "For-
eigners," and answered her question.

Historian Haines quotes a Review Staff member describing Pike
Committee staffers as "flower children, very young and irrespon-
sible and naïve." This description fit some, but not all Pike staffers.
Several, over time, came to respect CIA, and in fact three of the Pike
staff tried to join CIA upon completion of the investigation. (None
were accepted.)

The job I shared with others on the CIA Review Staff was to
fight off unrealistic, or even outlandish, requests for information.
We could not stonewall the committee's requests, particularly those
that came with an indication of a certain congressman's interest,
but we were deeply concerned by Chairman Pike's assertion that

his committee had the unilateral authority to declassify intelligence documents.

Given the tensions and personalities involved, dealing with the Pike Committee was the most difficult and unpleasant job I ever had at CIA. Having total strangers brusquely demand some of the Agency's innermost secrets with the full expectation of receiving comprehensive replies was traumatic, and ran counter to my deepest instincts as a CIA case officer.

After months of arm-wrestling with the Agency, the Pike Committee produced a report so biased and inaccurate that the House of Representatives voted by a two-to one margin not to release it. This caused Chairman Pike to refer to his committee's work as "an exercise in futility." The Pike Report was promptly leaked to the *Village Voice* and later published in Britain, with a foreword written by that CIA officer gone bad, Philip Agee.

Agee's systematic revelation of the names of hundreds of undercover CIA case officers serving overseas led to the passage in 1982 of the Intelligence Identities Protection Act, under which Lewis "Scooter " Libby, Dick Cheney's former chief of staff, was in 2007 convicted of perjury relating to public testimony he gave about a CIA officer serving under deep cover.

In early 1979, after thinking long and hard about my experiences with the Pike Committee, I wrote an unclassified article in *Studies in Intelligence* called "Congress and the Directorate of Operations— An Odd Couple?" I decided that what had happened from 1976 to 1979, though painful and difficult, still gave hope for a stabilized relationship between Congress and the Directorate of Operations that could allow essential intelligence functions to be carried out with both the understanding and support of Congress.

Deep "cultural" differences between the Directorate and Congress have always hindered the development of a strong oversight relationship. In the intelligence business, great premium is placed on clarity and precision in what is communicated and on the need for "getting it right the first time." If a case officer in the field knowingly reports the same piece of information twice, he knows he will be criticized.

This discipline has caused the Directorate to believe, erroneously, that once something has been said, particularly in testimony before a congressional committee, the subject has been covered and need not be dealt with again. What the Directorate has only slowly come to realize is that members of our oversight committees have many subjects and personalities competing for their attention, may not fully prepare for hearings they attend, or believe that the subjects under discussion are high priority matters.

Another problem is that CIA testimony before Congress often gets into highly sensitive issues involving "sources and methods"—those things that must be protected at all costs. CIA tries valiantly to tell as few people as possible about such issues. Word leaks out, other members clamor for information, and the process gets repeated.

The Agency is well aware that being a member of a congressional oversight committee is not a highly desirable or sought-after position. With skeletons from the Agency's past being regularly dug up and displayed, a congressman gains little political benefit or publicity from serving on an oversight committee. The members become almost as vulnerable to after-the-fact criticism as the Agency has always been.

If Congress claims, as it does now, that it is giving careful oversight to CIA activities, it may then share the burdens and criticisms of future "intelligence failures." Conversely, when something covert succeeds and is going well, Congress must remain mute. This discipline runs counter to the instincts of elected officials, whose natural tendency is to keep their constituents abreast of their doings, particularly those that reflect credit upon them.

Despite all this, I believe that if the Directorate collectively recognizes Congress's "need to know," and if it conducts its difficult work with all the professionalism of which it is capable, oversight can and will work to the ultimate benefit of all concerned.

Bill Colby had been DCI during the very difficult period in late 1975 when both the Church and Pike investigations were underway. Colby believed congressional oversight could only work with greater degrees of Agency cooperation and transparency. Former Director Richard Helms opposed this view, believing that Congress could not keep secrets, and that CIA's ability to carry out covert actions would be jeopardized by Congress's endless demands for more information and its dangerous tendency to leak.

I admired both men and believed that the concerns of both were valid. Agency morale was at low ebb at the end of 1975. Senator Church's frequent use of the term "rogue elephant" to describe the Agency was deeply resented, and the December 1975 assassination of the CIA station chief in Athens, Richard Welch, only added to the gloom, as rogue agent Philip Agee had named Welch as a CIA officer.

In late September 2011, a film on Bill Colby's life was released. Made by Colby's son Carl, it was called "The Man Nobody Knew." It captures Colby's unflappability wonderfully well. I worked directly for him for two years and never saw him angry. I only saw him upset that once, when the two of us watched a clip on television as a Buddhist monk self-immolated as a profound protest of what was happening in Vietnam.

Most of the time, Bill Colby was inscrutable. I never knew what he thought, apart from the job that needed to be done at the moment. His nickname in the Agency, "the warrior priest," was fully deserved.

The film also captures, better than anything else I have seen, the virtually impossible task of every DCI—to deal with insistent demands for accountability from Congress, while defending CIA's vital secrets. Each DCI handles this issue differently, depending on the issues involved, the political atmosphere prevailing, and his own instincts. I think Colby handled it well, but some of his contemporaries, including Henry Kissinger, thought he gave too much away to Congress.

(Kissinger was at the height of his powers in the mid-1970s and had a powerful impact on Washington. He was then in his "Hollywood stage," when he had been linked to several dishy actresses. Meg remarked "Whoever said that political power is the greatest aphrodisiac had it right.")

The early and mid-1970s were a tumultuous period in the history of the CIA. On February 2, 1973, President Nixon fired DCI Richard Helms, because Helms had distanced CIA from the burgeoning Watergate scandal and had refused to impede in any way the investigations that eventually led to Nixon's resignation.

Nixon replaced Helms as DCI with James Schlesinger, who immediately ordered ill-considered reorganizations of the Agency and began to summarily fire some of its most experienced officers. As Agency opposition to Schlesinger strengthened, Nixon appointed him secretary of defense in July 1973.

In September 1973, Bill Colby, a career CIA officer, was appointed DCI. In August 1974, Nixon resigned as president.

In December 1974, Seymour Hersh of the *New York Times* published an article on sensitive and controversial CIA operations contained in the so-called "family jewels" report compiled by DCI Schlesinger. The reverberations of this report led to massive investigations of CIA by both houses of Congress, the Church and Pike Committees.

Late in 1975, President Ford felt that a new director, free of any association with the congressional investigations, could help restore Agency morale and asked Bill Colby to retire. With the investigations still underway, in January 1976, Ford fired Bill Colby and appointed George H. W. Bush as DCI. Bush served as director for a little less than a year; but he loved the job, respected the Agency's professionalism, and did much to put the Agency back into fighting trim.

I was sorry to see Colby go, as I respected him. I had no particular feeling for Bush at that time, having met him only once. I never directly encountered Bush during his brief tenure as DCI in 1976, as I was operating out of an office away from Langley. But I think Ford's decision was a good one. The fact that the CIA headquarters building in Langley is named for George H. W. Bush supports Ford's decision. I quickly sensed Bush's positive impact on the Agency.

In November 1976, after Ford lost the presidential election to Jimmy Carter, Bush asked the president-elect to keep him on as director for at least a few months, to show that the DCI's position was not tied directly to politics. But President Carter was anxious to make a break with past patterns and so, for the first time, a new director came into office with a new president. His choice, Admiral Stansfield Turner, a Rhodes Scholar and Annapolis classmate of Carter, brought with him a large staff of Navy officers, a deep belief in the efficacy of all forms of technical intelligence, and skepticism toward what he called "the traditional human spy." Turner proceeded to operate much as his DCI predecessor James Schlesinger had, firing many of CIA's best operators.

I had been made head of a small Agency staff designed to ease Admiral Turner's move into the DCI role. My job did not go well. Turner's staff showed a mixture of disdain and hostility toward operations officers. I sent a staff memo to Turner saying that Clandestine Service officers felt that they were taking casualties from "friendly fire" coming from his office.

Turner ignored my memo, but certainly remembered me. In August 1977, he announced that over 800 Agency operations officers were to be retired over the coming two years, and that about 150 had to go immediately. Many of the people fired were among the most experienced people in the operations directorate.

I was not among that unhappy group. But Turner rejected my nominations to two or three very senior positions. I was given a series of staff positions that did not appeal to me at all, and the next two years were deeply unfulfilling. My bottom line on Stansfield Turner was that he was bright enough to steer a submarine by telling a helmsman which way to turn, but that he totally lacked the ability to inspire others to follow him out of the trenches and "over the top."

In June 1979, fate intervened in my favor, just as it had in October 1951, when by chance I met Meg in a shared taxi in Washington, D.C. At the White House, a CIA officer seconded to the National Security Council suddenly resigned, not liking President Carter's foreign policies or his attitude toward CIA. This created a slot that needed to be filled immediately.

I learned, many years later, that the late Paul Henze, a renowned Middle East CIA expert also seconded to the NSC staff, had put my name forward to national security advisor Zbigniew Brzezinski. I did not know Henze well, but his office was next to mine, and we got along very well once I moved to the White House staff. I never learned why Henze recommended me, but I am eternally grateful to him.

Brzezinski interviewed me and immediately offered me the job, which I was delighted to accept. Zbig took me to meet President Carter, who received me rather coolly. He seemed to regard CIA as something of a necessary evil. Zbig and I got along well, and I respect him to this day. We are almost the same age, and I admire the way he has kept fully in touch with global foreign policy challenges. He makes a great deal of sense whenever he speaks publicly.

So I stopped driving to Langley and began taking a bus to the White House, where I was put in charge of intelligence issues and Far East policy matters on the NSC. I had a fine office in the old Executive Office Building (EOB) looking south. I was delighted to be there.

There was a parochialism to some of President Carter's staff, holdovers from his staff in Georgia, who seemed to think their view of the world could become a transcendent force in Washington. But I prefer to remember the warm hospitality of Jimmy and Rosalyn Carter. In 1979, Jimmy Carter invited Meg and me to our first event at the White House—a movie. As they changed reels on the projector, we staffers and wives, including Bob Gates and his wife, were invited forward to stand around a huge punch bowl in which opened bottles of Coca-Cola were stuck in ice. We drank the Cokes out of the bottle and returned to our seats. The Carters were there, and acting very friendly. We were being entertained "Plains style."

In the autumn of 1979, after I had been on the NSC staff for a few months, the Brzezinskis invited Meg and me to a tennis party at their home in the Washington suburbs. Zbig asked Meg and me to play a set or two of doubles with him and a young man on the NSC staff. It became quickly apparent that Meg and I could win quite easily.

As we changed ends during the first set, Meg quietly suggested to me that we might be wise to throw a few games, saying: "Don't you think we ought to ease up a bit?"

I rejected this idea, feeling that Zbig would sense what we were doing and be insulted by it. So we won rather quickly. Zbig complimented us on our play, but we were invited back to no more Brzezinski house parties.

About nine months later, in July 1980, Prime Minister Ohira of Japan passed away, and Zbig was one of the leaders of the high-level American delegation sent to the Tokyo funeral. I was also included. On the long flight out, Zbig came to my seat and asked if I played chess. I said I knew how but hadn't played in years. He invited me to play.

We played two games. In game one I played way over my head and had Zbig on the ropes, until I made a truly bad move that undid all my previous good work. Zbig quickly took full advantage and won. As we reset our pieces he said, correctly and succinctly, "You had me until you made that stupid move with your knight." Zbig easily won the second game and, as I was about to retreat to my seat, he said very pleasantly: "That evens it up for the tennis."

I include these incidents, which Meg frequently reminds me about, because they are so revealing of Zbig: intelligent, tough-minded, competitive, and with a long memory. When he left office, he sent me a signed picture on which he wrote that I had been as good at my work as I had been on the tennis court. In the decade I worked at the White House, I saw seven national security advisors perform in that difficult role. Zbig was by far the best.

Over at the State Department in late 1979, the late Richard Holbrooke was appointed assistant secretary of state for Asian and Pacific affairs. In February 1980, soon after being appointed, Holbrooke embarked on a tour of several Asian countries. It was normal procedure for the NSC staffer responsible for the assistant secretary's area, to go along on such trips.

Holbrooke and I had different backgrounds and had never met. He announced that he did not need to have me accompany him. Brzezinski would have none of this and told Holbrooke in no uncertain terms that he would take me along.

I thus met Holbrooke for the first time as his plane took off from Andrews Air Base. He was perfectly civil, but did not ask me up to talk near his seat in the front of the plane, as we flew across the Pacific. Our trip began in Seoul, which was familiar territory for me, and I was able to introduce Holbrooke to several key Korean officials. We went from there to Singapore for a Chiefs of Mission conference.

As we approached our landing, one of Holbrooke's aides announced that he was looking for someone to play tennis with during breaks at the conference, adding that Holbrooke had been on the tennis team at Brown and wanted someone "who could give him a good match." I did not react to this announcement. But when it was repeated some time later, indicating that no one had responded, I offered my services, which were accepted. Shortly after landing in Singapore, we met on an embassy court.

Holbrooke was a good player, with a strong serve, but he was erratic, and I beat him quite easily. His attitude toward me changed as our match progressed, moving from surprise to frustration to friendly determination. We played whenever possible during the trip. During our stop in Bangkok we played a quick set on grass. Holbrooke's serve was a killer on grass, and he beat me in the one set we had time to play. When he won the set, he threw his racquet in the air and jumped over the net. That was the only time he ever beat me, and he never forgot it.

We became good friends and worked together well on difficult Asian policy issues, such as refugees from Vietnam and Cambodia and the Philippines' determination to oust us from Clark Air Base and from another strategic base at Subic Bay. Holbrooke could be difficult to deal with, but he was a magnificent public servant. His death in 2010 was a great loss to the country.

On November 4th, 1979, in an outrageous violation of international law, Iranian radicals seized our Embassy in Tehran and took sixty-six members of the embassy staff hostage. That issue became increasingly oppressive as time passed. Gary Sick, a retired Navy officer and the NSC staffer responsible for Iranian developments, became drawn into prolonged discussions about how to get the hostages released. I took part in initial discussions about the situation in Iran, but as time passed, and sensitive plans for rescue options were discussed, the circle narrowed, and I was excluded.

In mid-November 1979, the Iranians released thirteen hostages, women and African-Americans. In late January 1980, six American diplomats who had not been in the Embassy when it was seized and had found refuge in the Canadian Embassy, escaped from Iran by using Canadian passports, which had been issued to them under a special law passed by the Parliament in Ottawa.

The hit movie *Argo* depicted this escape, perhaps in exaggerated terms toward the end of the film. The essential point, however, is that the Canadian government went to bat for us, spent money, and took risks that resulted in the freeing of six of our diplomats. The Canadians, like the Australians and New Zealanders, are courageous allies, and we are fortunate to have such friends.

But the Iranians' release of the thirteen hostages and the escape of six more increased pressure on the Carter White House to free the remaining fifty-two hostages. A clandestine rescue attempt, called "Operation Eagle Claw," was planned and approved at an April 10th, 1980, meeting of the National Security Council.

Secretary of State Cyrus Vance, who had consistently opposed the operation, was on leave on that day and was angered by the decision. He returned from leave, protested the decision, but was alone in his opposition to it. Brzezinski's relationship with Secretary Vance, never close in the first place, was put under great strain. Brzezinski was consistently more hawkish than Vance, and they frequently clashed on issues involving human rights.

On April 21st, when it became clear that the operation was to be launched, Cyrus Vance resigned. The operation's tragic failure three days later seemed in a way to vindicate Vance's resignation and increased the darkness of the pall that hung over the Carter White House.

A storm of criticism erupted about the type and small number of helicopters used in the disastrously long flight across the desert toward Tehran. Extreme operational security during the planning stages had also excluded people who might have contributed to better planning.

The final six months of the Carter presidency was a dismal period for everyone involved, and in November 1980, when Carter was up for reelection, I was moved to vote against him. It was the first time I had ever supported a Republican ticket, and my decision was based largely on my favorable impression of George H. W. Bush, the vice presidential candidate.

As I've mentioned, I had only met Bush once—in Tokyo in 1967—but my impression then had been highly favorable, and I had heard good things about Bush in his role as head of the CIA.

PART THREE

WHITE HOUSE YEARS

17

The White House Years with Reagan and Bush

The transfer of presidential power from Jimmy Carter to Ronald Reagan did not proceed in a particularly smooth or friendly fashion. Carter's staffers did not seem interested in imparting their collective wisdom to the incoming Reaganauts, who, for their part, seemed uninterested in listening.

I was not at all sure what my fate would be. The CIA had let me know that it would be perfectly happy to have me stay in place at the NSC, but I knew no one in the incoming administration and had no idea how they would feel about keeping me on.

One specific issue on which the transition worked well was that of keeping Korean political leader Kim Dae-jung alive. Kim had been accused of treason by hardline President Chun Doo-hwan, the former general who'd seized power in a coup following the assassination of President Park Chung Hee in October 1979. Chun falsely accused Kim of stirring up social unrest in response to the coup and of secretly supporting North Korea. In May 1980, an uprising took place in the city of Kwangju, Kim Dae-jung's hometown, in response to Chun's draconian actions. Chun crushed this uprising with great brutality, killing more than two hundred citizens. Kim was quickly put on trial, convicted, and sentenced to death by a military tribunal in Seoul.

President Carter was well aware of the situation in Korea, as early in his presidency he had strongly considered pulling all U.S. troops out of that country. Carter and Park Chung Hee had had a difficult relationship on that issue. Carter was no fan of the military establishment in Seoul and strongly admired Kim Dae-jung, who had been a staunch supporter of democracy and human rights for many years.

In early December 1980, Carter sent Secretary of Defense Harold Brown to Seoul specifically to caution Chun not to execute Kim and to seek his release. I accompanied Secretary Brown on this trip and developed great respect for him. I found him erudite but approachable, and a good traveling companion. Brown wondered how we best could raise the subject of Kim's incarceration, in case Chun was reluctant to discuss it.

We need not have been concerned. Chun, a very direct and outspoken Korean, immediately raised the issue in our private meeting with him and an interpreter. He said he knew that Kim was popular in the United States and that his execution would be strongly condemned. Chun went on to say that virtually every Korean general wanted Kim dead, seeing him as a constant source of political unrest and a strong supporter of policies favored by North Korea.

Brown forcibly countered Chun's presentation, citing the American intervention that had kept Kim alive in 1973, and Kim's growing importance as a civilian political leader, whose execution would be devastating to South Korea's international image.

This made no impression on Chun. I was equally unsuccessful in raising the point that we knew through intelligence that North Korea expected Kim to be executed, and that they planned to make an effective propaganda issue out of his death. Chun was interested in this information, but chiefly because it seemed to him to illustrate Kim's close ties to the North.

I left the meeting feeling we had failed, and that Kim would soon be executed. I had trouble sleeping on the long flight back and recognized that Chun had seen us as representatives of a weak and unpopular American president who would soon vanish from the White House.

The Brown mission was given no publicity, but the State Department was made aware of what had occurred. Assistant Secretary Dick Holbrooke and his deputy, Michael Armacost, recognizing the suspicion and mistrust that hobbled relations between the Carter and Reagan administrations, took it upon themselves to quickly reach out to Richard Allen, President Reagan's designated national security advisor. In a Brookings memorandum, issued in December 1997 at the time of Kim Dae-jung's election as president of South Korea, Holbrooke and Armacost made their important meeting with Allen public for the first time.

During the transition, they told Allen in a meeting that although the Carter administration "had managed to keep Kim Dae-jung alive for the last few months," only a message to Chun in President-elect Reagan's name, warning him not to execute Kim, could keep Kim alive for much longer.

Allen knew Korea well, and acted quickly. Working through the Korean Central Intelligence Agency station chief in Washington, Jangnai Sohn, a well-connected former major general, Allen sent a message to Chun, saying that President-elect Reagan strongly opposed Kim's execution.

Through his dialogue with station chief Sohn, Allen learned that Chun hoped to be invited to Washington to meet President Reagan as soon as possible after his inauguration. It was subsequently worked out that such a visit would take place *if* Kim was freed. Kim was released, accepted a fellowship at Harvard, and Chun came to Washington in February 1981. (More on that later.)

During the transition period, to my great surprise, Stansfield Turner approached me and said he wanted to talk. (I doubt we had spoken even once before during my eighteen months on the NSC.) Turner said that he had been impressed with my NSC work, that he hoped to remain on as DCI, and that he had a high-level CIA position in mind for me if President Reagan kept him in place. Turner asked me to put in a good word for him with the Reagan administration.

I thanked him for his kind words, wished him well, and said nothing to anyone about our conversation. It soon was announced that Turner would be replaced at CIA by William Casey, who had been Reagan's campaign manager. Casey had once been an important figure in the OSS—the precursor of the CIA.

As the transition period progressed, Carter's staff steadily moved out of the White House and the Old Executive Office Building. It was rumored that some left nothing behind in their files that might be helpful to their Republican successors, and that some even scrawled vulgar graffiti on their desk blotters.

One day in early January, I was suddenly visited by three incoming Republicans, led by Richard Armitage, later assistant secretary of defense for Asia and the Pacific under President Reagan. Armitage and his companions quizzed me about my past assignments at CIA and my political leanings. I didn't particularly mind; it was all part of the game.

I said that within CIA the atmosphere was basically apolitical, but that I had voted for Democratic presidential candidates until the 1980 election, when I had voted for Reagan. My guests left, giving no indication of what my future might be. Armitage had seen combat in Vietnam and had worked with CIA while there. We had that in common. The other two officers appeared bland and noncommittal.

As the days remaining in the Carter presidency "dwindled down to a precious few," I was made aware by Brzezinski of frantic efforts being made by the administration to gain release of the remaining fifty-two hostages held in Iran. These efforts came to naught. The Iranians vindictively waited until Carter was out of office, then immediately sent a message to President Reagan telling him that the hostages would be freed. That was a bittersweet moment for Carter, but a triumphant way for Reagan to begin his presidency.

The Iranians hated Carter for having tried to rescue the hostages and wanted to get on the good side of Reagan, whom they saw as an activist Republican who might consider mounting a coup against them, as had his Republican predecessor, Dwight Eisenhower, in 1953.

As President Reagan prepared to move into the White House, his incoming Republican staff acted like the Visigoths at the sack of Rome. No space assignments had been made, and there was an unseemly scramble for choice office locations. On two or three occasions after Reagan took office, complete strangers burst into my office. Disappointed that this rather choice space was clearly occupied and operating, they demanded to know who I was and what I was doing. I stressed that I was on loan from CIA, and that I was not from Plains, Georgia. In the end, as I recall, only Bob Kimmit, then an Army major, Gary Sick, and I were permanently kept on at the NSC.

About a week after he took office, Richard Allen, the national security advisor, summoned me to his office and told me that the decision had been made to keep me in place. As before, I retained the Asian and intelligence slots on the NSC staff.

I had started working at the White House in June of 1979 and would continue working there until February of 1989—almost a decade.

The new NSC had quite a different look to it, as all members of the Department of State had been released, and none had been replaced. I was told in effect that "State is always late with its opinions and its papers, and we don't need them." It did not take Richard Allen long to discover that not having State represented at the NSC was unworkable. Within the first four or five months of the Reagan presidency, FSO Jack Matlock came over to the NSC. Matlock, an extremely able officer, later became U.S. ambassador to the Soviet Union. Other State Department officials quickly followed him to the NSC.

Very early on, I bumped into Vice President George H. W. Bush in one of the narrow halls of the White House. He looked at me and said in a friendly manner, "I've seen you before, but I don't remember your name."

I introduced myself and reminded Bush of our 1967 meeting in Tokyo, with our mutual friend Tom Devine. He immediately recalled that occasion and asked what I had been doing in the intervening years. Thus began a relationship that changed the trajectory of my life, and which continues to this day.

Soon thereafter, George Bush invited me to go with him on his first visit to CIA headquarters as vice president. He was cheered to the echo in the dome-shaped auditorium and was moved to tears by the power and warmth of his welcome. It felt great to be with him, and to be recognized by so many friends. On the ride back, still emotional, Bush said that his year as DCI had been the best job he had ever had before becoming vice president. I think that meeting was the foundation of our friendship.

That CIA headquarters is named for Bush is eloquent testimony to the Agency's appreciation of his leadership. In his polemical history of CIA, *Legacy of Ashes*, Tim Weiner had this to say about George H. W. Bush when he was president: "He was one of them. He loved them. He understood them. He was, in truth, the first and only commander-in-chief who knew how CIA worked." And George Bush understood that to do good intelligence work, you must be able to think vicariously. That seems to be almost a lost art today.

I did not know what to expect from President Reagan, whom I had never met until he came into the White House. I had first heard of Reagan when he was governor of California. I had an aunt, Leah Gregg, who lived in Los Angeles at that time. She was a retired university professor, living on a pension that allowed few luxuries. She disliked Reagan, whom she felt was indifferent to low-income people.

Despite this, I was prepared to like President Reagan. I had enjoyed one or two of his films. His performance as a presidential candidate had been appealing, and his upbeat view of America's potential looked good to me, particularly in contrast with Jimmy Carter's stress on American malaise in his unfortunate 1979 speech.

My first encounter with the president was outside the Oval Office, at the end of a meeting he had held with a foreign dignitary. I'd been asked to make notes to be used for the president's parting remarks to his guest as he was about to get into his limousine and leave the White House grounds. My notes were on three-by-five-inch cards that had been sent to the president the previous day.

I was waiting outside with a group of reporters when the president appeared and walked to a microphone with his guest. He had nothing in either hand, walked right up to the microphone, and recited the lines in my notes perfectly, giving them more resonance and impact than they deserved. President Ronald Reagan was a strong role player.

He also had a great sense of humor. In one of the first Oval Office meetings I participated in, the president's guest was a second-level Japanese politician who had somehow slipped through the screening of his neophyte scheduling office. Mr. Iseki, as we shall call him, was allotted fifteen minutes, the shortest possible time for a meeting. But Iseki settled into the Oval Office as though he were a head of state and, after being greeted by the president, never stopped talking. As everything had to be translated, time passed very quickly.

The Japanese ambassador, a real pro whom I knew well, quickly saw that the meeting was going badly but could not stop Iseki's ramblings. The ambassador rose and declared that the time for the meeting had expired. Iseki reluctantly stood up.

President Reagan addressed him, saying, "Mr. Iseki, your visit reminds me of the story about a man who had a horse to sell." As this was translated, Iseki looked rather uneasy, as he sensed that something was coming that he hadn't expected.

The president amiably told of a potential customer approaching the horse, and after inspecting its teeth and hooves, asking the owner if he could take a ride. The owner readily agreed, went into his stable, and returned with a saddle in one hand and a two-by-four in the other. After saddling the horse, the owner took the two-by-four and clubbed the horse between the ears. The shocked customer asked why, and the owner replied, "That's how you get his attention."

The president then courteously handed a rather confused Iseki a small White House memento and ushered him out of the Oval Office. The president laughed, shook his head, and said the only good thing about the meeting was that it had given him a chance to tell one of his favorite stories.

Later in my office, I received a call from Kyodo News, asking about the Iseki visit. I was appropriately evasive, saying only that the president had enjoyed the meeting. Kyodo pressed on, saying they had heard that the president had told a story about a horse. I confirmed that he had and asked if they had a question about it. "Who was the horse?" they asked.

"Who do you think it was?" I replied.

After a rather awkward pause, they said they were not sure. I ended the conversation by saying that I was not sure whom the President was talking about either, but that it might have been either the press in general, or certain members of Congress. Kyodo thanked me profusely and hung up.

My first major assignment was helping to plan the White House visit of South Korean President Chun Doo-hwan, which took place on February 1, 1981. Seoul had pressed for an early meeting with President Reagan to validate Chun's importance in his own country. In return for being welcomed as Reagan's first significant foreign visitor, Chun had guaranteed Kim Dae-jung's safety and release.

The White House, for its part, had a low opinion of the draconian Chun. Had he not held Kim's life in his hands, he would not have been invited to the White House. I was thus involved in an effort to downplay Chun's visit in every way possible. Chun's staff sought a state dinner and were given only a lunch. Chun's time in Washington was limited, as were the number of high-ranking officials with whom he met officially.

Despite such efforts, the Koreans got what they wanted out of Chun's visit. Reagan's natural hospitality shone through in the official pictures, and Chun returned to Seoul with his stature enhanced.

In late April 1982, Vice President Bush embarked on a long trip to Asia, and I was invited to accompany him in my capacity as NSC staffer responsible for Asia. On that long trip, I first met Christopher Buckley, who was speechwriter for the vice president. Christopher and I quickly became good friends, and he later married my daughter Lucy. To this day, Christo remains very close to President Bush, and paid him a visit in Kennebunkport in 2013. We both regard Bush as the finest senior official we have ever known.

A question hung over the trip: Would Bush visit China? China was registering its strong disapproval of the Taiwan Relations Act (TRA), passed late in President Carter's presidency, which called for our selling weapons, including aircraft, to Taipei and maintaining some sort of military balance across the Strait of Taiwan.

In 1979, China and the United States had established full diplomatic relations. This caused us to break diplomatic relations with Taiwan, which we had previously called the Republic of China. Conservatives in Congress had then insisted that the TRA be enacted, to allow us to communicate directly with the Taiwanese and to maintain economic relations with them.

Our first visit was to Japan, where we met with Prime Minister Kantaro Suzuki and had a lunch with Emperor Hirohito. The empress was feeling too poorly to appear, but the crown prince and princess were there and greeted me by name, recalling our tennis games at the Tokyo Lawn Tennis Club. Meeting the emperor was a vivid experience for me, as I had lived in Japan for ten years, gotten to know citizens at every level of Japanese society, and had become well aware of the World War II atrocities committed in the name of the emperor.

When I was introduced to the emperor, I told him, in Japanese, that I had enjoyed playing tennis with his son. He smiled and nodded his understanding. When he shook my hand at the luncheon's end, the emperor commanded me, using a verb form that only he could easily employ, to return safely to my home country. But behind the formal words "*Anzen ni kai-rei!*" his tone was friendly.

General Douglas MacArthur's postwar decision to keep the emperor in place greatly aided Japan's ability to quickly rebuild its society. But it has made it very hard for the Japanese to honestly face up to past depredations, such as the 1937 "Rape of Nanking." Germany has done far better on that score, as its top Nazi leadership was virtually obliterated by the war itself and by the Nuremberg Trials, leaving the Germans free to move into an entirely new set of relationships with its neighbors.

With the emperor system still in place, as a direct connection with its militaristic past, Japan has not been able to do that. The seeds of imperial thinking remain alive in Japan, and Yasukuni Shrine has now emerged as a full-blown, jingoistic attempt to both justify and glorify Japan's past military actions. There is a phrase in Japanese, *shima guni konjo*, "the prejudice of island people," that speaks to that national characteristic, and which partially causes the deep mistrust of Tokyo that still exists in Beijing, Seoul, and Pyongyang.

Our next stop was Seoul, where I heard from Korean friends that Chun Doo-hwan had become more repressive than Park Chung Hee had ever been. Vice President Bush gave an address at the National Assembly in Seoul, trying by his appearance there to help the assembly become something of a counterbalance to the all-powerful presidency.

Five years later, in 1987, prolonged and widespread riots in South Korea forced Chun to agree to a direct popular election of his successor. That was a major step toward South Korea's becoming what it is today, Asia's most vibrant democracy.

Next came a stop in Singapore, highlighted by a meeting with Prime Minister Lee Kwan Yew, one of the most quotable men I've ever met. In a discussion of America's role in Asia, Lee said, "It's all right for you to be the sheriff of the Pacific. But just be sure that your posse is Japanese, not Chinese."

In Australia came a celebration on the fortieth anniversary of the Battle of the Coral Sea (May 4–8, 1942), which had largely removed the threat of a Japanese invasion of Australia. Vice President Bush also played a tennis match with John Newcombe and other Australian notables.

I was desperate to play, as I'd played with Roy Emerson when he and other Aussies had come through Tokyo in the late 1960s. But Mr. Bush was unaware of my level of play; and, for several months more, I did not make what he called "the traveling squad."

During a short stop in Auckland, New Zealand, Bush made the decision that we would go to Beijing. I had favored our going. The vice president had served previously as U.S. envoy to China and even as a sort of de facto ambassador between the two countries. With that experience in Beijing, George Bush seemed to me the best equipped of any senior American official to explain to the Chinese that the Taiwan Relations Act, passed in 1979, did not violate our previous agreements with China, particularly the Shanghai Communiqué of 1972. Bush was not looking forward to the visit to China: he knew he would be severely tested by the Chinese. His interlocutor was 69-year-old Foreign Minister Huang Hua, a formidable, very senior Chinese official, fluent in English, who had negotiated with Henry Kissinger during his secret visit to China in 1971. Huang wanted to weaken U.S. support of Taiwan, particularly military sales, which would make it easier for Beijing to coerce Taipei back into full integration with China.

The argument over American support of Taiwan lasted for about two hours, with a break in the middle. I have a picture taken during that short respite; it shows the vice president looking a little like a pummeled boxer sitting in his corner between rounds. Huang Hua accused us of having adopted a "two-China" policy and of trashing the Shanghai Communiqué.

The Bush line of argument was that, while we clearly recognized that Taiwan was part of China, the Chinese should acknowledge that we had some very old friends on the island who were worried about a military confrontation with mainland China—a confrontation that would be in no one's interest. Our support to Taiwan, Bush asserted, was our way of being true to an old friend, a trait that the Chinese themselves asserted in their relations with countries along their border, like North Korea, to which they asserted that they were "as close as lips to teeth." Bush repeatedly noted that both Washington and Beijing should be committed to reunification of Taiwan with China and that maintaining a military balance across the Straits of Taiwan made it more likely this would one day take place in a peaceful manner.

In the end, Huang Hua backed off and said he would report fully on his conversation to Deng Xiaoping. Bush had a meeting with Deng the following morning, scheduled for an hour. Only he and the U.S. ambassador to China, Art Hummel, attended; the rest of us nervously milled about.

The meeting lasted far longer than expected, and Bush and Deng emerged all smiles. Deng shook the hands of all the Americans. I was amazed at how tiny he was—and how friendly. He made an immense impression on me as the embodiment of the cosmopolitan Chinese. I knew of his role in opening China up after the Nixon-Kissinger gambit of 1972, I recalled his wearing a huge cowboy hat when he formalized U.S.-China relations with Jimmy Carter, and I knew he was a highly expert bridge player.

Of all the Asian leaders I have met personally since 1952, I would rank Deng number one. If Richard Nixon is primarily responsible for the opening to China, Deng is the man who most capitalized on that new relationship.

The May 1982 visit of Vice President Bush to Beijing resulted in a joint communiqué that established the framework for a solid new course, over twenty years of constructive relations between China and the United States.

The vice president's discussion with Huang Hua was the first time I'd seen him in action as a diplomat and negotiator. I was strongly impressed with his intellect, his patience, and his humor. He also had a rare ability to put himself in the shoes of the man with whom he was negotiating, to see how the world must look from that man's vantage point.

On our final night in Beijing, I had a chance to talk one-on-one with Huang Hua, who was relaxed and friendly. I asked him when China had first become aware of Japan. He looked at me, smiled, and then spoke as though he were an astronomer who had been the first to discover a distant and obscure planet. He said, "I think it was about in the third century A.D. by your calendar that the wreckage of Japanese boats began to wash up on our shores. Later we encountered pirates from Japan. But it was a long time after that before we had any direct relations."

We were then interrupted, but it was clear what an innate sense of superiority he, as a distinguished Chinese, felt toward Japan. I also sensed how tough it had been for him, a man born in 1911, to have witnessed the immense destruction Japan had inflicted on China in the twentieth century.

Shortly after the end of that trip, Admiral Dan Murphy, Bush's chief of staff, asked me if I would like to become the vice president's national security advisor. Murphy said that my performance on the long Asian trip, and my support for the visit to China, had led to his making me the offer on behalf of the vice president.

I was delighted to accept, and retired from CIA. I was glad to end my CIA career on a high note and was happy to leave the NSC staff, which had changed under the leadership of Reagan's second national security advisor, Judge William P. Clark, a neoconservative if there ever was one.

On December 8, 1982, I received the CIA's Distinguished Intelligence Medal from Director William Casey. My mother, aged 92, attended the presentation ceremony, and I remember thinking that in her long life she had probably never met a man more different from herself than the swashbuckling director.

18

Travels with Bush

In the six-and-one-half years that I worked as the vice president's national security advisor, I traveled with him to sixty-five different countries, on more than twenty overseas trips, some of which lasted for two weeks.

Air Force II became a home away from home, and it was a marvelous way to travel. Always on time, no hassles with customs, excellent food, and wonderful traveling companions, particularly Vice President and Mrs. Bush. The Air Force crew was highly skilled in having just the right sort of food awaiting us when we boarded after a foreign visit. They knew when "comfort food" was what we wanted, and when a more elaborate repast was appropriate.

Some of our stops were "one-night stands," which were pretty hectic. We'd get to the capital city, meet the country's leader, unpack at the hotel, dress up—often in black tie—for the usual dinner, go back to the hotel, repack, and leave luggage outside our hotel room door for 5 a.m. pickup. Then more meetings in the morning and a rush to the airport. A two-night stay was much easier, and the rare three-night stay was luxurious, allowing time to think, to write reports, and even to do a little shopping.

Most of the countries we visited I had never been to before, but I was amazed at how much I learned during our short visits. This was mostly due to the vice president, who always set an agenda for his meetings that got us directly involved with the key issues of the moment. I normally sat in on all meetings and watched the vice president deal skillfully with a wide range of foreign leaders, ranging from the absurdly bad (Mugabe in Zimbabwe and the Ceauşescus in Romania) to the truly distinguished (Deng in China,

Thatcher in the UK, Kohl in Germany, King Hussein in Jordan, and Pope John Paul in the Vatican).

Bush was both a good listener and a probing conversationalist. He carried questions into every meeting and invariably emerged with answers, some good, some bad. Relaxing on Air Force II at the end of each visit, Bush was humorously pungent in describing how he felt about those he had met, including the local American ambassador.

Whenever possible, he quietly met with the CIA station chief to express his admiration for the Agency's work, and often to ask probing questions, if he felt that he was getting evasive responses from others. When it was not possible to meet the COS, due to cover considerations, I was sometimes sent to carry the vice president's good wishes and to ask any significant questions on his mind.

The distances the vice president and I traveled were enormous. On one trip in March 1985, we went to Sudan, Niger, Mali, Switzerland, Russia (Moscow), Grenada, Brazil, and Honduras. The reason for going to Moscow was the sudden death of Soviet Premier Konstantin Chernenko, who passed away on March 10, 1985, when we were in sub-Saharan Africa.

In all, Vice President Bush attended three funerals in Moscow. Leonid Brezhnev died when we were in Nigeria in November 1982. (We stopped en route in Germany to pick up warm clothes sent by our families.) Only President Yuri Andropov, who died in February 1984, had the courtesy to pass away when the vice president was in Washington, allowing a quick, overnight trip.

As Bush liked to put it: "You die, we fly."

Each of the three Moscow funerals had a different feeling about it. There was no great sadness at Brezhnev's funeral, as he had been in failing health for some time, and there was a real sense that Yuri Andropov, his successor, might bring something new to the Kremlin's leadership. The funeral itself was long and dreary, with not a whiff of religiosity to it until, just before Brezhnev was interred, Mrs. Brezhnev was observed to quickly cross herself as she bent and kissed her husband good-bye.

Bush commented on this when we flew back to Zambia to resume our African trip. At our first meal on the ground, when a Zambian cleric said grace, Bush jumped to his feet and said how much it meant to him to hear such words, after watching Brezhnev being pulled to his tomb behind a tank carrier, and seeing his wife's final gesture of crossing herself as the only Christian gesture made in the entire funeral procedure.

Yuri Andropov died after less than fifteen months in office, and there was a real sense of sadness and loss in Moscow, sharpened by the recognition that his successor, Konstantin Chernenko, was an aged political hack who would bring nothing new or imaginative with him to the presidency.

President Chernenko lasted only a little over a year. At his funeral, I sensed real Russian embarrassment that three of their top leaders had died within twenty-nine months. The vice president and his senior staff were excited about what Mikhail Gorbachev represented, thanks to what we'd learned from the Finns. (More about that in Chapter 21.) I felt we were probably ahead of the Russian in our hopes for what the future might hold.

Each of the funerals attracted a large gathering of top-level officials from around the world, including many heads of state. At each of the funerals, the ranking visitors and their senior people were gathered into a large waiting room and given a chance to talk with each other. Some of us realized immediately that the Soviets would have had the room thoroughly bugged and would be listening carefully to everything we said. Led by people like Lee Kwan Yew of Singapore and Hosni Mubarak of Egypt, simple verbal codes were quickly devised to mask what was being said. Notes were passed around so that those less alert to the danger of bugging were aware of what was being done. By the time of the third funeral, the process had become routine to the visitors, and most of us enjoyed the idea of confusing those listening behind the walls.

Certain other trips and incidents stand out in my mind. Of all the countries I visited, Nigeria, in November 1982, remains the worst. There was a pervasive, almost overwhelming, sense of corruption. The Nigerians have a bicameral legislature, based on the United States Congress. The speaker of their house openly bragged to us that he had spent over $7 million in "special payments" during the year—bribes.

The Holiday Inn in Lagos, where the staff stayed, symbolized Nigeria to me. Holiday Inn, Inc., had long since withdrawn any connection to the Lagos establishment, but it still brazenly used the name. I was ushered into a shabby room, with a nonfunctioning air conditioner. It was very hot and difficult to sleep.

About one a.m. my hitherto silent air conditioner emitted an array of sparks and burst into flame. There was no fire extinguisher, and I beat out the flames with a pillow. There was no open room for me to transfer into, and so I spent the night in the room that stank of the material that had burned in the air conditioner.

There was an infamous acronym in wide use in West Africa at that time. It was "WAWA," meaning "West Africa Wins Again." I felt I had endured a clear example of WAWA. In the morning, we left for the long flight to Moscow for Brezhnev's funeral, glad to have an excuse to leave Nigeria a day early.

Once back from Moscow, we visited Zimbabwe, the former Rhodesia, which had recently fallen under Robert Mugabe's rule. Our entry into Harare was upbeat and hopeful, as the roadway was lined with both black and white school children, happily waving at us. But that was the only bright spot in our visit.

The vice president immediately spotted Mugabe, a severe presence, as trouble on the rise. We met with white businessmen and ranchers, who spoke of a growing tide of pressure, verging toward terror, to get them out of the country. We left Zimbabwe with an uneasy collective feeling. What has happened there since 1982 has been worse than anything we might have imagined. The economy is ruined, inflation is staggering, and still Mugabe clings brutally to power.

In January 1983, Bush embarked on one of his most important trips. It was to Europe, to persuade our European allies to deploy the Pershing missile, the so-called Intermediate Range Nuclear Force (INF), to counter proposed Soviet deployment of powerful SS-20, multi-warhead missiles. He went to nine European countries to make the case for INF deployment. Bush repeated the same, hard-hitting speech at each of his stops. We in his "traveling squad," as he called us, grew tired of hearing the speech, but it was effective.

Upon his return, the *Washington Post*, usually restrained in its praise, especially of Republicans, on 13 February 1983 printed an editorial entitled "George Did It!" from which I quote:

He listened carefully, and he elaborated Washington's approach to the missile question in a way that allowed open-minded Europeans to consider that the administration is not missile-happy, not bent on confrontation … but that it is determined to assert American leadership and to deserve the confidence of the allies."

In June 1983, we visited Oslo and saw the stunning Norwegian exhibit of the Nazi occupation during World War II. To enter, one goes down steep stairs to a narrow entrance framed by the muzzles of hundreds of German Mauser rifles. Inside are depictions of the Nazi horrors; imprisonment, interrogation, torture, and constant propaganda. Vidkun Quisling, the Norwegian politician who sold out to the Nazis and became their cruel puppet, is vividly portrayed, and I could sense Norway's eternal loathing of the man. Coming up from that exhibit, I felt I had to take several deep breaths to fill my lungs with clean air.

Later in that same trip, we flew to Germany, where the vice president met with Chancellor Helmut Kohl to discuss technical and political problems associated with actual deployment on the INF missiles. Kohl knew that the Dutch, in particular, were wavering about deployment, and he recognized how important it was for Germany to deploy on schedule. He spoke of his very frank dialogue with Soviet Premier Andropov on the subject and promised to come through. Bush and Kohl had a strong relationship that was most helpful on this difficult issue, which was deeply unpopular with some Germans.

On 25 June 1983, in traveling by road from Krefeld to Bottrop in Germany, the vice president's motorcade was attacked by a mob that had lain in wait along the way. The motorcade was stopped briefly. The attackers were skulking, dark figures with a medieval look. One man in a hooded garment ran up to the car in which I was sitting and screamed at me as he smashed at the window with a rock.

No one was injured, but we all had had a direct look at the face of opposition to the INF deployment, and it was not a pretty thing to see. The Germans, particularly Helmut Kohl, were deeply embarrassed by the event. Bush made light of it and, in so doing, strengthened his friendship with the chancellor.

As a result of European decisions made after the Bush trip, which showed the Soviets that threats to dominate Europe would provoke an American response, on December 8, 1987, an INF treaty between Moscow and Washington was signed that banned all INF forces from Europe.

In September 1983, Bush went to Morocco, Algeria, and Tunisia, before going on to four countries in Eastern Europe. The stops along the southern shore of the Mediterranean were deeply fascinating. The Tunisians were open and sophisticated. They spoke of the countless invasions, wars, and occupations they had undergone, starting with the Phoenicians. I visited the sunken remains of Carthage that had been unearthed by archaeologists. The utter defeat of Hannibal at the Battle of Zama in 202 B.C by Scipio Africanus had led to many centuries of Roman occupation.

I asked a very polished Tunisian which of the past occupations had been the cruelest. Without hesitation he said it had been the Spanish, after they had driven the last Moors out of Grenada in 1492 and seized large portions of the North African coast. He said that each family was allowed by the Spanish occupiers to have only one knife, chained to a kitchen wall, for cutting bread. Anyone carrying a knife was subject to instant killing.

In Algiers, I was discussing Algeria's struggle for its independence from France with several military officers. One of them, who spoke English well, said that at times the Algerian people's discouragement had been "deeper than Hannibal's despair." To this day, I don't think I have ever heard an expression that so echoes down the long corridors of history.

In December 1983, Bush went to Buenos Aires for the inauguration of President Raúl Alfonsín, the first democratically elected president of Argentina after eight years of military rule. My most vivid memory of that visit was the strange noise that greeted the vice president's delegation as we stepped out onto a large balcony overlooking a large plaza near the capitol. We had just met and greeted the new president, and loudspeakers announced us as the U.S. delegation to an immense crowd packed into the plaza below us. A wave of sound engulfed us unlike anything I had heard in previous travels with the vice president. I looked down and saw that half the crowd was cheering us, while the other half booed us with even greater fervor.

The cause of this bifurcated reaction was the still simmering issue of the Falkland Islands, which, in 1982, Argentina's previous military regime had tried to seize from the British, with disastrous results for Argentina. Alfonsín's election resulted from this military debacle, but many Argentines deeply resented U.S. support of Margaret Thatcher's energetic response, and they showed their feelings that day through vigorous booing.

On our way home, we stopped in El Salvador on December 11, 1983, where the vice president gave one of his strongest performances as an American leader. Our ambassador, Tom Pickering, a brilliant diplomat who remains active to this day, had made it clear in dispatches to Washington that the El Salvador military was conducting a brutal and totally counterproductive military campaign against an insurgency with its roots in neighboring Nicaragua. Entire villages were being slaughtered on the mere suspicion that they sheltered hostile insurgents. Pickering asked the vice president to make the case to the El Salvador military that they were losing control in their country largely due to the indiscriminate severity with which they were conducting their counterinsurgency campaign.

Bush spoke to about twenty of El Salvador's top military leaders and did not pull his punches. He said that our experience in Vietnam had taught us the tragic consequences of emphasizing "body count" over winning the hearts and minds of the people. He also stressed the need to be certain that the people being attacked by government forces were actually hostile insurgents, not innocent civilians.

One officer put up his hand and said, in effect, that it was easy for the vice president to say what he had said, but the man himself had had both his father and his son killed by insurgents. He felt that only a kill-or-be-killed approach had any chance of winning.

Bush expressed sympathy for the man, but stated flatly that the government must hold itself to a higher standard. The vice president asked: "If you fight them with the same methods they employ against you, how are you different from them?"

A strained silence followed that question, and the meeting ended.

Ambassador Pickering reported later that the vice president's words had sunk in and that his visit had marked a turning point in our relations with El Salvador.

At that meeting, I noticed the American defense attaché listening intently. He was in uniform, and his familiar array of ribbons indicated service in Vietnam. After the meeting I asked him about the patterns of insurgency that the embassy was seeking to deal with. He said that they were very similar to what he'd seen in Saigon in the late 1960s.

This led me, a year or so later, to arrange for Felix Rodriguez to go to El Salvador, to advise its military forces on the efficacy of intelligence-based helicopter operations against specifically targeted guerilla units. Felix was successful in his mission, but his presence in El Salvador had unintended consequences for me. More on this later.

In May 1984, Vice President Bush visited India and Pakistan and did all he could to address and assuage chronic tensions and hostility between Islamabad and New Delhi. In a variety of other meetings around the world, Bush had developed good relations with Prime Minister Indira Gandhi of India and President Zia ul Hak of Pakistan. But the chaos in Pakistan resulting from the 1979 Soviet invasion of Afghanistan, and Indira Gandhi's assassination by Sikh extremists in October 1984, rendered the vice president's efforts moot.

The torrent of tragedy continued, as President Zia was himself killed in the mysterious crash of his presidential aircraft in August 1988. This crash also killed U.S. ambassador to Pakistan Arnold Raphel and several other senior Pakistani officers. Three years later, in May 1991, Tamil Tiger terrorists from Sri Lanka assassinated Rajiv Gandhi, who had replaced his mother as India's prime minister. To this day, the fear and loathing that Pakistan and India feel toward each other are thwarting American efforts to bring stability to Afghanistan.

In October 1985, Vice President Bush and his entourage paid a highly successful visit to China. En route we made a quick stop on Saipan, in the Marianas Islands, and I was able to visit a few haunts where I'd lived for my last year as a bachelor, and my first, wonderfully happy year, as Meg Curry Gregg's husband.

In China, we visited four cities, and made a picturesque one-day voyage down the Li River. Its winding course through lush green rice paddies, shoreline fishing villages, and mist-shrouded conical hills has been the inspiration for Chinese ink paintings for thousands of years. To me, it was the eternal heart of China.

In Beijing, there was a highly publicized tennis match involving the vice president and me against two senior Chinese officials whom Bush knew well, and with whom he had played tennis in his 1974–75 tour as head of the U.S. Liaison Office. We won handily, to the great satisfaction of us both.

I had first been invited to play with Bush a year or so earlier, and we had rarely lost since then. Bush had a very good net game, with excellent reflexes and the ability to make snap judgments, correctly, about which balls to put in play and which to let go by. In that sense, tennis is not so different from diplomacy. The match in Beijing was our first overseas venture, and it got considerable press coverage.

The fruits of the vice president's previous visit to Beijing, resulting in the 1982 U.S.-China Communiqué, were clear to see. All the Chinese officials we met, in every city, were relaxed, showing Bush great respect, and warmth.

In July 1986, en route to Jordan and Egypt, the vice president stopped in Israel. I was sent ahead of him to plan some specific meetings. I had hardly checked into my hotel room when I received a call from Tom Friedman of the New York Times, who was then posted in Israel. He invited me to a meeting with Theodor "Teddy" Kollek, the longtime mayor of Jerusalem and one of Israel's great political figures. The three of us spent more than an hour together. It was a fascinating introduction to the complexities of Israel, its size and shape, its neighbors, and its inner tensions.

Kollek's major fear for Israel's future was of internal fanaticism, as practiced by the rapidly growing ultra-orthodox Jewish population in Jerusalem. Kollek also worried about the settlements on the West Bank. But I was struck by the fear and bitterness he expressed about the ultra-orthodox, saying they neither served in the Israeli Army nor paid taxes, but would lash out violently at those they perceived to be threatening their holy days, their customs, or their dress codes.

I was reminded of Mayor Kollek's words in February 1994, when a Jewish fanatic, born in Brooklyn, machine-gunned twenty-nine Muslims as they worshipped in a mosque in the city of Hebron. In November 1995, a right-wing Jewish extremist killed Yitzhak Rabin, prime minister, defense minister, and war hero, for his support of the Oslo Accords, which sought to bring peace between Palestine and Israel by returning to the Palestinians some of the West Bank seized in the 1967 Six-Day War.

Such issues still haunt and divide us. I continue to read Tom Friedman's articles on this difficult subject with great interest, and am most grateful to him for introducing me to Mayor Kollek, who died in 2007.

The vice president's visit to Egypt in August 1986 left me with the strongest visual impressions of any I acquired in all my travels with him. We flew into Egypt from Jordan and, a few hundred miles south of Cairo, first saw the Nile, a great, green snake writhing through the desert sands.

The next morning, Mrs. Bush was given a one-hour guided tour through the cavernous Cairo Museum. Her guide was a handsome Egyptian woman, an articulate archaeologist, who took us through selected corridors more or less at a dogtrot. It was fascinating but frustrating, with so little time allowed.

I was able to get very close, almost nose to nose, with a partially completed bust of Nefertiti, Egypt's glorious queen from the fourteenth century B.C. Her beauty leapt across the millennia and hit me hard. I stood, entranced, until our guide gestured at me to come along with a smile and shake of her head. She got us to the entrance of the museum on schedule, but the motorcade for Mrs. Bush was stuck in traffic, and there was a wait of several minutes.

Everyone crowded around Mrs. Bush, and the guide was left standing alone, so I went over to her. I thanked her for the expert tour and asked if she thought the statuary we had seen were idealized representations of Egypt's ancient kings and queen.

Our guide replied that this was an issue frequently discussed among her colleagues. She personally believed that the statues and

carvings we had seen were honest depictions. As evidence, she cited the case of the homely King Akhenaten, who is shown with a
long chin, thick lips, and a wrinkled face.

I asked about Nefertiti, and she said she had seen me gaping
at her, and laughingly said, "Don't worry, that's how she really
looked."

I asked our guide if she had a favorite object in the huge museum. "Of course," she replied.

I asked her if she had shown us that object, and she said she
had not. I asked why, and what the object was. She said that her
favorite was a delicate wooden carving, which she appreciated not
only for its beauty but for the fact that it had survived for so many
millennia.

She said, "Why did you ask me that question?"

I recalled that Meg and I had had to rush through the Uffizi
Gallery in Florence, and that I'd had to be dragged away from one
object that stopped me in my tracks. She asked what it was, and I
replied that it was Michelangelo's bust of Brutus. She laughed and
said she also admired that piece. We parted as good friends.

Far up the Nile, in the Valley of the Kings, opposite Luxor, we
were allowed into a recently discovered tomb with wall paintings
of particular beauty that was rarely open to visitors. Our way down
into the tomb was lit by sunlight reflected from a series of mirrors
held by men at each bend of the descending tunnel.

The light was fresh and clear but wavered a bit, as it was passed
through the hands of five or six men, standing many yards apart,
who shouted at each other to help keep the reflected light on target.
We were told that this smokeless light, also used in ancient times,
had been crucial to preserving the fragile wall paintings.

On our final night in Egypt, we stayed on an island in the Nile.
The Egyptian ambassador to Washington was a friend, and that
night he invited me to come aboard a felucca, a traditional boat
with a lateen sail that quickly swung us out into midstream. The
ambassador suggested that I lie on my back and look at the stars.

For the next few minutes, I lay on deck, with the sway of the
sail and the rocking of the boat, and felt in touch with one of the
planet's eternal flows. Of the sixty-five countries I visited with vice
president Bush, Egypt was the one I most wanted to return to with
Meg.

In 2006, that hope was realized when she and I returned to Cairo and the Nile with a delightful group that included Spencer and Mia Kim, joyous companions with whom we have traveled twice to Spain, and also to Turkey.

Vice President Bush had three meetings with Pope John Paul II; in February 1984 in Washington, and in June 1985 and September 1987 at the Vatican. Zbigniew Brzezinski, himself born in Poland, had often spoken to me of his admiration of the "Polish Pope," calling him the strongest strategic thinker in Europe. The pope was tremendously impressive physically, even after he was severely wounded in a May 1981 assassination attempt.

Cardinal Agostino Casaroli, the Vatican secretary of state, was convinced that Soviets had told the Bulgarians to kill the Pope, but this was never proven, and the pope never expressed such suspicions in his talks with the vice president. In 1983, he had visited his Turkish assailant in jail and pardoned him. The pope's magnanimity on this issue was quite extraordinary, a true measure of the man. The Soviets had reason to fear the pope's influence; I believe he played an important role, particularly in Poland, to end Soviet domination of Eastern Europe.

In late September 1987, the vice president visited Poland. In Warsaw, he attracted the largest crowds I'd seen on any of my many trips with him. Ambassador John Davis gave a dinner for the vice president that included opposition labor leader Lech Walesa, the head of Solidarity and winner of the Nobel Peace Prize in 1983.

At the dinner it was arranged that they would meet "by chance" the next day at a Warsaw church, where a memorial service was being held for a Catholic priest killed by the police. Huge crowds gathered in the streets, and wildly enthusiastic cheers arose when Bush and Walesa appeared together.

By then it was known that the vice president would run for president in 1988, and Walesa shouted that if he had the chance to vote in America, he would strongly support Bush. More cheers erupted. Later that day, General Wojciech Jaruzelski, the Communist president of Poland, was asked whom he would vote for, and his answer was that he, too, would vote for Bush. One could sense that Poland was on the verge of abandoning totalitarian rule. Two years later, Jaruzelski legalized Solidarity, paving the way for Lech Walesa to become Poland's president in 1990.

After a short visit to the ancient capitol of Krakow, we flew to Bonn, where the top German leaders were delighted to hear our impressions of the evolving atmosphere in Poland. German president Richard von Weizsacker, in particular, spoke of the Poles with real affection. As one who had clear memories of the brutal Nazi invasion of Poland in 1939, I was deeply moved by this total change of German attitude.

In the spring of 2010, as I prepared to write this book, I found among my papers a full-page letter to me from President Reagan, dated January 6, 1989. It said great things about Vice President Bush, including this:

> When January 20 arrives and George Bush is sworn in as the 41st President of the United States a landmark will have been achieved. For only the second time in our history, and the first time in over 150 years, a sitting vice president will have taken office as the man chosen by the American people to lead them into a new era. That is a tribute to the remarkable character and abilities of George Bush....
>
> The Reagan-Bush team has worked side-by-side from the very first days of the journey we began together in Detroit back in 1980. From the start, we've enjoyed an unusual partnership of philosophy and practice, doing the tasks the American people called upon us to accomplish: rebuilding a faltering economy, rescuing our sagging defenses, defending family values, and unleashing once more the enterprising spirit of our people. Vice President Bush readily accepted some of the toughest assignments we faced in reaching these goals, from regulatory reform and the fight against terrorism to the anti-drug campaign and sensitive missions overseas. I've called George Bush the best Vice President America has ever seen....

I sent a copy of Reagan's letter to George H. W. Bush and quickly received the following reply, handwritten on June 26, 2010, from Maine.

Dear Don,

Thanks for your good letter. I don't believe I have ever seen the January 6th letter President Reagan sent you. I was very pleased, of course, by his words about me and equally pleased by what he said about you and our staff. What a kind, good man he was.

Give Meg a hug. I often think of our glory days of which you were an integral part.

Love from the Atlantic shore.

George B

I've received many presidential notes but I particularly value these two for what they say about the Reagan-Bush relationship. I spent all eight years of Reagan's presidency in the White House. I saw at close hand the issues swirling around the president and the strongly conflicting personalities he had to deal with. It was a tumultuous presidency, particularly in the foreign policy arena, where Reagan had six different national security advisors.

Through all of that, Vice President Bush acted like the rudder on a racing boat, an unseen but vital part of a fast-moving presidency, where much was accomplished in foreign policy, the area where Bush excelled. I hope that eventually historians will shed more light on this still largely neglected aspect of the Reagan era.

Though the president and vice president got on very well, with their wives it was another story—a different chemistry. I never got to know Nancy Reagan, but I did know that it was very unwise to arouse her ire. She had strong feelings about anyone who was close to the president, and somehow she never seemed at ease with either the vice president or Mrs. Bush. I regretted that, but it was far beyond my capacity to do anything about.

In 1988, President Eisenhower's devastating putdown of his vice president, Richard Nixon, continued to cast a shadow over the vice presidency. When asked, in 1960, to name a key role in presidential decision-making that Nixon had played, Ike had said: "If you give me a week, I might think of one."

The vice presidency started to change when Jimmy Carter gave more responsibility to his vice president, Walter Mondale, than any previous president had done. George H. W. Bush and later Al Gore took the office to new levels of significance. I believe Dick Cheney was allowed to take it too far.

In concluding this chapter, I feel it's only fair to mention my worst day on the tennis court with George H. W. Bush. It came at Kennebunkport, Maine, in the summer of 1988. Meg and I were thrilled to be invited to see the summer retreat of the Bush family that meant so much to them all. I took my tennis racket, "just in case."

I was taken on a ride in Bush's high-speed "cigarette boat" and was given a chance to steer it. His familiarity with the coast and his love of the sea came through strongly. At lunch, as part of a constantly changing flow of relatives, sons George and Neil appeared. To my great surprise, the vice president said to me, "Don, I think we can beat those two."

We both took naps after lunch, and went forth about 3 p.m., on a very windy day. In the small audience was Dorothy Bush, the vice president's mother, then in her late eighties. She gave me a strong, skeptically appraising look, which somewhat unnerved me, as it was clear that she wanted her son, not her grandsons, to win.

The vice president and I played two sets against his sons—both of which we lost. I played miserably, truly embarrassing myself. The elder George Bush, as always, was gracious about my play, but his son George W., grinning as he came to the net to shake hands, said: "What possessed you two old farts to think that you could beat us?"

I slunk off the court, not even daring to look at Dorothy Bush.

There were other, later games with the vice president when I somewhat redeemed myself. But that afternoon at Kennebunkport stays in my mind, not only because of my poor play but also for what it revealed about differences between Bush father and son.

19

Denis Thatcher and the Missing Brassiere

In January and February 1983, as noted, Vice President Bush undertook one of his most important and successful trips. To nine European countries he brought the message that American intermediate-range nuclear missiles had to be deployed in Europe in order to counter the threat of missile deployment by the Soviet Union. The trip went well, for George Bush always rose to the occasion in diplomacy, just as he did on the tennis court.

Our final stop was in London. On February 9, Margaret Thatcher invited the vice president's party to have dinner with her at Number 10 Downing Street, the official residence of the British prime minister.

I went to dozens of banquets and dinners during my travels with the vice president, but never anything quite like that at "Number 10." Going upstairs to the rooms where we talked and had dinner, I passed a stunning procession of portraits of those who had lived there, including Arthur Wellesley (the Duke of Wellington, who defeated Napoleon at Waterloo), Benjamin Disraeli, Arthur James Balfour, David Lloyd George, Neville Chamberlain, and Winston Churchill. The echoes of empire were powerful.

Prime Minister Thatcher was an imposing, handsome woman—blonde hair beautifully coiffed, unwrinkled complexion, and strong facial bone structure. I once sat next to Pamela Harriman, Winston Churchill's former daughter-in-law, at the Kennedy Center in Washington. She reminded me of Margaret Thatcher in coloring and physique.

But while Harriman was warm and flirtatious, Thatcher was all business. Sitting next to Harriman, I thought of her affairs. Sitting at the table with Thatcher, I thought of her battles with the trade unions.

There were about a dozen of us at dinner. I was particularly struck by Michael Heseltine, Thatcher's newly appointed secretary of state for defense. He was a large and rather imposing figure (think of Donald Trump less 50 pounds and with a much better haircut), and I expected to hear a lot from him over dinner. But he spoke hardly a word, and seemed almost cowed.

The prime minister dominated in every way. She was very pleased with what our vice president had accomplished; she was sure of herself, called on none of her advisors to supplement what she said, and clearly was gratified that Washington and London were so well synchronized on the missile deployment issue.

We left the dinner feeling that everything that needed to be said had been said, mostly by the prime minister. I left feeling particularly uplifted by a glass of port wine, vintage 1924.

Almost exactly a year later, the vice president was back in London, this time to talk about erupting problems in Lebanon, where 241 U.S. Marines had been killed by a terrorist attack in October 1983.

Since February 12, 1984, was a Sunday, Prime Minister Thatcher invited Bush and his traveling squad to meet at Chequers, a lovely country estate that has been the official country residence of British prime ministers since 1921.

A serious discussion of the Middle East took place, led by Field Marshal Edwin Bramall, in which Secretary Heseltine participated expertly. Mrs. Thatcher listened intently, obviously disturbed by the emergence of terrorism as a major threat, but largely content to let her military leaders lead the discussion on current military trends and events.

When the subject of nuclear weapons arose during the discussion, Thatcher made plain that she was strongly opposed to their total elimination. Born in 1925, she clearly recalled as a schoolgirl during World War II the growing fear in Britain that Hitler would develop nuclear weapons before anyone else, and would put them on the V-1 and V-2 rockets with which he was already pounding London.

Thatcher said that only allied possession of nuclear weapons

had kept the Soviets from using theirs and that, with growing insta-
bility in the Middle East, it was imperative that a nuclear deterrent
always be maintained by the U.K. and its allies.

A delightful lunch followed for about thirty people. Mrs. Bush
was with the vice president on this trip, and she sat next to Denis Thatcher, who laughingly called himself "the first male prime
ministerial spouse in the history of Britain." He and Mrs. Bush got
on extremely well. They both had a powerful sense of humor, and
their laughter often filled the dining room.

I was at Heseltine's table, and we both recalled the fact that
we'd said very little a year before at Number 10. Heseltine admitted
that at first he'd been somewhat overawed by Thatcher, and that
adjusting to her was a very delicate process.

Two years later, in 1986, Heseltine broke with Margaret Thatch-
er and challenged her for the leadership of the Conservative Party.
He later served as deputy prime minister under Prime Minister
John Major, who was elected in 1990.

Following lunch, I introduced myself to Denis Thatcher and
found him easily approachable and a great raconteur. He had an
array of humorous golf stories and enjoyed talking about a game he
played often and well. The Thatchers were quite obviously devoted
to each other, and I later learned that she referred to him as her
"golden thread." Perhaps it was Denis Thatcher's highly successful business career that left him so comfortable in his own skin and
happy to play his role as his wife's strongest supporter.

On July 4, 1985, Charles H. Price II, U.S. ambassador to England, gave a glittering dinner marking the 200th anniversary of the
appointment of the first American ambassador to London. Vice
President and Mrs. Bush were at the end of a seven-country swing
through Europe and were able to join in the festivities, which began
the day before with a luncheon at Number 10 for sixty-four people.

Everyone was in a festive mood. Mrs. Bush again sat next to
Denis Thatcher, and I could see how much they enjoyed talking
and laughing together.

The reception and dinner the next evening at the ambassador's
residence had the most interesting array of guests of which I had
ever been a part. At least 200 people attended, from the U.K., the
United States, and leading countries of Europe.

After all the guests had gone through a receiving line, Mrs. Bush approached me with a wicked gleam in her eye. She had noted that a handsome and sometimes aggressive female guest (we shall call her Emma Bovary, with apologies to Flaubert) was wearing a low-cut and very loose-fitting gown. Mrs. Bush said, "Don, you know Emma Bovary. She has forgotten to put on her brassiere, and I want you to go over and remind her."

I replied, "Mrs. Bush, I would charge a machine gun nest in your defense, but I do not have the courage to do what you have asked me to do."

With a great grin, she said, "I am deeply disappointed in you,' and turned to other mischief. As soon as possible, I checked out Emma Bovary and saw that Mrs. Bush had been correct.

At dinner, I sat next to Cary Grant's fifth and last wife, a beautiful brunette named Barbara Harris, who was having as much fun as I was. After dinner, Grant came over to me and thanked me for talking so cordially with his wife. He was then about eighty and looked marvelous. Having met him, I enjoy his old films even more, especially *North by Northwest*.

I also talked to Charlton Heston, and our subject was tennis. He told me his knees were bothering him, and I touted the value of running backwards. He said, "People must think you're crazy." I told him the results were worth the derision aroused, and he said he would try it.

It was that kind of rare evening.

The following morning, I asked the vice president how he had enjoyed the dinner. He laughed and said, "Denis Thatcher came over to me and said, 'I was sitting near Emma Bovary, and could hardly keep my eyes off her right tit.'"

I have a picture of me with both Bushes, taken just after our return to Washington. Mrs. Bush is grinning at me, and wrote "I'm thinking of dinner in London," with a smiling face drawn below her words.

Denis Thatcher was a decade older than his wife and died in 2003. He was perfectly at ease as the husband of a brilliant and formidable woman, and I remember both of them with affection and admiration.

I did not enjoy the recent film *The Iron Lady*, which largely depicts Thatcher in decline. But it did capture the intensity of her loneliness and love for Denis, which I saw in full flower at Chequers and at Number 10.

PHOTO GALLERY III

On Air Force 1 with Ronald Reagan and other White House staff, 1981.
Reagan is talking with National Security Advisor Richard V. Allen.
White House photo

An annoying visitor to the Oval Office. Note Reagan's expression. February 1982. *White House photo*

Reagan wishing me well when I joined Vice President Bush as his national security advisor, July 1982. Robert "Bud" McFarlane and Gaston Sigur, my replacement at the NSC, are in the background. *White House photo*

Ambassador to China Arthur Hummel at left of VP Bush (seated on rail) in Beijing, at rest between tough rounds of talks with Chinese foreign minister Huang Hua on "the Taiwan problem," May 1982. *White House photo*

Official photograph of me as national security advisor to the vice president, 1985. *George H. W. Bush Presidential Library photo*

Receiving a back rub from Barbara Bush, Wellington, New Zealand, May 1982. (from left:) Speechwriter Christopher Buckley. Kim Brady, me, and Mrs. Bush. *White House photo*

On Air Force 2 with Vice President Bush, talking with assistant secretary Richard Burt, on "INF trip" to Europe, February 2, 1983. *White House photo*

Two Yalies. CIA officer Jack Downey, Yale '51, held over twenty years in prison by the Chinese, with George H. W. Bush, Yale '48, in the vice president's office, August 1983. *White House photo*

Kim Dae-jung recounting his kidnapping experience at my first meeting with him. Washington, D.C., December 1983. Photo by Fumio Matsuo, *Kyodo News*

Briefing President Reagan on the new CIA Executive Order, December 1981. *White House photo*

"Go for it McEnroe!"
What a team — Thanks partner
Gzy Bush

Tennis with VP Bush, Houston, 1986. One of the few matches we lost.
White House photo

20

The Puzzling Case of Richard Nixon

I had never liked Richard Nixon. As a college student in the late 1940s, when I first read of his actions on the House Un-American Activities Committee, I was totally turned off by his hard-edged tactics. My animus increased when, in 1950, Nixon won a U.S. Senate seat in California after accusing his Democratic opponent, Helen Gahagan Douglas, of pro-Communist tendencies.

My parents were both on the liberal side. My father was quite proud of the fact that in 1928 he'd voted for the Socialist Party candidate, Norman Thomas, liking neither Herbert Hoover nor Al Smith. In late 1951 and early 1952, while in Washington, I lived with my aunt, Charlotte Phinney, in Georgetown. She was an ardent supporter of Adlai Stevenson and told me a lot about him.

I admired General Eisenhower greatly but was appalled when he chose Nixon as his running mate in 1952. I thus was disappointed when Stevenson lost the election, and Ike and "Tricky Dick" started their eight-year run.

In the mid-1950s, while living in Tokyo, I did quite a lot of hiking and skiing in the Japanese Alps in Nagano prefecture. One summer, the British diplomat Richard Burges Watson and I were hiking in the Kamikochi Valley, one of the most beautiful spots in all of Japan. Snowy peaks there surround a verdant valley with a river running through it. The Kamikochi Valley also sported a luxurious branch of Tokyo's Imperial Hotel, which was still functioning just as Frank Lloyd Wright had intended.

We had a strenuous day on the steep slopes. It was more than hiking but less than true climbing—call it scrambling. Burges Watson and I descended for dinner and saw a solitary foreigner sitting by a fire in the lobby of the hotel. We introduced ourselves and learned that he was Douglas B. Maggs, dean of the Duke University Law School.

The three of us had dinner together. We found Maggs very engaging. As it was his first trip to Japan, we were able to answer some of his questions.

As a distinguished American lawyer, Maggs was well aware that Japan was a country where for many years the word of the emperor had been law, and that the result had been chaos and war. He was interested in aiding the construction of a legal framework that would aid Japan's shift from military dictatorship to democracy. We wished him well, but we all realized Japan had a long way to go.

I knew that Vice President Nixon had graduated from Duke Law School in 1937, and, toward the end of dinner, I screwed up my courage and asked Douglas Maggs what he thought of our vice president.

Maggs leaned back contemplatively in his chair, shook his head and said, "He is the smartest man who ever went through Duke Law School." Silence settled on the table.

I ventured, "What do you think of him now?"

Maggs looked at the ceiling and said, "I truly do not know what to make of him." He paused. "I saw him recently and said to him 'Dick, you knew that Helen Gahagan Douglas was no Communist. Why did you accuse her of that?'" Another pause.

Maggs continued: "Nixon sort of hung his head and said 'Well, I wouldn't do it now.'"

Maggs looked at us as though we might have some enlightening comment to offer. Neither of us did, and so we said goodnight and goodbye.

In 1960, I rejoiced when Kennedy defeated Nixon. In 1962 I was delighted when Nixon was defeated in a race for the California governorship. And in 1968 I was deeply disappointed when Richard Nixon defeated Hubert Humphrey to win the presidency. I went off to Vietnam in September 1970 full of gloom about the war and Nixon's role in continuing it.

I was astonished to hear, in February 1972, that Nixon and Henry Kissinger had gone to China. "What the hell is he up to now?"

I asked myself. I was still in Bien Hoa, "Vietnamization" was well underway. But the military mantra was still that we were in Vietnam fighting to fend off the Chinese-engineered "domino" effect that would have country after country in Southeast Asia fall under Beijing's sway.

In June 1972, just as I was about to leave Bien Hoa, I first heard of the Watergate break-in. I immediately felt that that ill-conceived caper would blow up in Nixon's face, and that he would never be reelected in November 1972.

How wrong I was. The favored Democratic candidate, Ed Muskie, was seen to be weeping in the snows of New Hampshire, his campaign died, and in came George McGovern as the Democratic presidential nominee. Nixon won every state but Massachusetts in defeating George McGovern.

Thanks in large part to brave and indefatigable reporting by the *Washington Post*, the truth of Watergate was revealed, and in August 1974, Nixon resigned in disgrace.

Vice President Gerald Ford became the new president, and on September 8, 1974, pardoned Nixon of all actions taken while he was president, saying that the nation needed to "heal." Ford's pardon was extremely controversial and clearly contributed to his loss to Jimmy Carter in 1976.

My view of Nixon improved somewhat as time passed. The strategic benefits of his opening to China began to emerge, enabling the United States to head off what at times had appeared to be an inevitable clash between Taiwan and China. As we came to recognize that tremendous strains existed between China and the Soviet Union, our stance toward Moscow grew more confident, as we worked for strategic arms control agreements.

I think it's clear now that Nixon's opening to China is the single greatest U.S. diplomatic achievement since World War II. Over the past thirty years I have gotten to know Henry Kissinger fairly well, and I admire both his sagacity and his sense of humor. On a couple of occasions, I have had the honor of introducing him at large dinners in New York and managed to work in the fact that Kissinger and I have something in common—we were both sergeants in the U.S. Army. Beyond that, my respect for the role he played in reaching out to China grows stronger with time. That truly was a world-changing diplomatic achievement.

During my travels as national security advisor to Vice President Bush (1982—88), it became evident how much Nixon had been admired overseas. In country after country, we heard positive references to Nixon and to the clarity and balance with which he had represented American interests.

In August 1988, Vice President Bush called me into his office and told me that Nixon wanted to see me. To the great amusement of the vice president, I was clearly flummoxed by this news. I should not have been, as by that time it was clear that Bush would be the Republican nominee for president, and Nixon wanted to see what kind of person I was and what kind of advice I might be giving him.

Bush said Nixon was particularly interested in our continuing relationship with the Soviet Union, and so the vice president asked me to share with Nixon a paper I had written for him offering suggestions on our future stance as the Soviet Union under Gorbachev entered a transitional stage. So, a few days later, off I went to New York to see a man who had been my *bête noir* for decades.

Nixon had a comfortable but inconspicuous office on Federal Plaza in lower Manhattan, and there were only two or three other people with him in the suite. I was amazed at how well Nixon looked, how relaxed and happy he appeared. He hardly seemed to have aged at all since his tumultuous departure from the White House fourteen years before. The man's inner strengths must have been remarkable to have carried him through all the vicissitudes of his extraordinary career.

I was entirely alone with Richard Nixon for a fascinating ninety-minute meeting. Nixon was upbeat and friendly, with a self-deprecating sense of humor that astonished me. There were no references whatsoever to the problems of his presidency; it was as though they had never taken place. I gave him my paper, which we discussed, but which he did not immediately read, I think out of courtesy to me. His admiration for Vice President Bush appeared strong, and he seemed to recognize what an important role Bush had played as a stabilizing foreign policy advisor to President Reagan.

At the end of our meeting, Nixon showed me to the door. As we shook hands, I felt that I had made a new and unexpected friend. He thanked me for coming and for my public service. He also expressed strong admiration for Vice President Bush.

In a very courteous letter he wrote to me on August 16, 1988, Nixon said: "As long as he [Bush] follows the three guidelines you set forth in the conclusion of the memorandum you wrote him after your trip to Moscow, he will continue to steer a straight course between the super doves who would agree to anything with Gorbachev and the super hawks who will agree to nothing." Nixon also sent me a copy of his book *1999*.

A decade later, I was writing an article for the magazine *Orbis* and needed a forward-looking quote on America's role in the twenty-first century. I found what I thought was a very good passage in Nixon's book, and began my article with it.

The *Orbis* editor bluntly rejected this, saying "If you start your article with a quote from Nixon, no one will read the rest of it." That was as harsh a judgment of Richard Nixon as I've heard.

So, after all this, what do I think of Nixon? I feel a certain empathy with Duke University's Douglas Maggs when I asked him that question more than half a century ago. And my answer would be very similar to his: a mixture of grudging admiration and deep confusion.

21
The Finnish Connection

On April 17-19, 1997, Hofstra University held a conference to discuss the work and times of President George H. W. Bush. I was there and spoke of Mr. Bush when he was vice president, as did Victor L. Israelyan, who had been Soviet ambassador to the Conference on Disarmament in Geneva in 1984.

In his remarks, Israelyan noted that former Russian president Mikhail Gorbachev would speak later at the conference. Israelyan then dwelt at length with an April 1984 meeting he had had with Vice President Bush in Geneva, when Bush said he was certain that Gorbachev would be the next Soviet leader and asked Israelyan to set up a secret meeting with him.

Israelyan was amazed at this question and recalled asking Bush: "How do you know the name of our next leader?"

Bush only smiled in response. Israelyan ended his remarks by saying, "Years have passed since that Geneva episode, but still there are many questions. Only President Bush can answer them.... I believe the explanation lies in Bush's astonishing political intuition."

The answer to Israelyan's question was quite simple. Since July 1983, Vice President Bush had been in close and direct contact with the office of the Finnish president and, through the Finns, had been well informed of Gorbachev's rise to power, of his governing philosophy, and of the changes that he was likely to bring with him.

Here is how that all began. For several years in the late 1970s and early 1980s, I had an early morning tennis game, two or three times a week before work, with Tapani Kaskeala of the Finnish embassy in Washington. I had never had anything to do with the Finns before that and found Tapani to be a wonderful friend, and a strong opponent. We played at the McLean Racquet Club in Virginia.

Tapani was twenty years younger than I, but I was playing the best tennis of my life and had won both the singles and doubles championship at the McLean Club. I won about 60 percent of the matches we played. Tapani was wonderfully competitive and swore furiously in Finnish when he made a bad shot, or when I made a particularly good one.

Finnish is one of the world's toughest languages, and Tapani refused to tell me what his curses meant in English. They had a very strange timbre—something between the barking of a seal and the yapping of a coyote. Tapani said, in his wonderful Finnish way: "If I tell you what I am saying, I will be so embarrassed that I won't be able to say it again." So he cursed away, and I enjoyed it all immensely.

We exchanged family visits, and I got to know others in the Finnish embassy. They began to invite me to regular embassy "salons," where current events were discussed. At one of those meetings, I met Max Jakobson, one of Finland's senior diplomats and former ambassador to the United Nations. In 1971, Jakobson was the candidate of the five Nordic states to become secretary general of the U.N., but he was vetoed by the Soviet Union.

I found Jakobson's view of the Soviet Union fascinating. He spoke to me eloquently and at length concerning the impact on the thinking of Joseph Stalin of Finland's ferocious defense against Soviet attack in the Winter War of 1940–41. Here is how he put it in his book *Finland: Myth and Reality*:

> In the summer of 1940, the three small states (Latvia, Lithuania and Estonia) were incorporated into the Soviet Union. But the Finns fought, and this seems to have made a profound impression on Stalin. Military prowess was probably the quality he admired most. He respected military power and nothing else, as was shown by his famous question about the Pope's divisions.... During a discussion on Finland in the Teheran conference in December 1943, Stalin told Roosevelt and Churchill, as recorded by Charles Bohlen, that "any country that fought with such courage for its independence deserves consideration."... Finland in his eyes had passed a crucial test of manhood.

Jakobson was deeply annoyed by the brickbat term "Finlandization," applied indiscriminately to countries living close to the Soviet Union and implying that they would never challenge Moscow's interests. Jakobson asserted vehemently that Finland had a muscular and independent neutrality and would brook no interference in its internal affairs, whether from East or West.

As I got to know the Finns better, I found they all felt that way. They knew they lived next door to a difficult and brutal neighbor, which they detested. They recognized that they had a bit more "wiggle room" than most of the Soviet Union's close neighbors because of the respect from Stalin they had won in the Winter War.

They also realized, from the Soviet veto of Max Jakobson's U.N. secretary general candidacy, that the appearance of strict neutrality was their best option. Thus, they publicly endured the sting of the slanderous term named for them when, in fact, they were by far the least "Finlandized" country in Eastern Europe.

In mid-1982, I happily left my Asian-focused position at the National Security Staff and joined Vice President Bush as his national security advisor. Since that job had a global focus, I began to ask my Finnish friends more pointedly what they were observing within the Soviet Union.

The name Mikhail Gorbachev immediately surfaced as a rising star whom the Finns were watching with interest and approval. Gorbachev was then in charge of agricultural development in the Soviet Union. His main rival in the Soviet hierarchy was a hardliner, Grigory Romanov. All of this was passed along to Bush, who received it with great interest.

In late June 1983, Bush planned a trip to Northern Europe, and I suggested that Finland be added to the normal itinerary of Denmark, Norway, and Sweden. Bush readily agreed, and a very successful visit to Helsinki ensued.

Mauno Koivisto was then president of Finland, and his aide-de-camp was Juhani Kaskeala, the brother of my tennis opponent in Washington. Juhani later became commander of all of Finland's armed forces. The atmosphere was informal and very friendly, with Bush and Koivisto hitting it off extremely well.

During the visit, Koivisto invited Bush to join him in a sauna, and I remember the two men, buck naked, running down a hall from the steam room and leaping side by side into the Baltic. Out of such things, close relationships develop.

At the end of the visit to Helsinki, we established a special channel between my office and that of Jaakko Kalela, Mauno Koivisto's office director, so that we could discreetly continue to fully exchange views on issues relating to arms control and the Soviet Union. I found the information we received from the Finns through this channel superior to anything we received from other sources, domestic or foreign. In return, Koivisto appreciated our sending both information and arms control experts to Helsinki.

The result of this fruitful exchange was that in March 1985, when Bush went to his third Moscow funeral in less than three years, he was fully prepared to meet Gorbachev, who was appointed general secretary of the Soviet communist party the day after Konstantin Chernenko's death.

I was not in the meeting between Bush and Gorbachev, but Bush showed me what he immediately wrote to President Reagan, which made clear that Gorbachev was a man ready to work for fundamental change in the U.S.-Soviet relationship. Reagan acted quickly on this advice. He held four pivotal meetings with Gorbachev during the 1985–88 period that paved the way for the end of the Cold War in 1989.

I believe the ending of the Cold War without a shot being fired was one of the great diplomatic achievements in our history. We were fortunate to have Gorbachev emerge when he did, with his clear desire to move the Soviet Union in new directions.

We were also fortunate to have a president in Ronald Reagan, who, as he recognized Gorbachev's objectives, was able to change the direction of his own thinking toward the Soviet Union from hostility to engagement, and to meet with Gorbachev four times during his presidency.

The December 1988 meeting in New York, involving Gorbachev with both Reagan and President-elect Bush, was a sort of "laying on of hands" that symbolized the strong continuity between the Reagan and Bush presidencies. After a year of delay caused by internal bickering between hawks and doves in his presidency, Bush and Gorbachev met at Malta.

In his 1997 Hofstra speech, Gorbachev, in referring to his meeting with President Bush at Malta in December 1989, put it this way: "Malta became a watershed. It became an epoch-making event in the second half of the 20th century. Malta was the end of the Cold War."

In September 1990, Bush and Gorbachev wanted to hold another summit meeting and chose Helsinki as the venue. In his memoirs, *Witness to History*, President Koivisto describes his reaction to that development:

> The choice of Helsinki was, of course, a tribute that we valued, and I said in a television interview that it was hard to hide our satisfaction....This was a good opportunity to talk (with Bush)....He recalled that throughout his term as vice president we had been in regular touch, exchanging views of Soviet developments and other matters. I said I had greatly appreciated this correspondence.

I know how highly Bush valued what he had learned from the Finns. He often spoke to me of his admiration for Koivisto and for Finland, and of his enjoyment of the visit to Helsinki, particularly the sauna. His establishment of the channel between my office and that of Jaakko Kalela was evidence of this, as it was the only special arrangement of that sort that we made during my more than six years of work in the vice president's office. When Bush wrote Koivisto early in 1993 saying he had "appreciated our dialogue," he really meant it.

On March 21, 2011, Meg and I attended a "Points of Light" gala honoring President Bush at the Kennedy Center in Washington. All four former U.S. presidents were in attendance. We sat close to Ambassador Pekka Lintu of Finland. I described to him the Bush-Koivisto relationship and how much we valued what we'd learned from it.

It was clear, from Ambassador Lintu's presence at the gala, and by what he said to me, that both presidents are remembered with respect and admiration in Helsinki.

Finland played its very difficult role as one of Russia's closest neighbors with great courage and deep intelligence. First they fought the Soviets, when Latvia, Lithuania, and Estonia did not.

Geography aided Finland greatly in its effort, but in such struggles geography is never enough.

They then took full advantage of neutrality, never joining the Warsaw Pact but building the foundations of their societal and economic policies. Finland's technical competence, high educational standards, and social tranquility now place them among the most admired and advanced countries in the world.

PART FOUR

DIPLOMACY AND ATTENDANT TRAVAILS

22

Ambassador in Seoul

Right after he was elected president in 1988, George Bush nominated me to be ambassador to South Korea. I had a long wait, over seven months, for a hearing before the Senate, as some Democrats were determined to defeat my nomination due to my alleged knowledge of the Iran-Contra scandal.

There was opposition to my nomination in Korea as well, particularly among American missionaries and Korean church leaders. My predecessor in Seoul, the late Jim Lilley, was also a former CIA officer, and some Koreans did not want two of us in a row.

On the other hand, I was welcomed by many Koreans who recalled positively my tour in Seoul as CIA station chief. I particularly valued a March 30, 1989, letter from Kim Dae-jung, president of the Party for Peace and Democracy, in which he said, "I am looking forward to working with you in our common task of realizing true democracy in the Republic of Korea. ...I am deeply indebted to you for saving my life in 1973 and 1980."

In September 1989, I finally got a hearing before the Senate Foreign Relations Committee. It began inauspiciously, with the late Senator Alan Cranston, Democrat of California, dumping on me for 45 minutes. If his endless diatribe had any organizing theme, it was that my stubborn persistence in demanding a hearing had doomed me to humiliation before the Senate. As Senator Cranston droned on and on, I felt like a man lying on his back at the foot of Niagara Falls, looking upward.

After the Democratic diatribes were over, the late Senator Jesse Helms, of all people, leapt to my defense. This also made me feel awkward, as I had never cared for Senator Helms or his policies.

The Senate finally confirmed my appointment by a vote of 66 to 33, thanks in large part to support from the chairman of the Foreign Relations Committee, the late Claiborne Pell, Democrat of Rhode Island, and the committee's junior member, Senator Charles Robb, Democrat of Virginia. I will always be grateful to those two fine men—their support opened up for me another chapter of my life, centered on the Korean Peninsula, that continues to this very day.

I learned after the vote that some of my friends had reached out to senators they knew, urging that they support my nomination. Tom Devine of New York and Walter Craigie of Richmond were effective in reaching out to senators Pell and Robb. For that, I am eternally grateful.

Looking back at the tours of those who preceded and succeeded me as ambassador to South Korea, I would judge that my time in Seoul was one of the most dynamic periods since the end of the Korean War.

I arrived in Seoul in September 1989 and served through February 1993. South Korea had a highly competent though underrated president, Roh Tae-woo, whose policy of reconciliation with North Korea was fully supported by Washington. I had a solid relationship with President George H. W. Bush, and Korea was not, like the Philippines, one of Secretary of State James Baker's Asian hot spots, so there was room for initiatives to be taken. I also had a close working relationship with Kim Chong-hwi, President Roh's astute national security adviser, who served the entire five years of that presidency. Kim's continuity and resulting perspective were immensely helpful.

Perhaps most important of all, in the summer of 1987, with Jim Lilley serving as ambassador, South Korea had taken a major turn toward democracy by allowing its presidents to be elected by direct popular vote. This was a deeply significant change, one that the Korean people desperately wanted. Jim Lilley was overly modest in describing his role in helping to bring this great change into being.

I owe a tremendous amount to Meg, who was always a great partner during our time in Seoul. She did me a huge favor when, as we first disembarked at Kimpo Airport, I cringed at the battery of press cameras facing me at the entry gate. My prolonged confirmation process, marked by difficult encounters with the press, had made me gun-shy. Meg poked me and said something like "Smile, we're glad to be here." I was able to put on a happy face, and our entry onto the ambassadorial stage was a successful one.

One of the first official visitors I had to deal with was Carla Hills, our able United States trade representative. Carla raised a number of thorny trade issues with the Koreans, including, as she put it, "the strong desire of the United States for more access to the tightly closed Korean beef market." She apparently convinced the Korean government to enlarge our beef quota.

A few mornings after Carla had departed, at about 6 a.m., Meg and I were awakened by a loud "bang!" outside our embassy residence. The residence guards immediately called us and shouted, "Students, students!"

My first thought was: 'Oh shit, I hope they're not armed.'

Six Korean college students had driven up from the southern port city of Pusan and had used their car as a sort of vaulting horse to get over the low wall surrounding the residence grounds. They threw some sort of large firecracker at the unarmed residence guards and were quickly able to break a window and enter our house.

I called the security officer and told him to get the Korean police on the scene. Almost immediately, I had a reassuring call from the Marine Security Guard at the Embassy, saying he and his men would "take care of things" if I needed help. I told them to stand by, as one of the first things I'd been taught at "Charm School" (ambassadorial training) was to never turn the Marines loose on unruly local civilians unless a truly mortal threat was involved.

Sounds from outside our bedroom indicated clearly to me that we were dealing not with a trained group of assassins but with young men surprised at how easily they had gotten into the house and unsure what to do next. They gently tried to open our stout bedroom door, then retreated down the hall when they found it locked. I could hear the smashing of lamps and crockery from the front of the house. We slipped out a back window and went to another embassy house on the compound.

The Korean police eventually arrived, and the students were hauled off to jail. Their main motive had been to protest U.S.

pressure on the beef quota issue. I called the protocol office at Blue House and urged that the students not be treated too severely. I gather that they served up to two years in jail.

I immediately went into my embassy office, about a mile away, to discuss how to respond to the torrent of questions coming in from both local Korean, and international media. A hurried press conference was held at the Embassy, and both Meg and I appeared on television to thank the Korean police for their help and to say that we were aware of the sensitivity of the beef issue. Meg was gracious and stressed how glad we were to be in Seoul. We heard from many sources that her TV performance had truly moved the Korean people who saw it.

I have since met four of the six students who "visited" us that early October morning in 1989. Two are now rising young stars in the National Assembly; one of the others owns an Italian restaurant, and one works for a French trading company. During a December 2006 visit to Seoul, I was visited in my hotel by three of the former students, all of whom apologized. They were accompanied by the press in large numbers, and a good deal of publicity resulted, all of which I considered positive.

This entire, two-part episode strikes me as being typically Korean. First a passionate protest, later a courteous apology. During my time in Tokyo, an extremely dangerous Japanese terrorist group broke into the Embassy, armed with swords. Some went to jail and emerged still dangerous and unrepentant. The contrast between these two events is complete and stark and favors the Koreans.

Early in my term, I learned that the USS *Missouri* was to pay a port call at Pusan, which was Korea's second largest city. I inquired of the Pentagon if I could host a reception on board the battleship for Korean VIPs. I got an enthusiastic response from the Navy and pulled together a guest list of about twenty National Assembly members, Foreign Ministry officials, and military officers.

All the Koreans I invited were eager to come, as they were well aware that it was on the deck of the *Missouri*, moored in Tokyo Bay in September 1945, that Japanese foreign minister Mamoru Shigemitsu had signed Japan's unconditional surrender, finally ending World War II.

I had never before been on the *Missouri*, and its physical impact was stunning, particularly the thrusting 16-inch guns pointing forward and aft. It was hard to imagine that this monstrous weapon had been rendered almost completely obsolete by missiles and air power. But such was the case, and the *Missouri* was decommissioned a few months later. It is now anchored permanently at Pearl Harbor, beside that other famous battleship, the sunken USS *Arizona*.

That night, the ship's great wartime achievements were celebrated, with the Korean guests paying delighted attention to the plaque on deck marking Japan's final surrender. That event remains one of the most glowing memories of my tour. It was the first time I had hosted senior Koreans, and I was delighted at how well it had gone. Koreans are naturally gregarious and appreciate being invited to attend any sort of special event. They have a great sense of humor, quickly lubricated by liquor, and any all-male gathering with them inevitably develops a certain raucousness that I thoroughly enjoy. I was really sorry to see the last guest depart unsteadily down the *Missouri*'s gangway.

Being the U.S. ambassador in Seoul involved much movement around the city. My official vehicle was an elderly armored Cadillac. My driver, Mr. Hong, was superb handling traffic and avoiding congestion. We had brought along an inconspicuous personal vehicle, which Meg often drove around Seoul, shopping at the Yong San U.S. Army base several miles from the Residence. She superbly organized a constant stream of events at the residence, some involving scores of guests.

We both hankered after our lost personal mobility and occasionally went out on our own, particularly on Sundays when our driver was off duty. A favorite place was Kanghwa Island, near the mouth of the Han River about twenty miles west of Seoul. The island was a fascinating microcosm of Korean history. The Mongols who invaded Korea in 1231 were great horsemen but utterly incompetent in dealing with the sea. A narrow channel of fast-moving seawater subject to major tidal fluctuations protects Kanghwa, and the Mongols never were able to cross it. So Kanghwa became a refuge for kings and other notables.

The island also guarded the entrance to the Han River and was fortified during Korea's "Hermit Kingdom" period. In 1866 the French attempted to enter the Han River to press the Koreans to open up to the world, but were repulsed. The Koreans had no such luck in 1871, when the United States sent modern warships with Marines aboard to penetrate the Han. Several hundred Koreans were killed in two mud forts along the shore.

One Sunday, giving no notice to anyone, we slipped away in our personal car to visit Kanghwa. As we drove over the bridge to the island, it became clear that a small van was following us. I turned into a parking lot and waited. The van pulled in. "Terminal Flower Shop" was painted on its side. Three men wearing black leather jackets got out, trying desperately to act nonchalant. I walked over and greeted them, and they sheepishly admitted they were police. We adopted them and had great fun driving around together. We never found out how they learned of our "secret" trip.

Our last trip to Kanghwa, in our official car, took us to the two forts where so many Koreans had been killed. The grounds were crowded with Korean families, who stopped milling around when they recognized us and stood silently watching. We walked up a hill to one of the forts, still surrounded by silence. I noticed a large burial mound downslope off the paved path. I approached the mound feeling every eye trained on me. I stopped, stood silently before the mound, and then bowed, paying respect to the dead. I heard a sound that I cannot describe as the crowd came alive. As we walked back to our car, people approached with smiles. Some reached out to touch me. The Koreans' sense of their history is powerful and constant, and we had just run headlong into it.

The U.S. embassy staff in Seoul was excellent, with Korean linguists and area specialists well placed. The local Korean staff at the embassy was also very strong. And many were still in place whom I had known in my previous tour. I quickly located the strong tennis players, mostly junior officers, with whom I tried to play at noon, in lieu of lunch.

Through contacts with the Korean staff and the young American FSOs, I quickly saw that in the fourteen years between my departure from Seoul in 1975 and my return as ambassador, the U.S. relationship with South Korea had markedly matured. The people of South Korea were far more self-confident. They had carried off the 1988 Olympics beautifully. They knew that their country had grown far stronger than North Korea, politically and economically, and they were ready to spread their wings diplomatically.

One area of remaining high-level tension involved university students, and campuses in general, where North Korean influence remained strong. I was never able to make a previously announced public appearance on a university campus. When radical students learned that I had been invited to speak on a campus, they would threaten to hold massive riots and my invitation would regretfully be withdrawn.

In one case, I made an unannounced appearance at an evening class taught by a close Korean friend at Korea University. The Korean police, still red-faced about their delayed response to the student break-in at our residence, had five hundred riot police massed just outside the Korea University campus, just in case.

In another case, I sponsored a conference at Pusan University on Korea's relations with Japan. I traveled to Pusan to kick off the conference and was told that it would not be safe for me to do so. Another American scholar, who had come from the United States to attend the conference, was stopped by students outside the university campus until he proved by showing his passport that he was not me. With me sitting glumly in a nearby hotel, the conference was launched and was judged to have been successful.

Toward the end of my tour, Sogang, a Jesuit university, awarded me an honorary degree. To avoid stirring up student violence, I received the degree one night during Christmas vacation, when no students were on the campus. Park Hong, Sogang's Jesuit president, had made a study of North Korean influence on Korean campuses. He said that supposed American involvement in the brutal 1980 suppression of the Kwangju uprising (see below) and my CIA background had made me a particularly juicy target for student radicals. My successor, Jim Laney, former president of Emory University, had no trouble appearing on Korean campuses.

Former German chancellor Willy Brandt was a greatly admired figure in South Korea for the way his policy of *Ostpolitik* had set the stage for the establishment of diplomatic relations between East and West Germany. Brandt made his first and only visit to South Korea in October 1989, as guest of the *Dong-a Ilbo* newspaper. I was fortunate to be invited to dinner with him just after he'd visited the DMZ. Brandt referred to the DMZ as a "time warp" and felt it was a far more oppressive dividing line between the two Koreas than was the Berlin Wall between East and West Germany.

One of Brandt's hosts asked when he thought the Berlin Wall would come down, and Brandt replied, without hesitating: "Not in my lifetime." In fact, the wall came down less than sixty days later, prompting a Korean fascination with the German reunification process that continues to this day.

Very early in his term of office, President Roh launched a diplomatic offensive designed to improve relations with North Korea. He called his policy "Nordpolitik" in honor of former chancellor Brandt, and it turned out to be extremely effective. When Roh took office in 1988, only one Eastern European country had an embassy in Seoul. When he left office in 1993, Russia, China, and nearly every eastern European country had recognized Seoul.

President Bush was a strong supporter of Nordpolitik. He arranged a meeting between President Roh and President Mikhail Gorbachev in San Francisco in 1990, which paved the way for Russia's recognition of Seoul in 1991. In 1992, President Bush also used his strong influence to get China to recognize Seoul and to drop its long-standing opposition to either North or South Korea becoming members of the United Nations. Both Koreas then quickly became U.N. members.

Presidents Roh and Bush had an excellent personal relationship that began in 1987, when Roh, as a presidential candidate, came to Washington and met President Ronald Reagan. When Roh met with Vice President Bush, they realized they had a strong mutual interest in tennis. In July 1991, President Roh paid a state visit to Washington, and a tennis match on the White House court was scheduled.

The Korean ambassador to Washington was Hyun Hong-choo, a brilliant, U.S.- trained lawyer, whom I had first met in 1974, when KCIA director Shin Chick Soo brought him onto his staff as part of his effort to change Korean intelligence from a draconian, polemical organization into something worthy of Korea's emerging democracy.

Hyun and I discussed the upcoming match and decided it would be wiser to have the presidents play as partners, rather than as opponents. And so it was arranged; the two presidents against their two ambassadors. The match was great fun, and as Vice President Dan Quayle said at a dinner that evening held in the Korean Embassy Residence, "The two ambassadors made career-enhancing decisions as to how the match came out."

It was a wise decision to play as we did. President Bush and I had played a lot of tennis together, and we were a strong pair. The presidents won the match, but everybody felt good about the results. That would not have been the case had it been the Americans against the Koreans. By making or missing key shots, I kept the score very close. Bush knew what I was doing and winked at me as we shook hands at the match's conclusion.

This pattern was repeated when President Bush visited Seoul in January 1992, with the same pairings, and the same good feelings as a result. When DCM Ray Burghardt and I saw President and Mrs. Bush off the next morning on their way to Tokyo, we both noted that he did not appear to be feeling terribly well. Bush commented that he had an upcoming tennis match with Emperor Akihito and the Crown Prince, whom we knew to be an excellent player. We learned later that Bush had picked up some sort of intestinal flu bug during his stay in Seoul.

A few days later, I got one of the hand-written notes for which President Bush is famous. After generously thanking Meg and me for hosting him and Mrs. Bush at our residence in Seoul, he went on to describe his visit to Tokyo. He said that he and Mike Armacost, our ambassador to Japan, had lost a tough match to the emperor and his son, (the United States vs. Japan), but, apart from that, the visit had been quite successful, "except for my throwing up in the prime minister's lap in front of millions of people." One of the many things I admire about President Bush is his tremendous sense of humor.

Back in Seoul, the Koreans were preparing for a visit by Russian President Boris Yeltsin, who had requested a tennis match with President Roh. The Koreans asked my advice, and I suggested that the two presidents play as partners. This was suggested to Yeltsin who refused, saying that he wanted to play with a partner he had in his entourage, one of Russia's better players.

A Korean friend described the match, which was colorful, to say the least. Yeltsin, bulky and slow afoot, was a very poor player, with a wild serve that seldom went in. He had obviously been drinking vodka and belligerently argued against line calls made by a Korean acting as informal umpire. My friend said that the Koreans were embarrassed by Yeltsin's conduct on court, but the Russians seemed quite accustomed to it.

The Koreans demolished the Russians in the first set, and then wisely threw the second and final set. Yeltsin was pleased to have won and stated emphatically that he would have insisted on playing on until he and his partner had taken a set.

I was invited to the state dinner honoring Yeltsin that evening. Red-faced and white-haired, he vociferously greeted each person in the receiving line, which moved very slowly. Yeltsin's handshake was large, warm, and damp, quite in keeping with his demeanor. I noted during dinner that his alcoholic intake continued. The Koreans put on some wonderfully rhythmic dances after the dinner, and Yeltsin indicated his enjoyment of the dancers' performance by vigorously keeping time, hitting a spoon on his wine glass.

Those were truly constructive days for the Korean-U.S. alliance. Seoul was grateful for President Bush's strong diplomatic support, and it was interesting for me to watch the diplomatic climate change between North and South Korea, and between South Korea and its communist neighbors, allowing a far greater degree of interaction and dialogue to take place than ever before.

Soon after the first Russian ambassador arrived in Seoul, in 1991, I invited him to accompany me on a visit to Kwangju, a city in southwestern Korea, where the U.S. image was very bad. (See below.) The ambassador, a sophisticated man with excellent English, was probably the first Russian to visit Kwangju since the Russo-Japanese war, which began in Korea in 1904. He was well received and made a good impression. I felt that the U.S. image was also enhanced, as the leaders of Kwangju saw me acting as friendly host for our former Cold War enemy's representative.

In 1992, China's first ambassador to South Korea came to call on me immediately after his arrival in Seoul. Having served previously as China's envoy to North Korea and being fluent in Korean, he was well versed in North-South issues. This was a friendly gesture on the part of the ambassador and acknowledged America's powerful role in South Korea's affairs. I received him warmly in my embassy office. He spoke English, so no interpreter was necessary, and he spoke frankly to me, one on one.

He had accompanied Kim Il-sung on his last visit to Beijing, which had taken place shortly after the overthrow of the Nicolae Ceauşescu regime in Romania. I knew that Kim and Ceauşescu had maintained a close personal relationship and that Ceauşescu had twice visited Pyongyang. Those two tyrants seemed to admire each other's dictatorial control—and also needed one or two foreign capitals to visit where they could be assured of high security and a friendly reception.

The Chinese ambassador told me that Kim was obviously shaken by the rapidity with which Ceauşescu had been overthrown in December 1989, and that after only a two-hour trial before a military court, he and his wife had been executed on charges of genocide and corruption. In that context, Kim told his hosts in Beijing that he was aware of the need for certain economic changes in North Korea. He asked for Chinese advice as to how to proceed. Explaining the concept behind their "special economic zones," the Chinese advised Kim to keep strong central political control but to allow certain enclaves in border areas, where economic regulations could be relaxed and foreign trade developed.

The Chinese ambassador told me that he expected North Korea to try to follow this pattern, and he urged the United States to encourage it. (After a couple of false starts, a successful special economic zone has been established in Kaesong, just north of the DMZ.)

Russian relations with both South Korea and the United States had improved rapidly during my time in Seoul. In late 1992, the famous Russian cellist Mstislav Rostropovich gave a concert in Seoul, and we invited him to a reception at our residence. We also invited the next Russian ambassador, Alexander Panov, with whom I had established a good working relationship. Panov greatly appreciated my having taken his predecessor with me on a visit to Kwangju.

When Rostropovich and Panov met at our reception, they literally fell into each other's arms. Rostropovich told me that it was one of the first friendly meetings he'd had with a serving Russian diplomat since his exile from the Soviet Union in 1974. I have a happy picture of the three of us, taken on that occasion, and I later heard from diplomatic friends that Panov displayed a copy of it in his office, even when he rose to be Russia's deputy foreign minister.

One continuing negative note in the U.S.-South Korean relationship was the issue of alleged American involvement in the tragic Kwangju uprising of 1980. President Chun Doo-hwan had brutally cracked down on protests in Kwangju in the wake of the arrest of Kim Dae-jung on charges of treason. Chun sent in Special Forces units, noted for their toughness, which killed at least two hundred people in the streets. Chun claimed that the United States had fully supported his actions.

This was not true, but many South Koreans believed it was, and hostility toward the United States remained strong in the city. We had a cultural center in Kwangju that was often attacked with fire-bombs by rioters trying to drive us out of the city. I talked with Kim Dae-jung about visiting the city, and he advised me to go there during the winter university holiday, when student activists would be scattered.

So, in January 1990, I arrived in Kwangju and was immediately asked if I'd come to apologize for the U.S. role in the tragedy. I said that we had nothing to apologize for but that I wanted to learn more clearly the reasons for the bitter resentment that persisted toward our presence in the city.

I talked to as many Koreans as I could—but none would admit to being actively involved in the anti-U.S. demonstrations. It was clear that the impact of the tragic uprising still hung over the city and that the United States had failed to convince the Koreans that we had not been complicit in President Chun Doo-hwan's brutal crushing of the uprising. A report written by the State Department almost ten years after the incident had been too little and too late.

On the morning of my third and final day in the city, I was again asked whether I had come to apologize for what we had done in Kwangju. Having seen the lingering sadness and anger in the city, I changed my answer.

"Yes," I said, " I do have something to apologize for. We have kept silent for too long."

Almost immediately, I received word that some leaders of the anti-U.S. groups wanted to meet with me. At first, they demanded a meeting in complete secrecy, which I agreed to. They then demanded that we meet in front of the press, which we subsequently did.

Six Korean men met me in the U.S. Cultural Center. Three had spent time in jail for their part in the uprising, and two had been wounded in the fighting. They were highly uneasy meeting me, but less bitter than I had expected. My excellent interpreter whispered to me that they had been somewhat disarmed by my willingness to meet with them, and on their terms.

They had appointed a spokesperson, but all listened intently to what was said and clearly showed by body language and facial expressions how they felt about what they heard. In two or three instances, they withdrew into a separate room to work out a common response to something I'd said.

After we were seated in front of TV cameras and members of the local Korean press, I told them I appreciated their willingness to meet with me, and that I would try to answer any questions they had.

Their first question was, "Who gave the order for the soldiers to shoot the Korean rioters in the streets of Kwangju?"

I replied that I had no idea and that only Koreans could answer that question.

Their spokesman fired back, "That's a lie! We know you have satellites that can read a newspaper from the sky. We know you were watching; you must know who gave the order to shoot."

I explained that we did have powerful satellites—but that they could not take us into men's minds. They could only show us some of the things men did.

This answer clearly did not satisfy any of them; they continued to attribute to us a technical omniscience we have never possessed.

The questioning went on, and I sensed that their anger at us was deeply tinged by a sense of betrayal, not unlike feelings shown by Hungarians after the uprising of 1956, when the United States did not rush to their defense as they'd been led to expect we would.

The Korean spokesman said to me, "We thought you were coming to save us when you sent an aircraft carrier to Pusan." I told them that had been a signal to North Korea not to intervene. I also tried to make clear our general distaste for the Chun Doo-hwan administration.

Another question: "Do you think we are a nation of field rats?" This was reference to an unfortunate comment in 1980 by a U.S. general, who had said that Koreans sometimes showed "a lemming-like quality." This insulting remark still reverberated a decade after it had been made. I knew the general who had made the remark. He was a very good man, who made a glib remark that he himself came to regret.

I assured them that I deeply admired the Korean people and that I had come to Kwangju to try to lessen the hostility that the people of that city seemed to hold toward the United States. Their nods and smiles when those words were translated made me feel good; I knew I had reached them.

The meeting lasted over three hours. Toward the end of the meeting, the spokesman said, "We know you Americans are very close to Chun Doo-hwan because he was among the first foreign visitors to call on President Reagan."

I replied, "Yes, he was among the first visitors, and the price of his visit was Kim Dae-jung's life." (As noted earlier, after much haggling with Korean officials, the Reagan administration had agreed to receive Chun at the White House if Chun agreed to lift the death sentence imposed on Kim, and to release Kim from prison.)

What I told the Kwangju questioners was common knowledge in Washington and in Seoul—but it had never been said in Kwangju. These words had a very strong impact on my interlocutors and were in the next day's headlines of all the Kwangju newspapers. I was delighted to see this happen.

When the meeting was over, they thanked me for coming, saying they could not accept all of my answers but that I had at least listened to them and had tried to answer their questions. My interpreter whispered to me that all six of the men expected to be arrested by the Korean police, who'd had me under their protection during my entire visit due to a serious kidnap threat.

I walked outside with the six men into a sprinkle of rain, put my arms around two of them, and told the tough police officer in charge: "These are my friends. I do not want you to arrest them." The police scowled but allowed the six men to slip away into the darkness. One turned and waved at me as he disappeared.

The fire bombings of the cultural center stopped, and we moved it to a more secure location so that we could remain active in Kwangju. During my tour I returned to Kwangju three more times, first to launch the new cultural center and later to take the German ambassador and then the Russian ambassador with me in order to hold well-attended public discussions on German reunification and Russia's new role in Northeast Asia.

My first visit to Kwangju was deeply valuable in showing me how Koreans can hold feelings of *han* (deep-seated resentment) when they are dealing with events caused by others and which they feel are unjustified, immoral, and unfair. When I made my first visit to Pyongyang in 2002, I encountered exactly the same feelings of *han* that I had encountered in Kwangju twelve years earlier. Lessons learned in Kwangju were especially helpful as I tried to establish dialogue and some degree of trust between my North Korean hosts and myself.

The key to my meeting with the Kwangju leaders was my apology for keeping silent for too long. They saw that I recognized that they had a legitimate grievance, and that I was willing to talk with them and listen. This somewhat defused their hostility.

The key to opening dialogue with the North Koreans lay in the letter I wrote to Kim Jong-il, in which I cited the need to restore broken dialogue, without blaming them for the breakdown. In my first meeting in Pyongyang, I sensed their resentment at having been put into the "axis of evil" by George W. Bush.

I answered their questions, and even got them to laugh at me. A human link was established through laughter, as it was when I put my arms around the Kwangju men and told the police to let them go. In both Kwangju and Pyongyang, I quickly recognized I was dealing with Koreans, not some strange breed of fanatics, and that they would respond to my humanity once they saw that I respected theirs.

Trade relations between South Korea and the United States often posed contentious problems for the embassy. Once, a rather unsophisticated minister of trade announced without warning the cancellation of long-standing purchase orders for commercial aircraft from both Boeing and McDonnell Douglas. The cancellation was the Korean official's attempt to avoid an anticipated spike in politically sensitive import costs.

I quickly received outraged calls from both U.S. companies, protesting the cancellation. As one executive put it, "The aircraft are virtually completed; we are about to paint the insignia on their tails."

I quickly made calls to Korean Air and Asiana, which had ordered the U.S. aircraft, to find out how the Koreans felt about the cancelled purchases. Both companies were just as angry as Boeing and McDonnell Douglas. They had purchased landing rights and built new facilities in anticipation of the arrival of their new jets, and they were facing heavy financial losses if the aircraft did not arrive on schedule.

Feeling very confident, I placed a phone call to the cabinet minister in question and told him of the bad feelings at Korean Air and Asiana. That was all it took; the minister quietly put the purchases back on track.

Another time, a U.S. company was locked in tight competition with a European firm to sell antisubmarine warfare (ASW) aircraft to South Korea. The sale was crucial to the U.S. company. The European aircraft competing for the contract was new, virtually untested, and attractively priced.

By great efforts at cost-cutting, the U.S. company was able to match the foreign aircraft's price. We assumed this would clinch the sale for the U.S. side, as the American aircraft was well known to the Koreans and had been flown by them for years. But such was not the case; news of the U.S. cut in price had been kept from the Korean minister of defense, and the American company was about to lose the sale. Our well-informed defense attaché told me of this development, and I immediately sought an appointment with the minister of defense, a man I knew well.

As diplomatically as I could, working through a Korean interpreter, I told the minister that, after some cost cutting, the U.S. aircraft was now as affordable as its foreign competition, and I urged him to seriously consider buying the U.S. aircraft.

A U.S. Foreign Service officer fluent in Korean had accompanied me to this meeting and passed me a note indicating that the interpreter was not fully transmitting what I had said and had deliberately left out the lowering of the U.S. price.

I chose not to make an issue of this at the time, and the meeting ended politely as I thanked the minister for his attention. If I'd immediately raised the interpreter's shortcomings, it would only have created a very bad scene in the defense minister's office. There would have been an argument about what I had said as the interpreter struggled to defend himself. The issue would have become the interpreter, not the sale of the aircraft.

But the next day I asked for another meeting, saying I had urgent news to convey, and this time I requested that a U.S. interpreter be used. The minister agreed to all of this, and as soon as he heard the news of the U.S. price reduction, he called for a review of the case. He subsequently ordered the U.S. aircraft.

As my posting in Seoul went forward, I became more and more involved in working with the Foreign Commercial Service in promoting U.S. sales of all kinds of products to Korea. I enjoyed doing it, and at the end of my tour was thanked by Secretary of State Lawrence Eagleburger for my efforts. Shortly after I finished my assignment in Seoul, I was invited to the U.S. factory where the ASW aircraft were being built and was given a warm reception by the workers on the assembly line in Marietta, Georgia.

December 7, 1991, was the fiftieth anniversary of the Japanese attack on Pearl Harbor, and President Bush invited Meg and me to attend a ceremony commemorating that tragic event. A large group of dignitaries was assembled in the U.S. Navy base at Pearl Harbor, including senior representatives of Japan.

It was a calm, sunny morning, just as it had been fifty years before. We stood with the rising sun at our backs, looking to the west. The ceremony began dramatically early in the morning, at 7:48 a.m., with planes flying in low over the harbor at the exact time that the attack had started half a century earlier. Several modern Japanese destroyers were anchored in the background, their flags clearly visible. They were strong symbols of the alliance that had been formed out of the ashes and agonies of the war.

President Bush spoke eloquently, saying that the war was history, and that he bore no rancor toward Japan. As he spoke, I thought, as I'm sure many did, of the fact that he had been shot down by the Japanese as an eighteen-year-old Navy pilot over the island of Chichi-jima, and had narrowly escaped both capture and death. That fact made his words of peace and reconciliation all the more moving. We could not have had a more perfect representative of our country at that ceremony of remembrance.

One of the great pleasures of being U.S. ambassador to South Korea came from living in the beautiful Korean-style Residence in Seoul, the construction of which had been arranged by Ambassador Philip Habib. When the very old Korean-style ambassadorial residence in Seoul became too dangerous to live in, Habib moved out and insisted—over objections from the State Department—that the new residence also be designed by a Korean architect and built by a Korean contractor. Eventually, it was.

Koreans of every kind, of every age and political orientation, seemed to love attending functions at the residence. Late in my tour, having seen what a tremendous representational tool the Residence was, I sent a cable to the Department of State urging that the Residence be named for Habib. Silence followed.

To my great sorrow, Philip Habib died of a heart attack a few months later. I sent a second cable urging that it be announced at Habib's funeral that the residence was being named for him. Again, silence in response. A third, angry cable from me evoked the bureaucratic response that it would take an act of Congress to formally name the building for Habib.

I decided to act informally and had handsome brass plaques placed at the outside gate and beside the front door. The Residence is now universally known as Habib House.

As "Nordpolitik" began to bear fruit, the South Koreans stepped up the pace and intensity of their contacts with the North. The embassy was fully supportive of this process, but there was a mixed reaction from the Korean and U.S. military establishments.

The annual Team Spirit exercise, held every spring, involved transporting thousands of U.S. troops to Korea, to conduct training exercises designed to repel a simulated North Korean attack upon the South. The North hated this exercise—it was an annual reminder to them of their humiliation in 1950, when President Harry S. Truman had shocked them by sending U.S. troops to repel their original invasion. In response to Team Spirit, North Korea always put itself on an extremely high military alert level, and sent out waves of propaganda against the "American warmongers and their South Korean lackeys."

After a good deal of pushing and pulling, General Robert Ris-Cassi and I got the Pentagon and the Korean Ministry of Defense to agree to cancel the 1992 Team Spirit exercise. They jointly announced this late in 1991. Shortly thereafter, the two Koreas signed a pair of significant agreements. The "Basic Agreement," signed on December 13, 1991, pledged both countries to work toward "reconciliation, nonaggression, exchanges and cooperation."

On December 18, President Roh announced that there were no nuclear weapons in South Korea. On December 31, North and South Korea signed the "Joint Declaration" calling for a denuclearized peninsula and pledging to allow inspections by the International Atomic Energy Agency.

The signing of these agreements ushered in a period of good feelings between North and South Korea. A series of eight prime ministerial meetings was held, and the prospects for a major reconciliation were higher than ever before.

Unfortunately, this happy period did not last long. At the annual security consultation meeting held at the Pentagon in the autumn of 1992, the Team Spirit exercise was reinstated for March 1993. Both military establishments had cited the invaluable training that this exercise provided, and Defense Secretary Dick Cheney reinstated the exercise without consulting either the State Department or me.

I was caught completely by surprise. The presidential campaign was coming to its bitter end, and any move by President Bush to override his defense secretary would have given a political issue to the Democrats. I was told by State that it was a "done deal" and that there was no use in protesting it.

I still consider this the single biggest mistake made by the United States during my time as ambassador. This was only the first of several destructive moves Cheney later made as vice president to undercut any move toward reconciliation with North Korea.

The bitter fruits of this decision appeared soon. The reinstatement of Team Spirit was immediately denounced in Pyongyang, and the pace of North-South contacts slowed. In March 1993, Kim Jong-il, as commander in chief of the Korean People's Army, placed North Korea on a "semi-war" footing during Team Spirit. And on March 13, 1993, North Korea announced it was withdrawing from the Nuclear Non-Proliferation Treaty.

In late February 1993, just before I left Seoul, I held a final meeting with Kim Chong-hwi, President Roh's national security adviser. Both of us were leaving government, and we both wished that we could have a bit longer to work as a team. Kim put it this way. "I wish we had had one more year to work together. If we could have kept the same people in Washington and Seoul working on the North Korean problem for twelve more months, I think we could have solved it."

I'm sure Kim assumed that had I stayed on as ambassador, I could have reversed the damaging Team Spirit decision that would have allowed the era of good feelings between Seoul and Pyongyang to have lasted much longer. He also recognized that Kim Young Sam, the incoming Korean president, was not nearly as pragmatic as Roh Tae-woo had been.

It was nice of Kim to say what he did, and I remember it with nostalgia. But a changing of the guard had taken place in Washington and in Seoul. The stage was already being set for the dangerous nuclear crisis of mid-1994, which my successor, Jim Laney, handled so well.

I look back on my time in Seoul with both happiness and satisfaction. The Korean-U.S. alliance flourished, thanks to the fine leadership of two talented presidents. And, for a short time, North-South relations blossomed. Whatever the future holds, I can say with confidence that the post of U.S. ambassador in Seoul is one of the most demanding but fulfilling positions in the entire U.S. government.

PHOTO GALLERY IV

Swearing-in ceremony as U.S. ambassador to South Korea, with Secretary of State James Baker, September 1989. *State Department photo.*

To Don + Meg — With Great Pride in You Both and Friendship, too — *Geo. Bush*

Saying goodbye to President Bush as we left for Seoul, September 1989. *White House photo*

Entrance to Embassy Residence, Seoul. *Family photo*

Embassy Residence, Seoul, notable for being built fully in Korean style.
Family photo

Golf with Korean president Roh Tae Woo (2nd from left), 1991. I won 1,000 won (not much money). *Blue House photo*

Hilarious mixed doubles with President and Mrs. Roh Tae Woo. I'm sure Meg and I lost, 1992. *Blue House photo*

242

Both sides of a North Korean leaflet dropped over South Korea in May 1991. It denounces me for plotting with President Roh against other South Korean politicians, particularly Kim Young Sam, who later became South Korea's president. I picked up the leaflet on a golf course near Seoul.

23

Iran-Contra: Snakes in the Cellar for Seven Years

In mid-January 1994, Tim Weiner of the *New York Times* called me to ask if I had any final words to say about the completed Iran-Contra report that would be issued in a few days. I said that it had been like "living with snakes in the cellar for seven years."

Weiner said he would use my quote in his article. I thanked him, and asked how long he had been following the Iran-Contra story.

"Since the day it first made the papers," he replied.

"Where do you put me in it?" I asked.

"You were royally screwed," was Weiner's succinct reply.

Nothing Weiner might have said could have made me feel better. I knew I had been "screwed," but the fact that *he* knew it was vitally important to whatever my future might be. If the press had any doubts about my truthfulness on Iran-Contra, I would be dogged by that story *ad infinitum*. Weiner's judgment meant that I could move on, free and clear, which I have.

Tim Weiner and I have become good friends. I have used his hard-hitting book on CIA *Legacy of Ashes* in teaching my course on intelligence at Williams College, and his verdict on my alleged involvement in Iran-Contra is one that I treasure.

The Iran-Contra affair, which at times overlapped with the "October Surprise," was the most difficult period of my life. My troubles grew out of my decision, made in late 1984, to assist Felix Rodriguez in going to El Salvador to help in the counterinsurgency effort in that country.

In my December 1983 visit with Vice President Bush, I had noticed strong similarities between the insurgency in Vietnam and the struggle in El Salvador, which was being cruelly and ineptly dealt with. I contacted Ambassador Tom Pickering in San Salvador and several military officials and, with their support, Felix moved south in March 1985, something he had wanted to do for some time.

He quickly established his credibility with the El Salvador Air Force and soon had the run of Ilopango Airport in San Salvador. Once again, he was flying low in small helicopters, directing attacks on specific insurgent targets, based on intelligence, not ignorance and prejudice.

Unbeknownst to me, Felix soon attracted the attention of National Security Council staffer Lt. Col. Oliver North, who was deeply involved in supplying Nicaraguan rebels, or Contras, with weapons purchased with millions of dollars derived from the Reagan administration's covert sale of arms to Iran.

The Contras were fighting a leftist Nicaraguan government that was seen by Washington as threatening the stability of Central America. Ilopango Airport in San Salvador was central to the secret landing, servicing, and takeoff of planes involved in parachuting arms and supplies into Nicaragua.

North correctly saw that Felix, who was admired by the El Salvador Air Force, could keep the secret operation running smoothly, an operation which was in direct violation of the Boland Amendment passed by Congress in three sections between 1982 and 1984. All were designed to prohibit U.S. military assistance to the Contras fighting against the government of Nicaragua.

On September 20, 1985, North's recruitment letter to Felix started as follows:

> Dear Felix,
>
> AFTER READING THIS LETTER PLEASE DESTROY IT. You may keep the photographs (of aircraft to be serviced) … Since this is a completely compartmented operation, being handled by the resistance, you are the only person in the area who can set up the servicing of these aircraft… You must not advise the CIA.

Felix told me later that North instructed him specifically not to tell me about what North had asked him to do. Since Felix, a long-time intelligence officer, believed in the need for compartmentation of covert operations and the "need to know" principle, he agreed to these terms. Felix did not tell me of North's operations until August 8, 1986, when he came to Washington to say that certain people North had hired appeared to be corrupt and that the planes they had provided were in poor shape.

I immediately called North, who would not speak to me. Unable to get in touch with North, on August 12, 1986, I called a meeting of six officers from State, CIA, and the NSC, including Ed Corr, our new ambassador to El Salvador, who had responsibilities in Central America. I passed along Felix's concerns to them, specifically including his references to the poor quality of aircraft being used in dropping supplies to the Contras.

North's deputy, Lt. Colonel Robert Earl, attended that meeting. He later testified to Congress that it was clear to him that I was trying to get official attention paid to a questionable and danger-ous operation in El Salvador over which I had no jurisdiction or responsibility.

On October 5, 1986, one of the covert supply planes went down in Nicaragua, and the entire operation swiftly unraveled. Reagan fired North in November. Reagan's national security advisor, John Poindexter, was allowed to resign. They were among six officials later pardoned by President Bush for a variety of criminal charges relating to the Iran-Contra fiasco.

Investigative reporters digging into the growing scandal soon raised the question of how much I had known about the covert operations that North had recruited Felix into. I was proud of my friendship with Felix, and respected deeply what he'd done in Viet-nam. He called me frequently from El Salvador, reporting on the progress of his air operations against the rebels in El Salvador. It was thus generally assumed by the press that Felix had told me of all that he was involved with, including resupply of the Contras.

Because I respected Felix, and because he had wanted to work to correct the military abuses Bush had spoken out against in De-cember 1983 in El Salvador, I introduced Felix to the vice presi-dent in January 1985. A brief and friendly meeting took place. At a second short meeting, in May 1986, Felix showed Bush pictures taken during his counterinsurgency operations in El Salvador. Also at that meeting was our ambassador to El Salvador, Ed Corr, who strongly praised Felix's efforts to the vice president.

These contacts heightened press interest in what Felix had been doing in El Salvador and whether the vice president had known of his connection to North's secret and illegal Contra operations. Democrats in Congress, eager to spoil Vice President Bush's presidential hopes in 1988, joined in the fray, alleging that the vice president had known of the entire Iran-Contra affair.

Several times in the fall of 1986, eager TV reporters gathered in our driveway at 6 a.m., seeking comment from me. We had an alert next-door neighbor who often spotted these interlopers before we did. My feelings when I learned of a stakeout were akin to what early settlers in the southwest must have felt when they saw Apaches surrounding their cabin. I learned, painfully, that to say anything to the press at such times was a mistake.

Meg, who offered coffee to the CBS crew that first staked us out, was much quicker to learn that lesson than I was. She strongly advised me to say nothing beyond "Good morning," but I failed to listen, feeling, since I had nothing to hide, that I could help my case by speaking openly.

The technique of the stakeout teams was to ask a friendly question as soon as I came out of my front door on the way to my White House office. I had undergone major surgery on one leg that September and was limping visibly. "How's your leg feeling today?" they would shout.

I would respond, and they would immediately follow up with a "When-did-you-stop-beating-your-wife?" kind of question that was impossible to answer briefly. They filmed my hurried answers in such instances. "Sound bites" taken out of context from those responses, badly distorted my meaning, but were shown on the CBS Evening News.

After two such embarrassments, I learned to keep my mouth shut. I also recognized, about that time, that I'd been slow to recognize the possibility that North had drawn Felix deep into his efforts to support the Contras in Nicaragua. I should have figured that out sooner.

In early December 1986, I went to the vice president and offered to resign from my position as his national security advisor, feeling that press inquiries into my relations with Felix and suspicions about my knowledge of the Iran-Contra operation were of potential danger to his political future. Bush firmly refused my offer.

On December 19, 1986, Lawrence Walsh was appointed independent counsel in charge of investigating the murky Iran-Contra case. (His investigation continued until January 1994.) His appointment raised both the stakes and the tensions involved.

In January 1987, I offered my resignation a second time, after the vice president had done a contentious interview with Diane Sawyer of *60 Minutes* that included references to me and Iran-Contra. I felt that Diane Sawyer called my honesty into question in that interview.

Sawyer had noted that on one occasion in giving testimony I had forgotten to mention a key meeting with Felix Rodriguez. Now she asked the vice president: "What's the difference between Gregg forgetting and lying?" Bush had handled the interview well, but it had been awkward for him. Again, Bush refused my offer to resign.

In April 1987, the pressure got to Nicholas Brady, an investment banker and close personal friend of Vice President Bush, who clearly expected to be named to a cabinet post if Bush became president. Brady invited me to have a cup of coffee at the Hay Adams Hotel, and told me that I should resign, as I had become a political liability that the press would continue to exploit as the Iran-Contra affair dragged on.

I told Brady I had offered to resign twice and that Bush had refused. He said he knew about those offers and that Bush was "too loyal" and would keep me on. I responded by saying that my resignation at that point, when things had somewhat quieted down, would suggest that I had been doing something wrong or had lied about my knowledge of the Iran-Contra affair.

Brady rejected that argument as being self-serving on my part. I said to him "Nick, I could not disagree with you more!" And so we parted. I did not particularly enjoy the coffee.

I then decided to take the issue of my status to the late Lee Atwater, who'd been appointed the vice president's campaign manager. I did not particularly like Atwater, and I suspected he felt the same way about me, as some critical remarks I had made about him had reached his ears. I thought him totally unsentimental and completely dedicated to the election of the vice president.

I told Atwater all that had happened, including my session with Brady, and asked for his advice. He told me I had three options: to stay on and be vindicated, to stay on and be found guilty of lying, or to "jump over the side." He asked me if I had been telling the truth, and I said I had.

He then said that my resigning would incite further press attacks, seeking to find out why I'd resigned and what I'd done wrong. His conclusion was that as long as I thought I could ride it out, it was better for me to stay in place. I thanked him, and we shook hands. I never saw him again. He died in 1991 at the age of 40, but his legacy lives on in Karl Rove.

(Nick Brady served as secretary of the treasury in President Bush's cabinet. He visited Seoul when I was ambassador, but neither of us made any mention of our meeting at the Hay Adams.)

The next Saturday morning, a time when the vice president and I met privately at his residence to go over the President's Daily Brief (high-level intelligence summation), I told him of my meetings with Brady and Atwater. He laughed and shook his head when he heard what Brady had urged me to do. Making a strong "stay put" gesture with both hands, Bush said in no uncertain terms that he wanted me to stay on. I was relieved and grateful for his decision.

The most famous, or infamous, incident of the vice president's prolonged encounter with the Iran-Contra affair came on 25 January 1988 in what the *Washington Post* called "the most explosive confrontation ever televised between a network anchorman and a high-ranking federal officeholder." Bush's opponent was CBS anchor Dan Rather.

The occasion was a live interview, with Rather in his studio, and the vice president sitting at his desk in the White House. CBS had billed the interview as one in a series of profiles of 1988 presidential candidates. But we in the vice president's office suspected otherwise.

George Bush had often seen his words "cut-and-pasted" by the media to cause a false impression, so we insisted that the interview be done live, so that Bush would have a clear chance to get his message across.

I had prepared a memo for Bush that listed eight questions we thought it likely that Rather would ask. The first question was: "If the president fired Ollie North and forced John Poindexter to resign, why didn't you take similar action with Gregg?"

The "interview" started with a five-minute set-up piece, which included shots from a CBS "stakeout" of my home, including carefully chosen, distorting sound bites from my answers to shouted questions from the reporters.

When the interview went live, Rather's first question was a prolonged dump on me, saying I had been "deeply involved in running arms to the Contras," citing Reagan's firing of North, and ending with the question "Why is Mr. Gregg still inside the White House, still a trusted advisor?"

Bush immediately took the offensive in his reply, claiming that CBS had not been honest in telling the White House what the interview would focus on. "If this is a political profile for an election, I have a very different opinion as to what one should be."

The hostility escalated from there, and went on for nine minutes. George Bush, who always preferred to be gentle and logical, could talk tough when he had to, and that was one of those occasions. I agreed with the *Washington Post* verdict: "It was electrifying television even if repulsive journalism....The instant analysis was that the interview had been a triumph for Bush and a wipeout for Rather."

Despite the vice president's "win" over Dan Rather, the cumulative impact of the Iran-Contra affair was not without its cost, to others and to me. Press probing, congressional inquiries, high-level resignations and indictments, and the broadly focused investigation of independent counsel Walsh all brought the Reagan administration to a rather dreary conclusion.

Sometime in the fall of 1988, when it appeared highly likely that Bush would be elected president, he called me into his office and quietly told me that it was the opinion of his advisors that, after his election, he should appoint Brent Scowcroft as his national security advisor. That was a painful but not unexpected moment for me, and perhaps also for him. I told him that that was the right decision to make, as Scowcroft had received universal praise for his role as national security advisor to President Gerald Ford. The moment passed. Immediately after his election, president-elect Bush nominated me to be his ambassador to South Korea.

In choosing me to go to Seoul, President Bush was taking a risk, knowing that I'd need to be confirmed by the Senate, and that if I was rejected a tin can would be tied to the tail of his administration. It was clear from the outset that the Democrats would do their best to defeat my nomination. The late Senator Alan Cranston (D-California) was majority whip, and he and his aide, Gerald Warburg, led the effort to discredit me.

Their first tactic was delay. I did not get a hearing before the Senate Foreign Relations Committee until June 16, 1989, more than five months after I had been nominated. During that period, I sought to meet and talk with member of the committee, which was controlled by the Democrats, 10 to 9. My meeting with Senator Cranston, repeatedly delayed, was very cold. I then met Warburg for the first time and took an instant dislike to him. I'm sure the feeling was mutual.

Five days after my committee hearing, the SFRC voted to recommend my nomination by a vote of 12 to 7. Committee chairman Claiborne Pell (D-Rhode Island) voted in favor of my nomination, as did Charles Robb (D-Virginia). Their votes were crucial, and the *New York Times* of June 21, 1989, noted that the committee vote "was a setback" for Cranston and Warburg, who had actively led the Senate investigation of me.

When the Senate approved on September 12, 1989, I thought that I had left Iran-Contra behind me. President Bush had graciously called to thank me for "taking the heat" as he put it, and Meg and I immediately flew off to Korea, a happy and liberated couple.

In July 1990, we flew to Newport, Rhode Island, for the marriage of our daughter Alison to Ned Corcoran. During this festive family occasion, I was pursued by persistent phone calls from one Craig Gillen, a person of whom I had never heard. I subsequently learned that he was a newly hired assistant to Lawrence Walsh, the independent counsel still investigating Iran-Contra.

I talked to Gillen, and he said he had been asked to go over the entire investigation. In doing so, he had noted that in 1986 or early 1987, when I was first contacted by an agent of the FBI acting on Walsh's behalf, I had been asked if I would take a polygraph test on what I knew about Iran-Contra and had said that I would. He asked if I would still be willing to do so. I said I would be willing to be tested, and a test by the FBI was quickly arranged in Washington, D.C.

I remember getting up the morning of my test in high spirits, putting on a red-white-and-blue necktie, and saying to Meg that the test would finally end the entire miserable affair. I had been polygraphed three times during my CIA career by expert technicians and was utterly confident that I would find the same expertise at the FBI and sail through the test without trouble.

I took a taxi to the FBI office at Buzzard's Point in Southwest Washington, where I was greeted by the female FBI officer who had first interviewed me and asked if I would take a polygraph test. She was very happy that I had been willing to do so and added that I was the only person associated with the Iran-Contra case who had agreed to be tested.

The polygraph officer was a large, friendly man. As he strapped me to the instrument, he said the case was complicated and that he'd had little time to study it. He then asked me a series of rather complicated questions, which covered long periods of time. I remember one that essentially asked, "At any time since 1986, did you mislead the vice president about Oliver North, Felix Rodriguez, or Iran-Contra?"

My answer, of course, was "No." At the end of the questioning, the polygrapher looked over his tapes and said that I had shown deception in answering every question, including one on the "October Surprise," which had come as a complete surprise to me.

I could not believe my ears. I asked to be questioned again. After asking me somewhat modified questions, the polygrapher said that my second set of answers showed as much deception as the first.

I walked out of the interrogation office in a daze of disbelief and discouragement. Going outside, I stood looking in vain for a taxi, when the agent who had greeted me stopped in her car and drove me to the State Department. I think she was almost as sad as I was. I heard later that she had resigned from the FBI. I wish her well.

As soon as possible that day, I called Gillen and told him straight out: "I want you to hear it first from me. I flunked the FBI test cold."

He was silent in response. I then said that I would for the first time hire a lawyer, as I knew I would be hearing further from Gillen and Walsh. He said "Yes, you will." I hung up at that point.

Meg took the appalling news with great aplomb, and agreed that while we were in the United States, we should immediately hire a lawyer. I called my Williams classmate, Bob Geniesse, and told him what had happened. Bob, a distinguished lawyer, was then in charge of the Washington office of Debevoise & Plimpton.

He leapt into action and put me in touch with one of his law partners, Judah "Judd" Best, who agreed to take me on. Their firm most generously agreed not to charge me for their legal services, but only for charges and disbursements incurred in my defense.

I met and liked Judd Best. He took a completely no-nonsense approach to my situation and told me that I had been "an idiot" to agree to take the polygraph test. He warned me that Gillen and Walsh would publicize the fact that I had failed the FBI test as an indication of my culpability and that the only thing to do was for me to take another polygraph test at the hands of a man Best said was the most respected person in his field. I was thus introduced to Richard A. Arthur, head of Scientific Lie Detection Inc. in New York City.

Arthur and I had a long talk before he hooked me up to his polygraph. He asked me what kinds of questions I'd been asked by the FBI, and how I had felt in answering them. I said that the questions had been long, and that many thoughts crossed my mind as I listened to them.

Arthur's questions were short, and this is how I remember them:

"Have you ever told one lie about Felix?"

"Have you ever told one lie about Ollie North?"

"Have you ever lied to the vice president?"

"Did you delay release of the American hostages in 1980?"

I answered "No!" to all questions. Arthur told me to rent a hotel room in New York and to come back to his office early the next morning, when he would ask me the same questions over again. That I did.

The next morning's questioning was an exact repeat of the previous day. When he had finished, Arthur excused himself, saying he was going to compare his two sets of results. He returned after a very few minutes, smiled at me, and said, "You're clean as a whistle."

I was so relieved that I choked up and could hardly speak. He sat me down and told me that I was extremely sensitive to the polygraph. (This I had suspected, as a result of taking and passing the polygraph tests during my CIA career.)

Arthur added that the questions I had been asked by the FBI were badly phrased and far too long. He said: "It is not your fault that you failed that test." Those words were balm to my very soul.

Meg and I returned to Korea the next day, and I was feeling better than I would have thought possible under the circumstances.

Over the next two and one half years, while I completed my tour as U.S. ambassador in Seoul, Judd Best, from his law firm in Washington, kept me generally informed of the ebbs and flows of the Walsh investigation. Incredibly, Walsh went after Secretary of State George Shultz, even though Shultz had opposed arms sales to Iran.

Nothing came of this investigation. Secretary of Defense Caspar Weinberger was indicted but not tried by Walsh, and President Bush pardoned him in one of his last acts as president. As Best had predicted, Walsh and Gillen notified him that they were going to make public my failed FBI polygraph test. He immediately told them of my successful test with Richard Arthur, which completely took the steam out of that issue.

The final Iran-Contra report had this to say: "There was no credible evidence obtained that the vice president or any member of his staff directed or actively participated in the Contra resupply effort that existed during the Boland Amendment prohibition on military aid to the Contras. To the contrary, the Office of the Vice President's staff was largely excluded from … meetings where Contra matters were discussed by Oliver North and others."

In dealing with me directly, Gillen and Walsh were reduced to saying that I should have done more, after the October 1986 crash of the resupply plane, to alert others to what I had learned about Oliver North's involvement in the Contra resupply operation through Felix's August 8, 1986, revelations to me. They accused me of "acts of concealment," completely ignoring the meeting I convened on

August 12, 1986, where I specifically alerted officials from State, CIA, and the NSC to the dangers of North's ramshackle operation.

Judd Best was contemptuous of this finale, and angered by it. I was glad to be done with Iran-Contra, and deeply grateful for Best and Richard Arthur's support, and for Meg's great courage and love. The darkest chapter of my life had finally come to an end.

There was real catharsis for me in writing the "October Surprise" chapter of this memoir, as the congressional hearings came to a clear conclusion that nothing at all questionable had taken place. There was little or no catharsis at all in my recent plowing through the Iran-Contra report and writing this chapter—only remembered pain, and rekindled anger at those who had contributed to my difficulties.

The report is all there, easily accessible through Google. There is much more I could have said about the report and the people in it, good, bad and incompetent. I have chosen not to; it was truly a bucket of worms. What shines through is Meg's love and support, and also Vice President Bush's unwavering decision to stick with me.

I'll never know what role I might have played in the Bush presidency but for Iran-Contra. I do know that the vice president's decision to send me to Seoul has led to a strong Korean connection that continues to this day, and now involves both the North and the South.

I might add that I now have friendly, professional relations with both Diane Sawyer and Dan Rather. I have been a paid consultant on Korean affairs to ABC News, where Sawyer is the news anchor. And three or four years ago, with my full support and approval, the Korea Society, where I was chairman and president, helped Rather travel to North Korea.

A long time ago, just at dusk, I was riding a train through a dismal, wasted landscape in Northern Florida. Rays from the setting sun hit my face and produced a reflection on the train window that I looked through as the train slowly moved forward. Then and there, I wrote my first poem, one that comes to mind as I close this painful chapter:

My reflection
Casts a pale, flat light
On events long past.
Tears have dried
Passions have receded
Blood has drained away.
All that remain
Are cardboard figures
Propped in the sand.

24

October Surprise

As a footnote to this account of the decade I worked at the White House, I feel I must make some reference to the so-called "October Surprise." The phrase has been generally used for the past several decades to describe last-minute political shenanigans designed to influence presidential elections in November.

But by far the most notorious use of the phrase "October Surprise" is a totally false series of outrageous allegations, originating with a scabrous array of Iranians. The charge was that, for political reasons, George H. W. Bush, William Casey, and I, in the fall of 1980, met secretly in Europe with Iranians to arrange the delay of the release of the fifty-two American hostages held in Tehran until after the November 1980 election. The writings of Gary Sick put a megaphone to the mouths of these scurrilous characters.

I first heard of these spurious charges during the presidential campaign of 1988. Coming on top of the long-running and equally false Iran-Contra allegations, this putrid array of accusations was very hard for my family to take. They were first sourced to one Richard Brenneke, a businessman from Oregon who claimed to have been a CIA contract agent.

In an unrelated criminal case in Colorado in September 1988, Brenneke testified under oath that he had been in an October 1980 meeting in Paris where Casey and I met with several others to discuss delaying the freeing of the American hostages held in Tehran, so that President Carter could not reap political benefit from their release in his reelection campaign. Brenneke also swore he had been told that George Bush had been involved in the Paris meeting or meetings. As a result of this statement, perjury charges were brought against Brenneke, and in April 1990 he was brought to trial in Portland, Oregon.

I was serving as ambassador to South Korea at that time and was suddenly summoned to appear as a witness against Brenneke by the Justice Department. The interruption was annoying and disruptive. But, as I brooded about it on the long flight from Seoul to Portland, I realized that I was delighted to be given a chance to testify against Brenneke and get him sent to jail, because he had lied about me and my family, and had accused me of the worst kind of treason—betrayal of friends.

I knew a number of the hostages that had been held by the Iranians. One man I had worked with closely in Japan was CIA's chief of station in Tehran, and I was very much concerned about how he was being treated by the Iranians. I feared he would be tortured as our chief of station in Beirut had been.

And indeed, in January 2010, when I taught a four week-course at Williams College called "Making Sense of CIA," I invited my friend to speak to the class. He told in detail of his prolonged torture at the hands of the Iranians: whipping with a rubber hose, stress positions, darkness, isolation, and threats of execution, to be filmed and sent to his family. So the idea that I would have done anything to prolong this man's captivity was, to me, utterly obscene.

At the Brenneke trial, I had dated NSC documents showing I had been in my White House office around the weekend Brenneke alleged that I had been in Paris. I also had dated family pictures of me on a beach in Maryland with Meg and our daughter Lucy taken the day of the alleged Paris meeting.

The young Justice Department lawyers, thinking they had a slam dunk case against Brenneke, did not ask me to go into detail about the evidence I had. I was introduced as the U.S. ambassador to Korea and was merely asked if I had secretly gone to Paris as Brenneke alleged. I was happy to deny this charge, and returned to Seoul.

Later, I heard that the poorly conducted Justice Department case had not been convincing to the jury, and that Brenneke was acquitted. I was deeply angered by this news, but there was nothing I could do about it.

Later investigative reporting by Frank Snepp produced dated

documents, signed by Brenneke, showing he had been in the Portland, Oregon, area at the same time he claimed to have been in Paris. Brenneke is now a totally discredited figure.

For reasons best known to himself, Gary Sick, the NSC staffer responsible for Iranian affairs during the Carter administration, produced an April 15, 1991, op-ed piece in the *New York Times* entitled, "The Election Story of the Decade," seeking to give credibility to Brenneke's hugger-mugger of false allegations and to equally spurious charges brought by shadowy Iranians whom Sick had found convincing. Later in 1991, Sick released an entire book entitled *October Surprise.*

I think of the Iran-Contra case as "living with snakes in the basement for six years." When I heard of the publication of Sick's book, I told Meg I felt "as though I had been walking along the sidewalk when a filthy hand reached up through a sewer cover and grabbed me by the ankle." The costs and risks of public service are often very high.

Largely as a result of Sick's publications, both houses of Congress held investigations in 1992 of the "October Surprise," and both concluded that there had been no attempt on the part of the Reagan-Bush campaign to delay release of the hostages. The more substantive House investigation cost taxpayers $1.35 million. It concluded: "There is no credible evidence supporting any attempt or proposal by the Reagan presidential campaign, or persons representing or associated with the campaign to delay the release of the American hostages in Iran."

In August 2009, former congressman James Leach (R-Iowa) and I were members of the U.S. delegation sent to the funeral of President Kim Dae-jung of Korea. Leach had been on the House Committee, co-chaired by Lee Hamilton and Henry Hyde, that had investigated and dismissed the "October Surprise" allegations. On the flight to Seoul I asked Leach about the committee hearings.

He said it had quickly become clear that Gary Sick had been taken in by his Iranian contacts and had not investigated their spurious allegations thoroughly. Leach said he fully understood my deep anger at Sick for having made these scandalous allegations.

The *Wall Street Journal* had this to say about Sick the day that the House report was released:

Yesterday marked the end of one of the most appalling episodes of conspiracy mongering and media gullibility in recent American history. ... Crucial sources cited by Gary Sick and other October surprise theorists were "utter fabricators."...Too often Mr. Sick and others regurgitated the circular, internally confirmed accounts of fabricators. According to Mr. Sick's own admission to the House task force, he interviewed only five of the fourteen primary sources, relying on October surprise proponents for the rest....As for Mr. Sick, it was his embrace of the conspiracy that prompted Congress to authorize two investigations.

It has been very hard for me to deconstruct the complex, hostile feelings I have held toward Sick, who worked with me at the NSC and who had neither the courtesy nor the courage to let me know that he was accusing me of treason.

More than ten years ago I ran into him at a large conference and remarked that "a lot of water has gone over the dam" and that perhaps we needed to talk. He seemed to agree, but never followed up. He appears not to care about the hurt he inflicted on my family by voicing and publishing his unfounded charges.

Gary Sick continues to teach at Columbia. How he rationalizes his inflation of the "October Surprise" farrago I do not know, and am uninterested in finding out at this late date.

I am content to leave it at that.

PART FIVE
BACK TO THE PRIVATE SECTOR

25

Korea Society Years

In 1992, Bill Clinton's election as president brought my government career to an end. Had President Bush been reelected, I would have moved on from Seoul to some other position in his administration. I might have been sent to Tokyo as ambassador, a position I would have enjoyed.

As it was, Bill Clinton sent former vice president Walter "Fritz" Mondale to Tokyo. I had gotten to know Mondale when he was vice president and liked him. In 1995, I went to Tokyo on a business trip and ran into Mondale at a meeting. He shook my hand, shook his head, and said, "Don, this job is very heavy lifting."

Japan was in a funk, economically and politically, and constantly searching for consensus on every issue. The Imperial Household Agency in Japan was still a suffocating influence. Being U.S. ambassador to Japan would not have been nearly as interesting as my time in Seoul had been.

Before I left Seoul, I was fortunate enough to be offered a job as head of The Korea Society (TKS), a small nonprofit organization dedicated to fostering better understanding between South Korea and the United States. At the beginning of 1993, TKS was located in New York City in a corner of a large office at the Asia Society. It employed three or four people. Virtually its only activity had been an annual dinner, which raised enough money to keep the organization afloat, but barely. I had been the speaker at one of those dinners held in New York at the Waldorf-Astoria. No expense had been spared in flying Meg and me back to New York from Seoul, and putting us up in an elaborate suite at the Waldorf.

The people offering me the job, a mix of Korean and American businessmen, gave me the option of setting up the society in Washington, D.C., where they knew I lived, or keeping it in New York. I opted for New York. My goal as ambassador had been to change the U.S.-Korea relationship from a military alliance into an economic and political partnership. I believed I could do more to further that objective in New York than I could in Washington.

I think that that was the right decision in 1993, and today as well. It is easier to attract an audience in Washington than it is in New York, but I believe audiences in New York have more economic clout and stronger overall influence.

I was offered quite a munificent salary, which surprised me. I accepted on condition that The Korea Society would acquire its own, independent office. That was quickly agreed to, and a small suite of four rooms was rented on the eighth floor of a large building at the corner of 3rd Avenue and 57th Street in Manhattan. In 2009, when I cut all active connection with TKS, it had grown in stages to occupy the full 8th floor and had a full-time staff of about twenty people.

Meg and I packed out of Seoul at the end of February 1993, returned to Washington, and moved back into our house on Keokuk Street in Bethesda. Meg stayed there while I went to reconnoiter the situation in New York. The TKS board of about fifteen Koreans and Americans was glad to see me and threw an elaborate and expensive lunch of welcome for themselves and me at the Jockey Club. That event, and my recollection of the Waldorf dinner a year or so before gave me the totally false impression that The Korea Society was in strong financial shape.

After lunch that day, I met the small TKS staff at and took my first look at its financial status. Its net worth was about $200,000, and the Jockey Club lunch had taken a significant bite out of that sum. The only good news was that the Korea Foundation had agreed to an exponential increase in its annual support to society, in an effort to raise it to a higher level of significance. It was only on the basis of that increase that I was offered the job.

It dawned on me at about that time that the high salary I had accepted would take an inordinately large proportion of the society's cash flow—it was larger than the current net worth of the Society.

So I cut my own salary by 40 percent before I received my first paycheck.

I'd had visions of the nonprofit world as a domain peopled by philanthropists looking for new opportunities to give, and by rich and generous widows with bulging bank accounts. I found it instead to be a tough world and quickly saw I had missed the golden age of philanthropy toward Asian issues and organizations, a great deal of which had flowed into the Asia Society and other worthy organizations in the 1950s and '60's.

I had two rather embarrassing rejections by the Ford Foundation (three years apart) and the best oral pitch I ever made, to a world-famous philanthropist from a renowned family, resulted in *le grande zero*. Korea was neither a place nor a subject that excited the urge to give among the well-heeled, traditional givers in New York. I remember more than once walking rather dejectedly along a New York sidewalk, wondering if TKS, or I, would ever have much of an impact in that great, seemingly indifferent city.

The best managerial move I ever made at TKS was to hire Fred Carriere as my deputy, with the title of executive vice president. Fluent in Korean, Fred had spent more than twenty years in Korea, the last ten as executive director of the Fulbright Commission. Fred has an unequalled ability to understand and relate to Koreans, both in the North and the South. Two wonderful Korean women, Yong Jin Choi and Sophia Kang, helped me greatly from the time I arrived and continue to work at The Korea Society, fostering educational exchanges, and program development.

In mid-1993, Meg and I found a cozy apartment in New York, at the corner of 61st Street and Lexington Avenue. We lived there for two years, really getting to know the city. In 1995, following the death of Meg's parents, we moved into her childhood home in Armonk, New York, where we continue to live very happily.

With Fred Carriere doing most of the managing of TKS, my life centered on fundraising, writing articles, making speeches, attending conferences, and travel. Between 1993 and 2010, I made fifty-one trips to Korea, which included visits to China, Japan, and North Korea.

It was a full and busy life, particularly during the presidencies of Kim Dae-jung, 1997–2002, and Roh Moo Hyun, 2002–2007. Both presidents pursued "the sunshine policy" toward North Korea, resulting in improved relations with Pyongyang and North-South summit meetings held in 2000 and 2007. The awarding of the Nobel Peace Prize to Kim Dae-jung in December 2000 brought great satisfaction to me.

My saddest trip came in 2009, when I was part of the U.S. delegation attending Kim's funeral. Madeleine Albright headed our group. As the funeral procession approached the reviewing stand, I noted a visibly limping male figure laboriously walking near the late president's casket, and asked who it was. I was told it was Kim Dae-jung's son, who had been crippled by KCIA torture. I remember thinking that at least President Kim had been spared that terrible indignity.

In 2013, while visiting Seoul, I called on Lee Hee Ho, Kim's widow, to present my compliments. She remembered that I had come to the hospital to visit her dying husband. She said to me: "Had he known you had come, he would have jumped out of bed to greet you." I can only hope that with the passage of time, President Kim's contributions to North-South reconciliation will be more fully recognized and celebrated by the people of South Korea.

The Korea Society staff eventually grew to about twenty full-time professionals, with many outstanding young people serving for two or three years before going on to graduate work or other more lucrative positions. The society put on highly successful annual dinners and other events in New York, for fundraising and general public relations purposes.

Around 1995, former President Gerald Ford did us the honor of speaking at one of the society's annual dinners. His staff had indicated to me that some suggestions on his speech would be welcomed, and so I did a bit of research on him.

It became clear that before meeting his wife Betty, Gerald Ford had had a powerful relationship with a beautiful model that lasted for several years. When Ford came to New York to make his speech, he invited me to accompany him to one or two other appointments he had made in the city. As we rode around together, I found him completely open and a delightful conversationalist.

I asked him about the model, and whether he knew what had become of her. He laughed and said that "life in Grand Rapids" was not what she had wanted. He added that she wrote to him periodically and had been divorced more than once.

Ford spoke of his wife, Betty, with great devotion. Emboldened by this bit of conversation, I asked if he'd ever had second thoughts about his pardon of Richard Nixon. His reply was direct and powerful. "I never had regrets about the pardon. The country would have torn itself apart if Nixon had been put on trial. I'm sure it contributed to my defeat in 1976, but I felt I had to do it." President Ford remains clear in my mind as a strong, ethical man whom we were lucky to have as president when we did.

Only once did the Korea Society come close to disaster in putting on a major event. That was in November 1995, when I succumbed to pressure from one of my Korean board members, who meant to put on a concert at Avery Fisher Hall, showcasing the musical talents of some of his friends. He had in mind a local conductor and the conductor's young daughter, who was a gifted violinist.

Avery Fisher Hall has over 2,700 seats and is difficult to fill with anything short of well-known musical performers. As soon as it got out that we were planning a concert featuring local Koreans, we were swamped by calls from proud parents, pushing their children forward with loud assertions that they were far more talented than those chosen by my board member.

We could not solve the parental squabbles—but we put them out of reach of the parents by hiring an established musician whose talents were fully known. He was Earl Wild, then about eighty years old and a noted specialist in Rachmaninoff's piano concertos. The American Symphony Orchestra was to play the entire concert. We launched a vigorous ticket-selling effort, and were encouraged by the response.

But when we assembled our concert performers for a dress rehearsal, three days before the concert, the results were explosive. Earl Wild, after hearing the local conductor's efforts from the podium for only a few minutes, got up from his piano and said he would refuse to play unless a better conductor was hired. What to do?

Earl Wild recommended that we get the late Kenneth Schermerhorn, the highly talented conductor of the Nashville Symphony, and Schermerhorn readily agreed. There followed a tempestuous scene with the local conductor, who insisted on conducting the opening piece in the concert. We settled for that compromise, and Wild agreed, as he would then in no way be associated with a conductor whom he could not trust.

Schermerhorn was a delightful man. I told him everything that had happened, and we had a good laugh about it. He knew Earl Wild well and was comfortable with conducting the long and very difficult Rachmaninoff concerto Wild had selected to play.

On the night of the concert, Avery Fisher Hall was filled, with hardly an empty seat. The local conductor got through the opening piece without difficulty. All seemed well. Then Wild and Schermerhorn appeared to strong applause and launched into the Rachmaninoff.

Well into the piece, Wild lost track of where he was and stopped playing. Schermerhorn was instantly beside him and signaled where they were. Wild immediately picked up the score and never lost touch with the orchestra. The entire incident was over in a few seconds, and I later spoke to a number of people in the audience who had not noticed anything going awry.

My close friend Sam Koo was in the audience, with his wife, Myung-wha Chung, the renowned cellist. Of course, they had not missed anything, and Myung-wha told me she almost "slid under her seat" at the thought of what would have happened had Schermerhorn not been there to correct the situation.

Wild knew what he was talking about when he refused to play with the local man conducting. Such was our narrow escape, and we never returned to the classical music scene until we encouraged the New York Philharmonic to visit Pyongyang in 2008. That was a total success.

Each year, the Korea Society presented the Van Fleet Award to an outstanding Korean or American who had done much to improve relations between the two countries. Distinguished award recipients and keynote speakers at our major events included three American presidents (Gerald Ford, Jimmy Carter, and George H. W. Bush), three Korean presidents, (Kim Young Sam, Kim Daejung, and Roh Moo Hyun), U.N. Secretary General Ban Ki Moon, Henry Kissinger, Brent Scowcroft, and Colin Powell.

I was indeed fortunate that Buck and Doreen Freeman, whom

I had known—but not well—years ago in Japan, had just retired and were starting their wondrous Freeman Foundation. To my surprise, Buck came to me in 1993, knowing that I was taking on the TKS job and offered his generous financial support, which I was delighted to accept.

Even though Buck and Doreen have now passed on, their work continues to this day through their Freeman Foundation. It remains the most stalwart and generous American supporter of the Korea Society and a wonderfully eclectic group of organizations. Long may it wave.

Lockheed was grateful to me for helping to save the sale of P-3 antisubmarine aircraft to Korea. The company gave TKS a generous three-year grant that was a real blessing.

But what really made the Korea Society a success was what happened in Korea itself. Its economic rise, its increasing political influence in Asia, and its performance as a sterling ally of the United States made it a name that carried the society forward on all fronts.

26

Kids to Korea

In 1992, in Los Angeles, four white LA. police officers were caught on videotape giving a prolonged beating to a black man, Rodney King. The grotesque videotape became a national embarrassment. Eventually, the four cops were brought to trial. But when a white suburban jury acquitted the officers on all charges, angry mobs made up mostly of African Americans rioted, in the process destroying hundreds of Korean-American shops and stores in black neighborhoods.

I felt that the Korea Society should somehow respond to this, and so it was that the first Korea Society project I started was called "Kids to Korea."

The idea of sending inner city black kids to Korea—to show them what Korea was really like—had occurred to me before I left Seoul. Before my departure, I asked the commander of U.S Forces Korea if I could get Army housing for up to twenty high school kids that summer. The answer was "Yes" and I quickly proceeded.

I was fortunate to be put in touch with Fred Newkirk, a Quaker pastor who ran Inner City Ministries in the Long Beach–Los Angeles area. His focus was on inner city gangs. He worked tirelessly to try to keep young black men out of jail in the first place and to reduce recidivism among those who had already served time in prison.

A walking tour in a very tough Long Beach neighborhood, led by a one-time gang member, revealed the varying threats of violence hanging over each city block. Korean-run grocery stores were particularly tense. In the wake of the 1992 riots, the frequently robbed storekeepers were naturally quite suspicious of black customers.

For their part, blacks did not like the Koreans for what blacks felt were their rude and suspicious attitudes. Many blacks were openly envious of the relative prosperity enjoyed by the Koreans, a result of the long hours the Koreans worked, their frugality, and what seemed to blacks their sharp-edged business practices.

Newkirk strongly supported the concept behind "Kids to Korea" and was instrumental in pulling together a group of ten inner city high school students from families at risk whom he knew and could vouch for. Working with high school teachers in New York, I was able to pull together a similar group.

The two groups met in Los Angeles and flew to Korea in August 1993. For many, it was their first airplane flight, and for all it was their first trip outside the United States.

Funding came from both Korean and American sources, and the project was a great success. The students visited schools and museums in Seoul, went to the DMZ and Gyeongju, the ancient Silla capital, and had a one-night home stay with Korean families. All this opened their minds.

The project continues to this day and is now called "Project Bridge." The Pacific Century Institute has taken charge of the Los Angeles end of the project and has made it far more sophisticated, while the Korea Society continues to support it from New York.

Project Bridge now sends Hispanics and Asian-Americans as well as African Americans to Korea. Over four hundred students have now participated, and some have returned as team leaders. One of my students at Williams had gone to Korea as part of the program three years earlier. For him it had been a life-changing experience, as it has for many others who have written letters of thanks to the Korea Society and the Pacific Century Institute.

The older I get, the more I enjoy talking to high school students. Their curiosity remains boundless, but texting and tweeting cannot adequately encompass what they want to know and need to learn. In June 2013, I gave a talk at the high school from which I graduated in 1945. Among the questions I took, the last, from a ninth grader, was the most memorable. He said, "Mr. Gregg, when you graduated from high school, there was so much less history than there is now. What did you talk about?"

That question haunts me. We must do a better job of liberating youngsters from the "bubble of immediacy" that limits so many of them. Project Bridge was a step in that direction.

27

Epiphany in Long Beach

A wonderfully bizarre event resulted from pulling together the first group of Kids to Korea from the Los Angeles area. Fred Newkirk had chosen Nate, a former member of the "Insane Crips," one of the toughest gangs in the Los Angeles area, to lead the L.A. kids. Fred and I took a risk in sending Nate to Korea, but he did a good job as group leader and is now free of gang life and doing well.

On a trip to L.A. in 1994, I was contacted by Fred Newkirk, who said he would appreciate my coming to Long Beach to speak to eight former leaders of the Insane Crips, all of whom were out of jail at the moment. Fred was trying desperately to keep them "on the straight and narrow."

I asked Fred why he wanted me, and he said that the only "government officials" these men had previously met were cops with guns pointed at them, and he thought it would do them good to talk with someone who had had a different kind of government experience. I was deeply indebted to Fred, and so I agreed to go to Long Beach.

On the afternoon before the dinner, I was taken on a walking tour of a gang-dominated neighborhood in Long Beach by a still-active gang member. As we walked around, cars with darkened windows slowed as they passed. "You're being checked out," said my guide.

The guide knew Nate, the gang member who had gone to Seoul with the first Kids to Korea group, and noted how hard it was to pull out of gang life. He said starkly: "Nobody wants you to succeed where they have failed."

My guide pointed out places where gunfights had taken place

and where some of his friends had been killed. He pointed out the clearly defined blocks that were the territory of one gang and explained the dangers that befell any intruding rival gang member. This grim walk prepared me for the dinner that followed and highlighted the need for me to find some way of connecting with the men I was going to meet.

That evening, we met at a modest, second-floor restaurant. Nate was there, smiling, but the others, all larger and older, seemed stiff and ill at ease. Fred asked us to hold hands as he said a blessing. We sat down and silence descended on the room.

I knew it was incumbent on me to say something, and so I led off by remarking that I had a close friend who had served in prison for over twenty years, and was now out and doing well. (This was a veiled reference to my CIA comrade, Jack Downey.)

After a silence, one of the men asked cautiously, "What did he do?"—meaning what crime had he committed. I replied that he had been shot down over China during the Korean War and had been imprisoned in Beijing.

A long pause this time. Then: "What was he doing in China?"

"Well, he was on a CIA mission," I replied.

More quickly-- "How did you know him?"

The cat was almost out of the bag: "I was with CIA, too."

Instantly: "What kind of gun did you carry?"

"I didn't carry one except in Vietnam."

"What kind was it?"

"An Uzi."

Suddenly, everyone relaxed. I had carried a gun, and this gave me credibility. I had been admitted into the group.

"How many times did you shoot it?" one asked.

Proudly—"I never shot it."

A disappointed pause. "How many times did you pull it?"

"I only had to pull it once."

"What happened then?"

"Things got very quiet."

"They usually do." Said with a laugh by a man who had himself carried an Uzi and had used it on several occasions.

From then on, talk flowed freely, about gunfights survived, families, and even hopes for the future. Their leader, a man known only as "Tick-Tock," had not been able to come to the dinner, as he was having "a job interview." All present hoped that I could see him in the morning before my noon plane took off for New York. With Fred's urging, I agreed to do so.

At dinner's end, we all shook hands, they looked me in the eye, and thanked me for coming. I told them I was glad to have met them, and I think they knew I meant it.

The next morning Fred drove me to Tick-Tock's noisome second-floor apartment. He was a huge man, wearing some sort of Oakland Raiders cape. He apologized for the state of his apartment, thanked me for coming, and said he had heard from some of his friends that we had had a good time at dinner.

He then grew profane as he described his futile attempt to get a job as a janitor. "They asked me for fucking references," he said. "Any references I had would scare the shit out of them."

After I expressed sympathy, Tick-Tock said this: "In fifteen minutes I can put ten men on the street with machine guns, and I can't get a job as a fucking janitor."

I encouraged him to keep trying for a new job. He thanked me for coming, I wished him luck, and we parted. Two years later, Fred told me Tick-Tock had been shot dead in the street "resisting arrest."

I often think of my dinner companions, and wonder how many of them are still alive.

28

Six Trips to Pyongyang

Where to start in discussing North Korea—a country that I have frequently referred to as "The longest-running failure in the history of American espionage?"

There has been little direct dialogue of any significance between the United States and North Korea since the election of Barack Obama in November 2008. Tensions between North and South Korea have been dangerously high, and Seoul seems to be hoping that sanctions, food shortages, and economic deprivation will bring about regime change via collapse in the North.

China has emerged as North Korea's major ally, and Beijing is far more worried about the possibility of either implosion or explosion in North Korea than it is about Pyongyang's growing nuclear weapons capability. This means that China and South Korea, huge trading partners, are essentially working at cross-purposes regarding North Korea.

On June 15, 2000, a summit meeting took place in Pyongyang between President Kim Dae-jung of South Korea and Chairman Kim Jong-il of the North, which appeared to open up a new era in North-South relations. I was asked to comment on the summit meeting by a Korean newspaper, the *Korea Daily*, and on August 1, 2000, in the article that I wrote included these remarks (in Korean):

How does the Pyongyang summit stack up against other significant events that have taken place in Asia since the end of World War II? Pyongyang would seem to bear comparison with Richard Nixon's breakthrough meeting with Mao Zedong in 1972. Judged somewhat differently, in terms of new challenges that it has produced for the United States, Pyongyang has similarities to the French defeat at Dien Bien Phu in 1954.

How can anyone draw a parallel between a catastrophic military defeat suffered by France in the jungles of Vietnam half a century ago and a signal diplomatic success scored by President Kim Dae-jung in Pyongyang last June?

The point is that both events marked the opening of new eras in their regions. The relevant question is whether the United States will do better in judging the changed situation in Northeast Asia that the Pyongyang summit is producing than it did in reacting to developments in Southeast Asia in the wake of France's defeat and withdrawal from Vietnam.

...We unsuccessfully fought a war in Vietnam because, in the decade between France's defeat at Dien Bien Phu and the introduction of the first American troops near Danang, we had chosen to deal with Southeast Asia in the stark and rigid terms of the Cold War, rather than seeking to understand the region in its more subtle post-colonial terms.

The Pyongyang summit is a success, not a failure, but it is starting a paradigm shift in Northeast Asia. Seoul's diplomatic activism and its new dialogue with Pyongyang will become more and more central in determining the future of the region. These new factors will gradually change the way Americans are viewed by countries in that area. This shift will also require us to reexamine our objectives in the region, and how best to achieve them. This will not be an easy task for Americans to undertake....

The next American president, whoever he is, can use President Kim's remaining two years in office as a time to create a new posture for the U.S. in Northeast Asia. How well he does this will largely determine the future patterns of America's relations with Korea and its neighbors in the new era that is now beginning.

The new American president elected in November 2000 was George W. Bush. His misguided, ideological approach to North Korea brought to a tragic and totally unjustified end significant progress made in the wake of the Pyongyang Summit meeting in developing new relations with North Korea by both Seoul and Washington.

Largely on the strength of work done in 1999 and early 2000 by former secretary of defense William Perry, in settling the so-called North Korean "missile crisis," North Korea's vice marshal Jo Myong Rok had visited Washington in early October 2000. Marshal Jo went to the White House in full uniform, was warmly received by President Clinton, and invited our president to visit Pyongyang. Vice President Al Gore hosted Marshal Jo at an elaborate luncheon at the Department of State, as high-powered an event as a vice president can arrange. At the luncheon, both sides expressed hopes for the establishment of friendly and secure relations between Washington and Pyongyang and for the signing of a peace treaty that at last would bring a formal end to the Korean War.

I attended that luncheon and to this day am motivated to do anything I can to bring to fruition the hopes expressed on that memorable occasion.

President Clinton wanted to accept the North's invitation, and sent Secretary of State Madeleine Albright to Pyongyang to assess the potential value of such a trip. Upon her return, Albright convened a bipartisan dinner for about thirty "Korea watchers," including me, on November 2, 2000, at the Department of State. I remember clearly the sharp divisions of opinion that emerged on the potential value of a presidential trip to Pyongyang. Only two of the thirty attendees urged that Clinton go to Pyongyang "no matter what." Three or four were strongly opposed to the trip, and the rest of us were spread out in between.

Albright said she'd had over ten hours of discussion with Kim Jong-il, whom she described as friendly and forthcoming. She was also highly impressed by Kim's intelligence. "He listens and is not a nut case," she said. President Clinton wanted to make the trip, but time ran out on his presidency and he was unable to go.

The first words on North Korea coming from the new Bush administration sounded hopeful. Secretary of State Colin Powell said that the new administration would in essence take up where Clinton had left off in dealing with Pyongyang.

President Kim Dae-jung, in an early visit to the Bush White

House in 2001, learned that this would not be the case. His efforts to have President Bush support a continuation of his "sunshine policy" were abruptly rebuffed in an Oval Office meeting.

I had dinner with President Kim that night in Washington. I admired his "grace under pressure" but could see his surprise and deep disappointment in what he had heard from the younger Bush.

A Bush administration review of North Korean policy, completed in May 2001, resulted in a cautious and basically hostile policy toward Pyongyang. Asked about his opening statement indicating continuity between the Clinton and Bush administrations, Secretary Powell ruefully said: "I got a bit too far forward on my skis."

Bush infamously gave the guillotine to Clinton's North Korea policy when he placed North Korea along with Iran and Iraq in what he called an "Axis of Evil" as part of his State of the Union speech in January 2002. Hearing that phrase, I was taken back to Vietnam in early 1962 and General Harkins's equally misguided statement to me that "We will be out of here with a military victory in six months."

My direct involvement with North Koreans had developed slowly in my early years at the Korea Society, beginning in 1993, where I was both president and chairman of the board. In 1995, I attended a meeting at Berkeley with some North Korean officials, arranged by the renowned professor on Asian affairs, the late Robert Scalapino. A man named Li Gun and I struck a few friendly sparks, particularly after a drink or two of Korean soju.

The Korea Society also helped sponsor the visit to New York of two North Korean officials who wanted to explain some of their policies. These officials were totally unprepared for follow-up questions to their rather inept policy presentations. They made no friends in New York, and I could only hope they learned something from their fractious and unsuccessful trip. The Korea Society was roundly criticized by hard-line South Korean officials in the Kim Young Sam administration who seemed to oppose any direct American dialogue with the North.

That attitude in Seoul changed completely with the election of Kim Dae-jung in late 1997. I was invited to President Kim's inauguration, and, in a private meeting, he personally urged me to "plant the flag of the Korea Society in North Korea." He added that for the society to be worthy of its name, it had to become involved in both North and South Korean affairs.

I was glad to oblige, and quickly increased the tempo of the society's contacts with the North Korean mission to the United Nations. Friendly, though informal, relations rather quickly developed. As a result I was asked to introduce the North Korean minister of foreign affairs when he visited New York's Council on Foreign Relations in September 1999.

Because of these contacts, following Bush's election, the North Koreans asked me to try to do something to rebuild a direct, but informal dialogue with Pyongyang. Our first idea was to have Professor Scalapino lead a group of former U.S. ambassadors to South Korea on a visit to Pyongyang. The strongly negative atmosphere that emerged in North Korea after the "Axis of Evil" speech doomed this plan.

With things at a stalemate, the idea of writing a letter directly to Kim Jong-il arose in my mind. At first I dismissed the idea, but it kept recurring. I discussed the possible value of writing a letter with Fred Carriere, my close friend and trusted deputy at the Korea Society. Fred pointed out that the North Koreans knew who I was and had recently approached me about reestablishing some sort of dialogue with the United States.

After stewing about it for several weeks, I drafted a letter, showed it to Fred, and on March 6, 2002, took it to the North Korean mission in New York. The letter stated my interest in visiting Pyongyang to talk about issues of mutual concern to our two countries, particularly those growing out of the terrorist attack of 9/11.

Li Gun was the official in charge. I told him I'd written to his chairman. He scowled and stuck out his hand for the letter. Li rapidly read my message and then asked harshly, "How dare you write a letter like this to my chairman? Who do you think you are!"

I said I thought that I knew what might be of interest and concern to Chairman Kim and had discussed some of these issues in my letter.

"How do you know what might be of interest to my chairman?" Li snapped.

I told him of conversations I'd had with Chinese, Russians,

Americans, and South Koreans—all of whom had talked with Chairman Kim, had been impressed with the chairman's intelligence, his interest in developing a stronger economy, and his desire for better relations with the United States. I named the people with whom I had talked.

Li thought a moment and said, "That is a good answer. I will send your letter." Within two weeks, I was invited to go to Pyongyang.

I then notified the Department of State of my letter, and of my invitation to visit the North. I had not done so before, as I had expected to be asked by the North Koreans to tell them who had instructed me to write my letter. I wanted to be able to say truthfully that it had been my idea to do so, and that my letter had no official status whatsoever.

The question had not been asked. My experience as ambassador had also left me with the feeling that if I had discussed the idea of writing a letter to Kim Jong-il with the Department of State, I would have been advised not to do it. Bureaucracy frequently stifles personal initiative.

To my surprise and relief, State appeared to be pleased with what had occurred and offered to send a young, Korean-speaking Foreign Service officer with me, an offer I happily accepted. FSO Julie Chung met me in Beijing and accompanied me to Pyongyang. She was a great help to me and a very sharp observer of all that took place.

We flew from Beijing to Pyongyang in an ancient Russian Ilyushin 62, loaded to the gills with people and massive amounts of luggage. We were driven to a large guesthouse deep in the countryside. I was ushered into a huge, high-ceilinged room and was proudly told that I was the privileged occupant of the "Robert Mugabe Suite," named for the president of Zimbabwe, a former visitor to North Korea. By 2002, Mugabe had emerged as one of the most monstrous dictators in Africa, so I was not particularly flattered.

The following afternoon, after some sightseeing around Pyongyang, I had my first meeting with my host, Kim Gye Gwan—the official that most Americans met when they went to Pyongyang. He was vice minister of foreign affairs and counselor at the Institute for Disarmament and Peace.

I presented Kim with three action films I had brought as presents for Chairman Kim Jong-il. (They were *The Patriot* on the American Revolution, *Training Day*, a tough police melodrama, and *Ronin*, a classic espionage thriller directed by my college classmate John Frankenheimer. I was told later that the chairman liked them all.)

Kim began our first long conversation by asking me three questions. First, "Why is George W. Bush so different from his father?" My answer was that Americans born and raised in New England, as the elder Bush was, are often very different from people raised in Texas, as his son was. There was no follow-up to my answer.

Kim then asked his key question. It was this: How can America function as a country when we elect presidents who have little or nothing in common with their predecessors? This was an obvious reference to the almost complete change in U.S. policy toward North Korea that had come about when George W. Bush replaced Bill Clinton.

I did my best to explain the democratic process to Kim and the several others in the room, stressing that public reaction to presidential policies often results in people of different persuasions coming into office. Their collective response to this was that it was very hard for a country like North Korea to build a stable relationship with a country that changed policies as often as we did.

Kim's final question was direct: "Why don't you understand us better?"

I gave a fairly long-winded answer in response, using the line that North Korea remained the longest-running failure in the history of U.S. espionage, because we had not been able to recruit North Koreans to be our agents, as we had with the Chinese and Soviets.

Kim seemed pleased with my answer. After a pause, he grinned and asked: "Were you wearing your *Op-Center* hat when you responded in that way?"

I was completely taken aback, as I knew that *Op-Center* was a 1995 paperback novel co-authored by Tom Clancy and Steve Pieczenik. I do not know Clancy, but Pieczenik had been a psychiatrist working as a crisis manager and hostage negotiator at the Department of State when I was at the White House. We had met and talked several times. The central character in *Op-Center* is named Gregory Donald, with long service in CIA and as ambassador to

South Korea. I had taken a lot of razzing from friends when the book came out, but was amazed that the North Koreans were aware of it.

I said, "I can't believe you people have read that lousy book."

"Of course we have," said Kim, implying that I should not think that they were as ignorant of us as we were of them.

"I have not read the book, but my wife has," I countered. "Would you like to know her opinion of it?" They said they would.

I said: "She thinks of it as a book only to be read on long, boring airplane flights. She did not mind that I died a heroic death at the end of the book, but she was furious that I had had a very young and beautiful Korean mistress!"

This evoked a good laugh, and our more formal talks got under way. By and large, the North Koreans received me with both seriousness and courtesy. I set the only guidelines for our talks: my hosts should not expect me to criticize my own government any more than I would expect them to criticize theirs.

In addition to Vice Minister Kim, I met with Lt. General Ri Chan Bok, a crusty man in his seventies, who was in charge of the central section of the Demilitarized Zone (DMZ) that included Panmunjom, where meetings between U.S. and North Korean military officers were held. General Ri was quite hostile when I first entered his office, saying: "Why are you here? You speak first!"

I told the general that on the day before I had been taken to the top of their impressive Juche (independence) Tower. I wondered how he would feel if he were to see one of his own commercial aircraft deliberately crash into the tower, reducing it to rubble. I said that the people of the United States had seen that happen twice in New York on 9/11 and that it had been an unforgettable, horrifying experience.

I said I had come to North Korea to try to make certain that neither North Korea nor any of its weapons would ever be involved in such an incident involving the United States. This got the general's attention, and we had a vigorous, uninhibited conversation, at the end of which he shook my hand, said he was glad I had come, and invited me to return to Pyongyang in the future.

In meetings with both Vice Minister Kim and General Ri, I expressed the hope that the positive experience of the Pyongyang summit meeting of June 2000 would be reciprocated a visit by Chairman Kim to South Korea. My hosts were evasive on that subject, but they repeatedly expressed their hope for high-level talks with the United States.

In marked contrast to the cynical belligerence I had encountered in talks with officials in the former Soviet Union and in Romania under Ceauşescu, my North Korean interlocutors showed a deep concern for the problems they were facing in their own country. Both men stressed the power shortages that crippled their economy and rendered almost impossible their efforts to produce more fertilizer and raise more food for their malnourished people.

They expressed considerable nostalgia about the last few months of the Clinton administration and deep regret that a U.S.-North Korean summit meeting had not taken place. They also appeared baffled about why the Bush administration was treating them so much more harshly than the Clinton administration had, particularly in terms of the rhetoric being used to describe their government and its leaders.

In response, I stressed that since 9/11 the United States had become a nation at war with terrorism, which made North Korea's possible production of weapons of mass destruction and long-range missile systems a far greater worry than they'd ever been before.

General Ri was particularly concerned about the high-tech military capacities that the United States was demonstrating in Afghanistan, saying that those weapons increased the likelihood of an American attack on his country.

I reminded the general of President Bush's statement during his February 2002 visit to Seoul that America had no intention of attacking North Korea. But this did not seem to ease his concerns.

General Ri said that North Korea wanted a peace agreement with the United States to replace the armistice agreement and that the refusal by Washington to move toward making such an agreement showed that America was open to another war on the Korean Peninsula.

I reminded Ri that the United States had removed all its nuclear weapons from South Korea. But he retorted, "That is just a trick to calm us down."

In the end, Ri agreed with me that there would be no winner

in a second Korean war but that, for real dialogue to begin, Washington would have to end its hostile policy toward Pyongyang. Ri said he hoped that the United States would not obstruct the good relations that had started to emerge in the wake of the last summit meeting. He thanked me for coming and hoped that I would return to Pyongyang in the future.

Kim Gye Gwan hosted a farewell dinner for me, during which I raised with him the possibility that the USS *Pueblo*, seized by North Korea in 1968, might be returned to the United States. This clearly surprised Kim, as he had assumed that America had lost all interest in that ship.

I told him that it was still listed on the roster of active U.S. Navy vessels, that I had met the skipper of the ship, Commander Lloyd Bucher, and that he, his crew, and the people of Pueblo, Colorado were very anxious to have the ship returned to them. For the only time in our talks, Kim took notes on what I said. It was clear that he saw the return of the *Pueblo* as a possible way to restart some sort of dialogue with the United States.

Our meeting ended on a friendly note. Kim made it clear that "working-level talks" such as we had held would never solve the major problems between our countries. But he'd been interested in some of the things I'd said.

On my way home, I stopped in Seoul and had a long talk with Lim Dong Won, former head of Korea's intelligence service and then President Kim's special advisor on reunion and national security. Lim and I were and remain close personal friends. He had been to Pyongyang just before my visit and had a long meeting with Kim Jong-il, who had mentioned my upcoming visit. Lim then gave Chairman Kim some of my background, particularly my work as U.S. ambassador to Seoul.

Lim also stressed to Chairman Kim the value of "Track II" approaches in helping to restart an American dialogue with North Korea that had been stalled by the Bush administration's hard-line approach. Chairman Kim specifically mentioned work of the Korea Society in this connection and asked what other Americans might be involved in such approaches, writing down those that Lim mentioned.

Lim told me that Chairman Kim's top priority was normalization of diplomatic ties with the United States. In this connection he had been amazed and disappointed by the "great disconnect" between the Clinton and Bush administrations. Kim ended his remarks on this subject by saying to Lim that if the United States avoided "further slander" toward Pyongyang, there would be great enthusiasm for a resumption of direct dialogue with Washington.

Upon my return home, I wrote a full report of my visits to Pyongyang and Seoul in the form of a letter to President Bush, which I sent to Deputy Secretary of State Rich Armitage, who was by then an old friend. I received not a word from anyone in response.

In early October, I received the following letter from Kim Gye Gwan, dated October 3, 2002;

> Mr. Gregg,
>
> I am writing to you with my graphic [sic] of our meeting in Pyongyang last April, which was productive and where we got to know each other.
>
> At the same time, I am greatly encouraged by your goodwill efforts to resolve bilateral issues back home and on our part. We have conducted serious examinations on the proposed issue in a positive way.
>
> I am taking this opportunity to extend my invitation to you to visit Pyongyang again at the earliest possible date to further our discussions.
>
> Sincerely,
> Kim Gye Gwan"

I asked Li Gun in New York what this meant, and he said, "The question is no longer if the *Pueblo* will be returned; it is when it will be returned."

I immediately called Deputy Secretary Armitage, an Annapolis graduate, to tell him this news. His lack of enthusiasm was surprising and disappointing. I came to learn, through other conversations with Navy officers and with members of the *Pueblo* crew, that the U.S. Navy regarded the case of the *Pueblo* as a continuing embarrassment that they wished would go away. A retired four-star admiral whom I met at the Naval War College at Newport put it this way: "That goddamn ship should never have surrendered; it should have been scuttled on the spot."

In striking contrast, the *Pueblo* crew, and the people of Pueblo, Colorado, were extremely excited to learn that the ship might be returned.

The North Koreans let me know that they would welcome my bringing along other informed friends on my return to Pyongyang. I invited economist Joseph Stiglitz, journalist Don Oberdorfer, and Fred Carriere from the Korea Society. All accepted, and Pyongyang invited us to travel to Pyongyang by crossing the DMZ, which would have made the trip far shorter and easier to accomplish than by having to travel to Beijing and wait for one of the twice-weekly flights to Pyongyang.

A day or so after receiving Kim Gye Gwan's letter, I learned that Assistant Secretary of State James Kelly had gone to Pyongyang, where he accused North Korea of secretly developing a second nuclear weapons development plan involving highly enriched uranium. The existing North Korean nuclear reaction was plutonium-based. The meeting had been emotional and highly charged, with the North Koreans saying that they were entitled to develop any weapons they deemed necessary in view of constant American military threats against them.

I expected my invitation to be canceled, but it was not. Our planning continued. Just before we were to leave, the U.S. government said that it would not allow us to travel to Pyongyang by crossing the DMZ. This caused Joe Stiglitz to withdraw from our group, due to the additional time required to go to and from North Korea by way of Beijing. Don Oberdorfer, Fred Carriere, and I changed our plans as required, and entered North Korea via an Air Koryo flight from Beijing.

We were warmly greeted by Kim Gye Gwan and, at a later meeting, by General Ri Chan Bok. We heard much about Jim Kelly's tumultuous visit, but no anger was directed toward us. The North Koreans clearly saw us as unofficial, "Track II" visitors with whom policy matters could be dispassionately discussed.

Our main objective was to try to get the North Koreans to send a message from Chairman Kim Jong-il to President Bush, offering to begin a high-level dialogue. We repeatedly cited the statement made by President Bush in Seoul earlier in 2002 that the United States had no intention of attacking North Korea and that better relations could be achieved through denuclearization of the Korean peninsula.

On the last day of our visit, Kim Gye Gwan asked to meet with me privately. He told me that he was happy to have me return to Pyongyang, but that the Kelly visit had "turned things upside down" and had made it impossible to return the *Pueblo*. Kim said he hoped to get a message from Chairman Kim for us to carry back, but that that was being decided as we spoke by First Vice Minister Kang Sok Ju in a discussion with the chairman himself.

After some delay, we met with Kang, who said that he had been authorized to give me a message from Chairman Kim Jong-il to be transmitted in secret to the White House. He quoted from the message and gave me a printed copy in Korean. He asked that no other Americans be told of the message until we got to the White House. I agreed to this and told Kang that, on the way back to Washington, I would be stopping in Seoul and that I would be meeting with Lim Dong Won there. Kang said it was "up to me" what I told Lim of our visit.

I thanked Kang and Kim and said I hoped that the message could open a new chapter in relations between our countries. We left Pyongyang on a high note.

In Seoul, I told Lim Dong Won that we had a message to deliver to the White House but did not show him the message or go into any detail about its contents. Lim congratulated us and said that we had done "great work" in getting the message.

Don Oberdorfer was most helpful in getting us into the White House. He knew Stephen Hadley, the deputy national security advisor. Upon receiving a call from Oberdorfer, Hadley agreed to see us. We were received in an office I knew well from my decade in the White House. Hadley took a quick look at a translation of the message and, checking with no one, said "We won't respond to this. That would be rewarding bad behavior." We were in and out of the White House in less than twenty minutes.

A few days later, the White House announced that it was stopping shipment of heavy fuel oil to North Korea that had been part of the Agreed Framework in place since 1994. No mention was ever made by the White House of the message Oberdorfer and I had delivered.

I made three more trips to Pyongyang, in 2004, 2005 and 2008. All trips involved hours of discussion on policy issues of concern to the United States and North Korea, all of which were reported in detail to the Bush administration. There was zero feedback.

The 2005 and 2008 trips had a special flavor involving Ted Turner and the New York Philharmonic. In 2005, Turner wanted to discuss the creation of a "peace park" in the DMZ. The Korea Society proposed the trip to Pyongyang, which was quickly accepted. Fred Carriere and I met Turner in Pyongyang, attended his meetings, where he was courteously received and listened to, and flew directly back to Seoul with him on his private jet.

The contrast between the somnolent, virtually deserted airport at Pyongyang and the teeming air traffic at Incheon International Airport near Seoul was stunning. Turner, an astute observer who had never been to Korea before, was amazed at the contrasts between North and South Korea. It was also interesting to note the near-reverence with which he was viewed by the CNN people encountered on the trip.

In 2008, the New York Philharmonic visited Pyongyang from February 25 to 27. The Korea Society had encouraged the trip. I had been invited to attend the inauguration of South Korean President Lee Myung-bak in Seoul, which took place the day before the concert in Pyongyang. A delegation from the Korea Society was allowed to go directly to Pyongyang by crossing the DMZ on the day of the concert, thus allowing us to attend both major events.

Former secretary of defense Bill Perry was part of this group. He and I shared an ancient Mercedes Benz sedan, which picked us up at Panmunjom and drove us through a fresh snowfall to Pyongyang. Villagers along the way were responsible for keeping the road open, and we counted over 1,000 citizens sweeping and shoveling along the way. The morning was bright, and the snowfall less than three inches. The people along the way seemed quite cheerful, waving at us as we passed, and often tossing snowballs at each other.

We drove directly to a luncheon hosted by Kim Gye Gwan, where Perry, a Democrat, urged the North Koreans to take steps toward reconciliation with the Bush administration in its last months in office. I regret to say that this did not happen, for a variety of reasons, for which all concerned share responsibility.

The concert was a great success. Lorin Maazel, a great conductor and an engaging showman, had learned some Korean phrases with which he introduced himself and his orchestra. The concert ended with the playing of the beloved Korean informal national anthem "Arirang," which delighted the audience. At the end of the concert, the applause was so prolonged that individual members of the orchestra returned to the stage to wave and bow to the audience.

The next morning, selected musicians from the orchestra gave master classes to carefully chosen young North Koreans. I watched several of these classes take place. The Americans were amazed at the high quality of the young musicians they were teaching, and the young North Koreans were thrilled to receive world-class instruction. It was a very happy morning for all concerned.

The Philharmonic then flew to Seoul where it gave another concert. The Korea Society delegation were given seats on the big Asiana jet, and so for the second time I enjoyed the direct flight, well less than an hour, from Pyongyang to Seoul.

On August 1, 2011, I met in New York with Kim Gye Gwan, newly promoted to first vice minister of foreign affairs, and several other North Koreans I had met on my previous trips to Pyongyang. For the first time in all my meetings with the North Koreans and other Americans, there seemed to be a mutual recognition that talking to each other is not "rewarding bad behavior," but a necessity, to keep a difficult and dangerous relationship from growing worse.

Too many pundits in the United States predict the imminent collapse of the North Korean government. Then, out of pride, these pundits feel they have to interpret all later events in a way that justifies their earlier extreme predictions. The result is a lot of uninformed blather when pundits discuss North Korea.

I am very glad to have become involved in this relationship and continue to hold hopes for its evolution into something more positive and more powerful.

North Korea will deal with whatever policy comes out of Seoul—and Washington. But there is a chance for vastly improved relations between the United States and North Korea—if only we have the intelligence to see it, and to grab that chance.

PHOTO GALLERY V

Chairman and president
of the Korea Society, New
York (1993–2009).
Korea Society photo

In North Korea with Lt.
General Ri Chan Bok, 2004.
Personal photo

The marriage of son John Gregg to Mary Ceglarski, in Middletown, Rhode Island, September 2006. From left: Ned and Alison Corcoran, Lucy Buckley, the groom and bride, and Meg and Don Gregg. *Family photo*

Three generations of Greggs on family trip to Japan on our 50th wedding anniversary, July 2003. *Family photo*

Colorado College president Richard Celeste bestows an honorary degree on the author, 2010. *Family photo*

With Meg at Syracuse University, where a professorship in Korean studies has been named for us both, 2012. *Family photo*

Arriving at Pyongyang with Pete McCloskey, February 10, 2014.
North Korea News Agency Photo

Pete McCloskey and Lt. General
Ji Young Choon, Pyongyang,
February 13, 2014. *Photo by Lynn
Turk, Pacific Century Institute*

29

Jazz

My introduction to modern American music started in the late 1930s. It came over the radio from *The Make Believe Ballroom* on station WNEW in New York, with disc jockey Martin Block presiding. The ballroom was on for two or three hours a day, broken into quarter-hour sessions during which Block would play four songs by the same artist, interspersed with commercials like "Barney's, at Seventh Avenue and 17th Street, the only store of its kind in New York," a phrase Block repeated so many times that I still remember it today.

The music was then mostly called "swing," as practiced by big bands such as those of Benny Goodman, Harry James, Glenn Miller, Tommy Dorsey, and Artie Shaw. Listening to this music every day prompted me to buy records. My very first was Benny Goodman's "Stompin' at the Savoy," which I played endlessly on our wind-up Victrola, which had an old rasping needle that quickly wore down the record.

The Paramount Theater in New York periodically presented big bands and vocalists on stage, teamed up with a highly rated movie. I dutifully stood in long lines on the street in New York waiting to hear the big bands and the big vocalists, including Frank Sinatra. It was great fun. I remember how thrilled I was when Harry James, on stage at the Paramount, played a tune called "The Mole," which I liked very much. My ability to name the tune increased my standing among Hastings School classmates with whom I had gone into the city.

In the summer of 1944, just after Dad died, the family went out to Colorado Springs for the summer and stayed at the Gregg family home on Tejon Street. I found they had an ancient gramophone, which led me to buy the Will Bradley Orchestra's wonderful arrangement of "Celery Stalks at Midnight," which I also played endlessly. My grandfather, Harry Renick Gregg, then 92, grinned and shook his head as I played that tune, but he never complained.

The music I listened to in those days was all meticulously arranged. Every tune always sounded just the same when it was played. I began to hear about jazz that featured improvisation, but it was rarely played on the radio programs I listened to, except as background music accompanying vocalists like Billie Holiday and Ella Fitzgerald. I was struck by their powerful rhythmic sense, whether they sang fast or slow. They really "swung."

My first direct encounter with jazz came at the Club Benghazi in Washington, D.C., in 1946 when I was stationed there in the army. The featured musician was saxophonist Ben Webster, who also played piano. The club was small and crowded, and everybody smoked except me. Cigarettes in those days smelled rather good, and I felt that the smoky atmosphere contributed to a free and easy atmosphere, where anything could happen. The audience was mixed racially, and everyone was very friendly

At about 8 p.m., Webster and his quartet sauntered in (piano, bass, and drums, plus Webster). There wasn't a sheet of music to be seen. Webster greeted the audience of about thirty people in a deep voice, and then off they went. Webster's sax had a breathy tone, and he played deliberately. Once he had established the basic melody, he went off into variations unlike anything I had ever heard. It was perfectly wonderful, and I stayed until the place closed about 2 a.m.

I was hooked. As I left the club, I asked one of the other customers where I could find more jazz in Washington. He told me of a place at 9th and V streets, Northeast, where there was almost continuous jazz, adding with a smile: "You'll find mostly black folks there."

He was right. The place at 9th and V (it had a number of names) was a center for jazz, and I went there frequently, often as virtually the only Caucasian in the place. The place was basically a gray-walled auditorium, with a big stage and rows of fixed seats that could hold several hundred people. It had a balcony running around the sides and back. One special night, sitting in the balcony, I watched Louis Armstrong and Ella Fitzgerald combine in an unforgettable night of jazz that rocked the house. The impromptu dancing in the aisles was spectacular and was rewarded by great bursts of applause.

One Sunday afternoon in early 1947, I went to a USO "tea dance," where I met a lovely blonde who was attending Mary Washington College in Fredericksburg, Virginia. We got along very well and, as a result, she missed a 9 p.m. bus to Fredericksburg that would have gotten her back on campus before the gates closed and the dormitories locked down.

I had accompanied her to the Greyhound Bus station, and she was clearly distressed, as the next bus to Fredericksburg left at 3 a.m. I suggested that we might go to 9th and V, where I knew that Lionel Hampton was playing. I also knew that he would be playing until about 2 a.m. She accepted my suggestion. My new friend was from Kingsport, Tennessee, and on our way I told her that we might be the only white people in the place. She looked startled, but agreed to proceed.

9th and V was packed, and we had to stand at the back. Hampton had a big band that night and was blasting away. "The joint was jumping," as they used to say. My friend was terrified at first, and had my right arm in a viselike grip as we stood against the wall. She gradually relaxed as she saw how friendly everyone was. A man I had met at earlier visits saw us, and we squeezed in at his table. From then on things loosened up.

We made the 3 a.m. bus, and, as I put her on board, she said, "I have never been as scared as I was tonight, but I thank you for taking me there. I learned a lot, and the music was fabulous." We saw quite a lot of each other during my college years. She went on to marry a man from Norfolk, and I hope she lived happily ever after. She was a lovely person.

During my years at Williams, 1947–51, New York had become a center for jazz. Fifty-second Street was loaded with small clubs where jazz luminaries played, but Bop City and Birdland were the crown jewels of the jazz scene. I frequented Birdland, established in 1949, and named for Charlie "Yardbird" Parker, one of the all-time great saxophone players.

Birdland was downstairs in a basement. It had a low ceiling

and was always smoky and crowded. But the audience went there to listen, not to talk, and the music could be heard clearly. The performers were announced by a very small man with a high, squeaky voice, dressed in a bellhop uniform. His voice filled the room, and he dramatically set the stage for whoever was to play.

And how they played! I remember in particular nights spent listening to pianist Errol Garner, Stan Getz, and "the Bird" himself. Often, piano players wearing hats at rakish angle, smoked as they played, somehow adding to the tempting insouciance of the place.

One night Bill Everett, my college roommate and lifelong friend, and I, went to Birdland with dates. My date was an attractive Canadian whom I had met at Camp Ahmek in Ontario. I was anxious to make a good impression. Bill felt the same about his date. We had to wait for a table, and the waiter asked what we would be drinking when we sat down. He strongly pushed champagne as the preferred beverage, and our dates seemed to like the idea, so we ordered a bottle. Shortly thereafter, we were taken to a table directly in front of the small stage. In fact, the top of our table was level with the surface of the stage.

Charlie Parker was playing that night, and he was superb. He was also "high" and moved actively around the stage, frequently stepping on our tabletop as he played. Our dates were dazzled. The jazz was unforgettable, and so was the bill when it arrived—$25 for the champagne, in those days a staggering price, at least for us. Bill and I went home virtually penniless but happy. I had carefully kept a dime for the toll on the Henry Hudson Bridge. That was literally all the money I had left.

In 1952, bandleader Artie Shaw wrote a book called *The Trouble with Cinderella*. That gave me my first insight into what being a celebrity was like. Shaw was famous for his wonderful rendition of "Begin the Beguine"; and wherever he and his band went, they were expected to play that tune, often more than once in an evening. I naïvely assumed that the band enjoyed playing the tune as much as I, and other fans, enjoyed hearing it. That was not the case. Shaw made clear that he and his band grew utterly bored by playing the same thing over and over. This led Shaw into other forms of jazz, including his small group, the Gramercy Five, where he could escape playing the Beguine. Shaw always felt constrained by the conventional, and his music was brilliant in any form that he chose to play it.

I pursued jazz overseas, whenever I could find it. In 1952, when I first visited Japan, I was delighted to find drummer Gene Krupa banging away to a full house in a huge cabaret in Yokosuka. Later in the 1950s, when Meg and I moved to Japan, we found quite a lot of pretty good Japanese jazz in Tokyo. Perhaps under Krupa's influence, Japanese jazz groups often featured endless drum solos that Meg in particular found rather dull and deafening.

Late in the 1960s, Lionel Hampton came through Tokyo on a tour that had taken him to Bangkok, where the Thai king, who played the saxophone, sat in with his group. A few days later in Tokyo, Hampton played at the ambassador's residence. I talked to him there, and recalled to him that I'd heard him play twenty-five years earlier at 9th and V in Washington. Hampton laughed and replied, "That place really jumped."

I then told him that the Thai king and I were born on the same day of the same year, and that I had often wondered how good a musician he was. "How well did the king play?" I asked. With a slight roll of his eyes, Hampton replied: "Not bad for a king."

When we returned to Bethesda in the mid-1970s, Meg and I had become very partial to the music of guitarist Charlie Byrd, who had been instrumental, along with Stan Getz, in bringing Brazilian jazz, called *bossa nova*, into the United States. Byrd often played in Annapolis, and we enjoyed driving over there to hear him.

In 1991, after we had returned to Seoul, Charlie Byrd came through on a State Department–sponsored tour. He was accompanied by his brother Joe on bass and Chuck Redd on drums. We invited them over to the Embassy Residence, where they played a wonderful concert for us and a group of close Korean friends.

After that concert, Redd told me he had never been to Seoul and asked me about the jazz scene there. I told him there was not much to it, but that I would be happy to take him out. We went to the Hyatt Hotel, where I knew there was jazz of some sort played every night. We found a Korean quartet in action, playing at about a B-level. The club manager knew who I was, and he also knew that Charlie Byrd was in town. When I introduced Chuck Redd to him as Byrd's drummer, he immediately invited him to sit in with the quartet.

The Korean drummer slunk off stage, and Chuck sat down. He introduced himself with a short riff on drums that woke everybody up. The musicians agreed on a tune, and off they went. Chuck's solid rhythmic foundation transformed the group, and they quickly went from B-level to A-level. Chuck lifted the music everyone played. Even the Korean drummer, when he returned, played much better than he had. The power and influence of one man's talent had clearly been shown.

In September 2012, I was in a bit of a funk about the state of politics in America, when Meg suggested that I "put on some music." I looked over a number of CDs, and chose Charlie Parker's "Star Eyes," recorded in 1950, a song I had heard him play at Birdland. After hearing just a few bars, my mood changed completely for the better. Charlie Parker is long gone, but the rhythm and lift of his music is undiminished. Jazz continues to enrich my life, and I am most grateful for that.

30

A Stint at Goldman Sachs

Just before we left Seoul in early 1993, Goldman Sachs offered me a job as a consultant on Asian affairs. I knew of the firm's high reputation, as exemplified by the work of John Whitehead, whom I had met when he served as deputy secretary of state from 1985 to 1989 under President Reagan.

Whitehead had joined Goldman Sachs in 1947 and rose to become senior partner and co-chairman in 1976. His principles for being an investment banking rang true to me in terms of competence, honesty, and integrity, and I was pleased to have been offered a position.

I told the Goldman representatives who contacted me that I knew virtually nothing about international finance. They were well aware of this, but they were interested in my experience in Asia dating back to 1952.

I was happy to accept the offer after I had returned to the United States. The salary I was offered was a pittance by Goldman standards but very generous by mine. I've said before how deeply I believe in "pertinence over affluence," and at Goldman Sachs it was much more important to me to make a difference than to make a buck. And I've met hundreds of other people along the way, in CIA, in the teaching profession, among our diplomats, and in the military, who believe that, too, and live by it.

Most of my work was done over the phone with the head of the Goldman Sachs office in Seoul. But, from time to time, I met with senior management in New York and occasionally in both Japan and Korea.

I had gotten to know Jon Corzine, who had served as Goldman

Sachs's chairman from 1994 until May 1998, when he invited Henry Paulsen to join him as co-chairman. A power struggle soon ensued over the future of the firm.

I was with Corzine in Seoul in early January 1999, when he got the word that he had been ousted by Paulsen and two other key rivals. I had just taken Corzine to Blue House to meet newly elected President Kim Dae-jung when the bad news came.

Corzine took it very hard, immediately returned to New York, and soon thereafter left Goldman Sachs. We remained friends as he became a New Jersey senator, and he subsequently spoke at a Korea Society dinner.

Around the year 2000, I introduced Goldman Sachs to a good Korean friend of mine, a senior economist and former government official who I felt could give the firm high-quality economic advice far beyond my capacity. He was hired by the firm, and I was let go.

It was all amicable and understandable. I had sensed a change in the firm since it had gone public in 1999, which brought far greater emphasis on trading instead of investing. I had met Lloyd Blankfein a couple of times and found him quite different from his predecessors. I was offered a stock option (called an IPO Award) when my services were terminated, and I accepted it.

Then came the financial crash of 2008, and word emerged that Goldman Sachs had played a major role in bringing that debacle about. As it became clearer and clearer what Goldman had done, essentially betting against masses of subprime mortgages it was urging its customers to buy, I grew disgusted and wanted nothing to do with the firm.

In September 2010, I sold all my stock and gave away the proceeds, some to my children. But the large majority went to the Center for Development Economics at Williams College; to a scholarship fund named for my parents at Colorado College (with a request that funds be used to offer more scholarship aid to Native Americans); and to Syracuse University's Korean Peninsula Affairs Center at the Maxwell School.

In the New York *Times* of March 17, 2012, columnist Joe Nocera put in words what I feel about Wall Street in general, and Goldman Sachs in particular:

This week we saw a different kind of American capitalism on display—the "rip your eyeballs out" capitalism of Goldman Sachs....A corporate culture that values only one thing: making as much money as possible, by whatever means necessary... Goldman bundled terrible subprime mortgages that helped bring about the financial crisis. Smelling trouble, it unloaded its worst mortgage bonds by cramming them down the throats of their clients.

It's been more than five years since I dumped my Goldman Sachs stock, and I still feel that it was absolutely the right thing to do.

31

The Dangers of Demonization

As I think back over the varying patterns of U.S. foreign policy that I have observed or been a part of, it seems clear that what invariably gets us into trouble is our tendency to demonize foreign leaders or foreign groups we neither like nor understand. In such cases, we fill our gaps of ignorance with prejudice, and the result is hostility fueled by demagoguery, and damage done to all concerned.

In my early days at CIA, James Jesus Angleton, head of counterintelligence, demonized our Soviet opponents by saying that their thinking was so occluded by the Soviet ideology that they could not be recruited as agents on an intellectual basis, but only through coercion and intimidation. This appreciation was totally wrong and led to embarrassing "flaps" such as that which took me back to Japan in 1966. Angleton was also convinced that Soviet "moles" had penetrated CIA. DCI Bill Colby finally got fed up with Angleton's paranoid misapprehensions and fired him in December 1974.

Ironically and tragically, the entire concept of counterintelligence had been so discredited by Angleton's misjudgments that Aldrich Ames, a member of the counterintelligence staff, was able to carry on his traitorous activities far longer than should have been the case. Before he was finally arrested in 1994, Ames had betrayed almost all of CIA's Soviet agents who had been recruited after Angleton's demise. Included in this group was an admirable GRU officer with whom I had dealt. He had retired, was taken from his dacha, and shot in his yard.

Three other cases of U.S. demonization of foreign leaders immediately come to mind: Ho Chi Minh, Saddam Hussein, and Kim Jong-un.

* * *

Late in World War II, OSS parachuted a paramilitary team into Indochina to support the Viet Minh, who were fighting effectively against the brutal Japanese forces that had invaded and occupied the region. Paul Hoagland was the medic on that team. (He later joined CIA and was stationed on Saipan, where I got to know him.)

Hoagland recalled vividly being rushed to a grass shack immediately after he had landed by parachute to treat the local Viet Minh leader, whom he described as "a bag of bones with a goatee." That was Ho Chi Minh, who was wracked by malaria and dysentery. Hoagland's medicines saved his life, and Ho was deeply grateful.

Ho was a sophisticated, convinced communist who had lived abroad for many years. He had strained relations with the Chinese and had twice been imprisoned in China. He was well impressed with the United States and admired Thomas Jefferson and our Constitution.

As Ho's political leadership grew stronger after World War II ended, he repeatedly reached out to the United States, hoping to build a friendly relationship. In 1945, Ho wrote a letter to President Truman asking that we recognize the independence of Vietnam, as we had done with the Philippines. That letter was never answered, and it was not declassified until 1972. Ho's efforts were doomed to failure, as America chose to help France reestablish its colonial control over Indochina in return for its joining the European Coal and Steel Community, which it did in 1951.

The French defeat at the hands of the Viet Minh in 1954 at Dien Bien Phu ended France's colonial hopes. As a result, Vietnam was divided at the 17th parallel in 1954, with a referendum, scheduled for 1956, that was never held. Ho Chi Minh led North Vietnam, and a southern puppet, Bao Dai, was quickly replaced by Ngo Dinh Diem in Saigon. The conflict between North and South Vietnam became inevitable.

Our tragic mistake was to equate what was happening in Vietnam with what had happened in Korea. We saw two divided countries, both bordering China, with the bad guys in the northern halves. I believe that in dealing with the issue of historical analogies, similarities are seductive, but differences are definitive. The

Chinese gave full support to North Korea, but they despised the Vietnamese. That was the definitive difference. Truman was right to intervene and eventually stymie the North Korean invasion, which had been fully coordinated among Stalin, Mao, and Kim. But Eisenhower, Kennedy, and Johnson were all wrong in getting drawn into the Vietnam conflict.

Ho's sole objective was to reunite his country. We ignored centuries of hostility between the Chinese and the Vietnamese and mistakenly saw Ho as China's cat's paw, with the aim of spreading communism throughout Southeast Asia. This misconception was the foundation for the so-called "domino theory," which drew us into the tragic Vietnam War.

When the war finally ended, Ho had achieved his objective, a reunified Vietnam, and we had lost 58,000 men and women and spent hundreds of billions of dollars in a futile conflict in which we never should have been involved. Estimates of how many Vietnamese died in this conflict vary greatly, running as high as 3.8 million in one British medical study. Whatever the number, it was far too many. In July 2013, President Obama met in the White House with the president of Vietnam, a country with which we now have full and productive relations. The Vietnamese people still deeply admire Ho Chi Minh.

Saddam Hussein of Iraq was a brutal dictator, but we had sided with him in his long war with Iran. When Saddam invaded Kuwait in 1991, President George H. W. Bush kicked him out via "Desert Storm," but left him in place in Baghdad. In the wake of 9/11, President George W. Bush decided that Saddam must be overthrown because he was viewed as a threat to Israel, had nuclear weapons, and was aiding Al Qaeda.

The result was an American war of choice, mismanaged in the extreme and undertaken without congressional support and with no planning for how it was to be paid for. Saddam was overthrown and executed, but he had no nuclear weapons, and was a bitter foe of Al Qaeda, which cheered his death.

In January 2005, I was invited to a conference in Britain, sponsored by the Ditchley Foundation. The title of the conference was "The Role of Intelligence in the Policy Making Process." One major purpose of the conference was to explore how both the U.K. and U.S. intelligence establishments could have been so wrong about Saddam Hussein and weapons of mass destruction. It was by far the most glittering international array of "spooks" I had ever been part of. MI6, MI5, CIA, NSA, DIA, and various French intelligence services were all represented, at or near the top, along with think tanks and distinguished university professors.

It emerged that in both London and Washington, the intelligence establishments had been put under immense pressure by Prime Minister Tony Blair's minions and by the George W. Bush administration, led personally by Vice President Dick Cheney, to come up with intelligence proving that Saddam had nuclear weapons. As one high-ranking British official put it, "We knew he had nuclear weapons, but we could not prove it in advance. But we knew we would find the weapons after we invaded Iraq." The clear, if unstated implication of this statement was that faulty intelligence was not properly questioned and became the rotted foundation for our invasion of Iraq.

A report issued by the Ditchley Foundation after the conference put the problem this way:

> The drawing of wrong conclusions over weapons of mass destruction was not considered a systemic failure: it was peculiar in the extraordinary context of the Saddam Hussein regime. ... Failure to delve more accurately into the mindset of the dictator himself could, however, be regarded as systemic. Hitler and, especially, Stalin offered well-documented models. History, as Churchill constantly reminded us, does offer clues on the deeper areas. The conference came back to this in its recommendations for more deliberate action on long-term analysis and strategic thinking.

The Bush administration's judgment that Saddam was aiding Al Qaeda was also totally off the mark. Saddam was totally secular, brutal though he was. In a recent year, one of my students at Williams College was Iraqi. She told me that her mother got her PhD in engineering at Baghdad University, under Saddam's rule, and that she was thoroughly Westernized in dress and thought.

The Ditchley Foundation's conclusion that our collective failures in analyzing foreign dictators' thinking are systemic applies fully to North Korea, which I frequently refer to as "the longest-running failure in the history of U.S. intelligence." That epithet, unfortunately, still applies, both in terms of organizational failures on the part of our intelligence agencies and our national failure to think intelligently about what is going on north of the 38th parallel.

There is no question about North Korea's status as a brutal dictatorship. Their gulags are notorious and horrifying, and their efforts to assassinate South Korea's leaders in the 1970s and 1980s are fully documented. I am frequently asked why I keep urging that we establish continuing communication with the North Korean leaders, despite their threats and prevarications.

My answer is that what has happened in China since Nixon's brilliant diplomacy of 1972 and what has happened in Russia since the collapse of the Berlin Wall in 1989 show that dictatorships will change, slowly and imperfectly, but peacefully when their leaders recognize that it is in their own interest to change. The more traditional U.S. approach of trying to force change through regime removal, as in Iran, Guatemala, and Cuba, leads to chaos and continuing conflict.

In the summer of 2009, when Kim Jong Un first began to appear on the Pyongyang scene showing clear indications of impending prominence, I wrote to Vice President Biden, suggesting that young Kim be invited to the United States for an "orientation tour," through which we could learn about him, and he could learn about us. I received a pro forma turndown from Biden's office, but later learned that my suggestion was brushed aside because of expected ridicule from the Republicans if an invitation had been extended to Kim.

Today, Kim is in power and appears to be adjusting to it well. But since his emergence he has been subjected to all sorts of spurious calumny, based largely on prejudice, such as the idea that he ordered the sinking of a South Korean naval vessel in March 2010, to show the North Korean military how tough he was. I think that Kim, educated in Switzerland for at least two years, shows clear signs of wanting to take North Korea in new directions, more in touch with the outside world.

Most "Korean experts" dismiss this idea as wishful thinking. We'll never know who is correct unless we talk with the North Koreans, directly and at length. I intend to continue working to set up such talks, designed to draw North Korea out of its extreme isolation, so it can more clearly see that it is in its own interest to bring massive changes into being, and that the United States is not determined to be its permanent enemy.

President George H. W. Bush proves a powerful exception to this pattern of demonization in his disciplined judgment of foreign leaders, and particularly in his relationship with Mikhail Gorbachev. Bush first met Gorbachev at Chernenko's funeral in 1983, had seen him several times in the following years, and had encouraged Ronald Reagan to meet with Gorbachev four times during his second term as president.

Thus, when the Berlin Wall came crashing down in 1989, Bush knew Gorbachev well and understood the tremendous pressures he would be under in seeking to take Russia in a new direction. He therefore refused to symbolically "dance on the Berlin Wall" as a means of celebrating victory in the Cold War. He knew that that would only make Gorbachev's job harder and our relationship with a "new Russia" more tenuous.

President Obama seems cut from the same cloth. He has been admirably restrained in his judgments of controversial foreign leaders. I hope very much that, before he leaves office in 2016, the president will reach out to North Korea and work with it to bring about real change in our relationship and in the way that North Korea treats its own people.

In the mid 1970s, there was a country in Northeast Asia that was routinely seizing and torturing those of its citizens who conspicuously protested its hard-line political policies, had started a covert nuclear weapons development project, and was secretly ordering high-tech weapons, including midget submarines, from foreign countries. That country was South Korea. Today, President Obama sees South Korea as our most reliable ally in Asia.

The transformation in our relationship with Seoul was the result of continuous dialogue and engagement—some of it emotional and contentious—that was maintained though thick and thin for more than thirty years. We need to start a similar process with North Korea. It will be prolonged and difficult, but unless we are prepared to fight them again, it's the only way to go.

In 2012, I became chairman of the Pacific Century Institute in California, near Los Angeles. I am working closely with Spencer Kim, PCI's founder, and Fred Carriere, my long-term friend and deputy at the Korea Society, to try to maintain open channels of communication with Pyongyang. Our goal is to open a way to the establishment of some degree of mutual trust, where none now exists. It is good to have such tenacious and well-informed friends to work with, and to have PCI, at least for now, as an organizational base from which to operate.

Early in 2014, as PCI chairman, I wrote a letter to Marshal Kim Jong Un in Pyongyang saying that I would like to lead a small PCI delegation on a visit to his capital. I said that we would have two purposes in making our visit. First would be to learn of North Korea's plans for its future economic development and to see if PCI could be helpful to them. Second was our hope to have former congressman Pete McCloskey, a highly decorated former Marine with extensive combat in the Korean War, meet and pay respects to a North Korean veteran of that same conflict.

We were quickly invited to come. We informed the State Department of our plans and departed. On February 10, 2014, four of us arrived in Pyongyang: PCI founder Spencer Kim, McCloskey, Lynn Turk (a senior PCI staff member and retired Foreign Service officer), and myself. We departed from Pyongyang on February 14 and returned to California. Here is how the *Los Angeles Times* described our trip, in a February 18, 2014, article by Lee Romney:

> For decades, former eight-term Bay Area Rep. Paul N. "Pete" McCloskey Jr. has dreamed of a Korean War battle moment he cannot shake: Peering into a trench he sees the terrified faces of his teenage opponents, clutching wicker baskets full of grenades.
>
> He empties his weapon.
>
> Last week, at 86, he at last had an opportunity for personal reconciliation. As a member of a small delegation led by Donald Gregg, a former U.S. ambassador to South Korea, McCloskey traveled to Pyongyang with a singular intention.

"My primary hope was that I could salute, shake hands and embrace one of those kids who fought against us," said McCloskey, a decorated war hero. . . . "It's something I've wanted to do for 50 years."

It wasn't easy. Many have died. But North Korean officials called around and found a retired three-star general, in full regalia, working as a docent in the North Korean capital's imposing Victorious Fatherland War Museum.

Ji Young Choon was a 17-year-old machine gun platoon leader when his division drove through the South Korean town of Inje and the county of Yanggu, McCloskey would learn. McCloskcy, a Marine second lieutenant who led six bayonet charges and came home to two Purple Hearts, the Silver Star and Navy Cross, was 23 and fought in the same theater.

Through an interpreter the men spoke, haltingly at first, in the museum courtyard. "He wondered, really, what we were doing there," McCloskey said with a laugh in San Francisco on Friday, after his long trip back to California. I said I had been in the American Marines. That didn't impress him."

But when McCloskey asked the 81-year-old Ji how many times he had been wounded (Ji answered "Three") and deferentially offered that he had only been wounded twice, the ice cracked. As McCloskey rattled off the ridges and other geographic landmarks of his 1951 ordeal, the two men acknowledged a shared experience.

He returned the following day to continue the conversation. Then, McCloskey stepped back and saluted.

"I told him how bravely I thought his people had fought, and we embraced," said McCloskey, who served in Congress from 1967 to 1983, became the first Republican to oppose the Vietnam War, and helped craft seminal environmental legislation.

"We ended up friends," he said. "We agreed that we don't want our grandchildren or great-grandchildren to fight, that war is hell and there's no glory in it." . . .

Gregg met McCloskey a dozen years ago at a war crimes

inquiry. When organizing the trip to Pyongyang, Gregg, now chairman of the Pacific Century Institute's board of directors, turned to his old friend, a man with a near-legendary reputation in military circles for his battlefield bravery who turned conciliation into the cornerstone of his career.

"He was known as the Beowulf of the 5th Marines. But he wanted to make peace," Gregg said in an interview. "So we thought, what a terrific addition he would be. And he was tremendous." . . .

Gregg, who last visited Pyongyang six years ago, said he was surprised at its vibrancy—new buildings, thriving restaurants, a flood of cellphones. Yet he said the most moving aspect of the trip was watching the personal bond blossom between two men who had battled on opposite sides of a painful war.

It was, Gregg said, "diplomacy of the best kind."

I am encouraged by the results of the February 2014 visit. What PCI has learned of North Korea's economic planning and objectives shows clearly that Pyongyang wants foreign investment to come into North Korea. I intend to remain actively in touch with the North Koreans, with the objective of helping them to emerge from their isolation into a more normal pattern of relations with their neighbors, particularly South Korea, and with the United States.

The continued division of the Korean Peninsula is a tragedy that can and must be ended. That will only happen when mutual demonization is replaced by dialogue, allowing reconciliation to emerge.

Gratitude

I remember that night long ago when I was four or five, teary and fearful, crying out for my parents, filled with the fear of death. They assured me I would live to reach the year 2000, and here it is, fourteen years beyond that. How lucky I am to have survived for so long.

It's been a very good run, and it's been great fun—much more laughter than pain. I've rummaged through my memories, sorted out the fragments that still have impact and meaning, and told them as best I can. What's left is gratitude. I'm deeply grateful to have recovered from tuberculosis and to be alive and well today.

How lucky I was to have met Meg, totally by chance, in a taxi, more than sixty years ago. What joy she has brought into my life, since the moment I first saw her. With three men crammed in the back seat, listening to every word, I chose not to introduce myself in the taxi. I did not want to devalue in any way what I felt to be an extraordinary encounter.

I was then reduced to driving past her house as often as I could, hoping to "bump into her" again. A couple of quick sightings on the sidewalk, with only a word or two exchanged, paved the way for our encounter in a CIA library, where it felt completely right to introduce myself.

My father's close friend, Branch Rickey, the man who brought Jackie Robinson into major league baseball, had a great saying on this subject: "Luck is the residue of design." I certainly had designs on Meg, from the very beginning, and our appreciation of each other continues to grow, wondrously.

I'm deeply grateful to Lucy, Alison, and John for the way they endured our long-range moves, to and from Asia; how they adjusted to exotic new places, and learned from them. Family moves are tough on everyone, particularly kids when they are pulled out of school and forced to make new friends in totally new settings.

All three of our children tell me they are grateful for their overseas years, and in 2013 Lucy returned to Burma for a bicycle tour and found the house we lived in on Wingaba Road, still with its tennis court intact.

They all handled our changes well, emotionally and academically, and as a result we had them at Williams College for twelve consecutive years, perfectly spaced. (The last time I skied was with Alison when she was at Williams. She was a jaw-droppingly fine skier who left me completely behind.)

I also love the wonderful people they married, Christopher Buckley, Ned Corcoran, and Mary Ceglarski; the children produced, Cat and Conor Buckley, Gregg, Alex, and Meggie Corcoran, and the Corcorans' ward, Tyquan Davis. These young people have brought to Meg and me happy new dimensions of family life with all its varieties and challenges; rugby, classical piano, military history, girls' basketball, and the demands of working at *Vanity Fair* magazine.

Sports remains a strong bond between my children and me. Lucy, like my mother, for whom she is named, has developed a great interest in baseball, the Washington Nationals in particular, and I am now rooting for them in the National League, on the strength of Lucy's enthusiasm. With Alison and John, it is the Boston Red Sox for whom we all root hard. Their winning of the World Series in 2013 was a great joy to us all.

For years, we all played tennis together. Now I love playing golf with Alison and John, and Lucy has also taken up the sport.

With all the children, there is a shared interest in reading, and we like recommending books to each other.

I was truly fortunate to have worked so long and so closely with George H. W. Bush. I learned so much from him, and could not possibly have had a better boss. He combined loyalty with toughness, and an earthy sense of humor with an ability to unerringly judge foreign leaders. He also dealt with adversity with patience and strength, and his example helped me get through the Iran-Contra and "October Surprise" episodes. Responding to a book I had sent him, he sent me a note, dated May 1, 2014, in which he commented on our past association. He ended the note saying, "Well done, good friend." Nothing anyone outside the family has ever written to me means more than those four words.

Many of the things I try to live by come from Williams College philosophy professor J. W. Miller. I teach a four-week course there in January on intelligence work and try to give back to my Williams students some of the ideas Miller gave to me:

> Man does not have a nature. He has a history, for which he is rsponsible.
> Cut behind appearance to reality.
> Never treat a human being like an object.
> Civility does not exist in the abstract; it comes as part of a shared human endeavor.

I'm still inspired by Professor Miller and, as a result, I want to continue teaching.

As I hope I made clear in the last chapter, I remain deeply concerned about trends and tensions on the Korean peninsula, and I hope to contribute to the solution of some of the problems that have existed there since the Korean War. Since I believe dialogue is the best antidote to demonization, I hope the United States will resume direct contact and conversation with North Korean leaders in Pyongyang.

I think often of my parents. A couple of years ago, under the eaves at Birch Hill, John and Mary's home built in 1940 in Westminster West, Vermont, we found a packet of letters that my parents wrote to each other during the time of my illness. Reading those letters was painful, as for the first time I fully realized how deeply they had been worried about me, how carefully they had camouflaged their concerns, how wonderfully they had cared for me, and how much my illness had changed the pattern of their lives.

We found another packet of letters that I have not and will not open. It is neatly tied, and my father wrote on it "Lucy's letters to Abel." They are both long gone, but I want to preserve the privacy of that packet of intimacy for them alone. I will leave it for another, later, descendant to discover.

My mother set a great example for me in the way she lived her life. She told me that her life got better and better until she was 85, when health issues intruded. She died gracefully, just short of 98.

I'll try to do as well.

Index

CPSIA information can be obtained at www.ICGtesting.com
Printed in the USA
BVOW07s0019030714

358070BV00002B/9/P